Governing Educational Desire

Governing Educational Desire

Culture, Politics, and Schooling in China

ANDREW B. KIPNIS

THE UNIVERSITY OF CHICAGO PRESS   CHICAGO AND LONDON

ANDREW B. KIPNIS is senior fellow at the Australian National University. He is the author of *Producing Guanxi: Sentiment, Self and Subculture in a North China Village* and *China and Postsocialist Anthropology: Theorizing Power and Society after Communism* and coeditor of the *China Journal*.

The University of Chicago Press, Chicago 60637
The University of Chicago Press, Ltd., London
© 2011 by The University of Chicago
All rights reserved. Published 2011
Printed in the United States of America
20 19 18 17 16 15 14 13 12 11   1 2 3 4 5

ISBN-13: 978-0-226-43753-8 (cloth)
ISBN-13: 978-0-226-43755-2 (paper)

ISBN-10: 0-226-43753-1 (cloth)
ISBN-10: 0-226-43755-8 (paper)

Library of Congress Cataloging-in-Publication Data

Kipnis, Andrew B.
    Governing educational desire : culture, politics, and schooling in China /
Andrew B. Kipnis.
        p. cm.
    Includes bibliographical references and index.
    ISBN-13: 978-0-226-43753-8 (cloth : alk. paper)
    ISBN-13: 978-0-226-43755-2 (pbk. : alk. paper)
    ISBN-10: 0-226-43753-1 (cloth : alk. paper)
    ISBN-10: 0-226-43755-8 (pbk. : alk. paper) 1. Education, Higher—China—Zouping
Xian. 2. Education and state—China—Zouping Xian. I. Title.
    LA1134.Z68K575 2011
    306.430951—dc22

                                                                                    2010017308

Contents

Illustrations

Acknowledgments

The research and writing for this book took place over most of the first decade of the twenty-first century. Many debts have been accumulated during this period, and trying to recount them all is a daunting task; I beg forgiveness from those I forget to mention. Institutionally I have spent this decade at the Department of Anthropology and the Contemporary China Centre of the Research School of Pacific and Asian Studies (RSPAS) at the Australian National University (ANU). As RSPAS and its constitutive units were officially restructured out of existence on December 31, 2009, I wish to acknowledge how wonderful an academic environment RSPAS created. An exciting mix of disciplinary and area studies research, of thoughtful colleagues, helpful staff, brilliant students, and stimulating visiting scholars, RSPAS was responsible for some of the world's best English-language writing on the societies, cultures, politics, and histories of the Asia-Pacific region. I am proud that this book is also a product of that school. Colleagues like Geremie Barmé, Assi Doron, Ben Hillman, Tamara Jacka, John Makeham, Andrew McWilliam, Francesca Merlan, Mark Mosko, Ben Penny, Kathy Robinson, Alan Rumsey, Sally Sargeson, Graeme Smith, Nick Tapp, and Philip Taylor have provided much input over the years. I especially thank Jonathan Unger and James Fox for bringing me to RSPAS in 1999 and Jonathan Unger, Luigi Tomba, and Janelle Caiger for working closely with me on the *China Journal* and other related projects. Students like Louise Simon, Alec Soucy, Juan Carlo Thomas, Michael Lickorish, Josaphine Wright, Nico Warrou, Hans Lim, Scott Pacey, Nanlai Cao, Adelyn Lim, Antonella Diana, Tom Cliff, Sin Wen Lau, Jenny Munro, Jamie Coates, Nguyen Thi Thanh Binh, Tina Liu, Lior Rosenberg, and Liang Chen have enriched my world by sharing their thoughts and projects with me. Staff members, including Heli Brecht,

Ann Buller, Fay Castles, Penelope Judd, Stephen Meatheringham, Sandie Walters, and Hong Yu have guided me through many bureaucratic mazes and practical problems. I especially thank Darren Boyd, who spent hours digitally converting my color images into the black-and-white prints used in this book.

In Shandong, many people facilitated my research. I have benefited immensely from my association with the Shandong Academy of Social Sciences. Yao Dongfang attended to the troubling task of organizing visas, while my good friend Li Shanfeng worked closely with me collecting data in several research sites and coauthored two papers with me. In Zouping, research assistance was capably provided by Julie Zhai, and bureaucratic support by my longtime friends Han Zhenguang and Yang Xueping. Many educators in Zouping, Pingyuan, and Jiaozhou counties discussed their lives and pedagogic strategies with me. I found their dedication to their profession inspiring and their friendship warm. Out of political caution I will not name them here, but they are surely among the greatest contributors to this project. Thanks are also due to the many Chinese parents and students who shared their hopes and fears.

Many scholars outside of ANU have shared their thoughts, insights, and friendship with me over the years. I thank Ann Anagnost, Joel Andreas, Joe Bosco, Susanne Brandtstädter, Lily Crumley, Gonçalo dos Santos, Louise Edwards, Bill Jankowiak, Fan Ke, Judith Farquhar, Stephan Feuchtwang, Vanessa Fong, Martin Forsey, Carl Gerth, Thomas Gold, Doug Guthrie, Dorothy Holland, Carolyn Hsu, James Lee, Bradley Levinson, Linda Li, Lin Qinghong, Kam Louie, Gordon Mathews, Helena Obendiek, Nyíri Pál, Frank Pieke, Charles Stafford, Stig Thøgersen, Tia Thorton, Emily Wilcox, Terry Woronov, Mayfair Yang, and Zhu Xiaoyang. I would like to single out Børge Bakken, whose underappreciated masterpiece, *The Exemplary Society*, was a particular inspiration for this book. Audiences at talks given at various conferences and institutions, including Cambridge University, Oxford University, Peking University, Nanjing University, the University of Manchester, the University of North Carolina at Chapel Hill, Aarhus University, Macquarie University, the University of Hong Kong, City University of Hong Kong, the Chinese University of Hong Kong, Hong Kong Science and Technology University, and the Max Planck Institute, provided valuable feedback.

Financially, research for this book was supported by research grants from the Australian Research Council, especially a Discovery Grant (DP0556422) but also a Linkage Grant (LX0775919) and a more recent

Discovery Grant (DP0984510). The University of Chicago Press has been a pleasure to work with. The anonymous reviewers for the Press provided many useful suggestions, most of which I have tried to incorporate and a few of which I have ignored at my own peril. One of these reviewers, Heidi Ross, revealed her identity to me. I have found her comments especially useful. Elizabeth Branch Dyson both read the manuscript from start to finish, suggesting many concrete improvements, and guided me through the Press's review process. Her help has made publishing this book a joy. Anne Goldberg and Susan Tarcov also provided much practical assistance and editorial advice.

My wife, Kejia, and son, Jonathan, put up with both the physical absences required to complete the fieldwork for this book and the absent-mindedness that results from too much attention to abstract projects. As much as anything, their tolerance for my academic preoccupations allowed me to write this book.

Introduction

In 2005 and 2006, during the course of research on education reform in Zouping County, Shandong Province, the People's Republic of China (PRC), I conducted a survey of households with a child in the sixth and final year of primary school. I surveyed over a hundred households, and my project design ensured that they included richer and poorer households, rural and urban households, parents engaged in a wide variety of occupations, and students with above and below average academic records. When I asked whether they wanted their child to attend college, one hundred percent of the parents that I interviewed in both rural and urban Zouping answered affirmatively. Many expressed this desire quite strongly, saying that it would be one of the most glorious dreams that they could imagine if their child were able to test into college. Many were even shocked that I could ask such a question: "Of course," "Isn't that what everybody wants?" and "How could someone not want that?" were common replies. The rural households, in which many of the parents had attended only a few years of primary school themselves, were just as enthusiastic as the urban households. Only three of the fifty-eight rural households that I surveyed even qualified their responses with asides like "if I can afford the tuition" or "if [so and so] is bright enough."

This book examines educational desire, in Zouping and elsewhere, in the broadest possible perspective, as what Marcel Mauss would have called a "'total' social phenomenon . . . at once legal, economic, religious, aesthetic, morphological and so on" (Mauss 1967 [1925]:76). The consequences of this desire are vast, influencing household and national economic priorities, birthrates, ethnic relations, patterns of governing, gender relations, and state ideologies. But for the most part this book focuses on the causes of this desire, not the consequences. Just where does this desire

FIGURE I. Map of China, as displayed in a Zouping primary school. Shandong province is highlighted. As with the following maps, the original was in bright colors.

come from? What are the specific cultural, economic, political, and social circumstances that frame its emergence?

When I asked parents why they wanted their child to attend college, some would mention better jobs and more opportunities, but others either could not reply or suggested that university attendance was an end in itself. In Zouping, it is not clear to me that college is necessarily a good investment. Many white-collar jobs pay no more than the blue-collar ones available there, and I knew quite a few university-educated Zouping residents who, because their work units had gone bankrupt, ended up in a worse financial position than the average factory worker. Moreover, over the past decade tuition costs have soared. Still, few in Zouping questioned whether a university education is a good investment. The aura of prestige that surrounds a university degree inhibited the application of strict economic reasoning.[1] As one parent put it, "If you attend college, no matter what happens in the rest of your life, no one can ever take that away from you." That many could not articulate a reason for their desire supports the notion that a university education has become an object of desire in itself. By recently erecting monuments to Song dynasty scholars in the county seat's central park (Thøgersen 2002:1–2), as well as by displaying the photographs, names, and universities of the high scorers on each year's university entrance exam on bulletin boards located at the busiest commercial street in the county capital, the county government echoed the desires of its citizenry.

Though the desire for educational success may be particularly strong in contemporary Zouping, it is illustrative of a wider cultural phenomenon. Researchers at the Shandong Academy of Social Sciences told me that survey data (which they could not share with me) indicated that Zouping was typical of the entire province in this regard. Though I was not able to duplicate my household survey outside of Zouping, interviews with teachers, principals, and education officials in my research trips to other Shandong counties, including ones in both the eastern and the western extremes of the state, which varied considerably in economic development, confirmed Zouping's typicality in this regard. Shandong, moreover, is not the only Chinese province where high levels of educational desire are evident. Though statistical data I gathered during the late 1990s suggest that desire for education in Shandong Province is higher than in

FIGURE 2. Map of Shandong, as displayed in a Zouping primary school. Zouping county is darkened.

some other provinces (Kipnis 2001b), researchers in Jiangxi Province, Hubei Province, Jiangsu Province, Henan Province, and Zhejiang Province
have told me that similar levels of educational desire exist there. In addition, in many nations outside of China, Chinese parents or, even more
generally, East Asian parents are known for pushing their children toward
college.

When I discussed this educational desire with educated Chinese parents, the suggestion often came up that Confucian culture (*Ruxue wenhua*)
or Chinese culture respects education. Such an explanation, however, is
unpopular among contemporary Anglophone anthropologists, even as a
form of shorthand. Attaching cultural traits, like educational desire, to
a particular, nonhistoricized, non-Western geographic space is usually
dismissed as an exercise in orientalism. This book attempts to work through
the theoretical impasse brought about by the conflict between these two
views.

The intersection of three major theoretical concepts forms the basis of
my response to this impasse: culture, governing, and emplacement. Of the
three, "culture" is the vaguest and most controversial and has the deep-
est genealogy. Many anthropologists, at least since the late 1970s, have
abandoned the concept for being static, ahistorical, holistic, and apolitical;
yet others have reflected on how difficult a complete abandonment of the
concept is.[2] Michael Fischer (2007) has issued a call for the relevance of
the concept, "[a]rguing that without a differentiated and relational notion of the cultural, the social sciences would be crippled, reducing social
action to notions of pure instrumentality" (43) and offering a complex
definition:

> Culture is (1) that relational . . . , (2) complex whole . . . , (3) whose parts cannot
> be changed without affecting other parts . . . , (4) mediated through power-
> ful and power-laden symbolic forms . . . , (5) whose multiplicities and perfor-
> matively negotiated character . . . (6) is transformed by alternative positions,
> organizational forms, and leveraging of symbolic systems . . . , (7) as well as by
> emergent new technosciences, media, and biotechnical relations. (1)

As with any definition, points of contention emerge. In particular, I
am wary of the notion of social wholes. The social, political, economic,
artistic, and cultural phenomena that surround the desire for educational
achievement intertwine in complex ways without forming a closed-off system. They interact with educational desire in ways that have the potential

to go beyond the reproduction of a singular social formation; parts may interact to reproduce a larger social dynamic, but the larger social dynamic never constitutes a single whole (Kipnis 2003b, 2008b).

Yet Fischer's definition still illuminates many of the social dynamics discussed in this book. As his definition suggests, as a product of culture, the desire for educational achievement is relational in many senses. It invokes a system of prestige in which those with educational accomplishments are marked as superior to the noneducated. This prestige relates in a complex manner to other forms of inequality (class, geographic, rural/urban) in China and beyond the national borders. Insofar as this desire comes to mark particular identities—Han Chinese, rural dwellers (Kipnis 2001b), Asian American, and so on—then it is further implicated in wider forms of social and ethnic relations. While disliking the language of cultural wholes, I agree that this desire is a complex phenomenon that influences many other aspects of social relationships inside and outside China, including those usually categorized by social scientists under the signs of economics, art, demography, politics, and geography. As Fischer's definition of culture suggests, educational desire is also quite literally mediated by power-laden symbolic forms, one of which is the necessity of learning how to write Chinese characters, with all the aura, performative political power, and cultural capital that are tied up with this now widespread art (Yen 2005). Educational attainment is further a form of social desire that is manipulated by political elites for various purposes and both transformed and reproduced by new forms of media. All of these themes will be taken up in greater detail in later chapters of this book.

Governing, the second of this book's key concepts, in the Foucauldian tradition refers to the "conduct of conduct." Within this tradition the focus is on how governing is to be carried out rather than on who, specifically, is doing the governing (Barry et al. 1996; Dean 1999; Foucault 1991; Gordon 1987, 1991; Hindess 1996a, 1996b; Rose 1996). This conception of governing has many advantages for an anthropological study of educational desire. First, it rejects a strictly top-down imagination in which a small group of state elites governs the masses. Rather, governing is carried out by various representatives of state agencies, by teachers and parents, by children vis-à-vis one another, and by everyone vis-à-vis him or herself. Second, a focus on the how of governing opens up consideration of specific disciplinary techniques as well as governmental manipulations of a wider social environment. Given that China has a long and explicit history of using education as a governing technique (Bakken 2000), a focus on the cultural specificities of Chinese governing is useful. Third, the conduct of conduct almost always takes as its goal the production of a governable subject (Dean 1999:17), what some anthropological theorists have called "subjectification" (Foucault 1983; Rabinow 1984), and modern educational discourse is usually quite explicit about the types of citizens its educational techniques are designed to create. Teachers, education researchers, and government bureaucrats argue endlessly over how to induce students to grow into patriotic, creative, "high-quality," entrepreneurial, responsible, moral, intelligent, and adaptable adults as well as over which of these qualities is most important. Examining such debates further illuminates the culturally specific aspects of Chinese governing. Finally, as Sam Kaplan (2006) demonstrates so well in the case of Turkey, the politics of educational policy are multiheaded, contradictory and complex; rarely, if ever, does "the state" speak in a single voice on this topic. This complicates rather than rules out state/society dualisms. For while the governing agents include state and nonstate actors, and while both extremes of the state/society continuum might engage in multiple and contradictory governing strategies, there are still clearly moments in China when someone who speaks with the authority of the state steps in to impose a major intervention on the governed population. To abandon the language of state and society entirely would lead this analysis to ignore these moments.

Some theorists of governmentality consider it inappropriate to apply concepts derived from Michel Foucault's lectures to dynamics of governing in premodern and non-Western contexts. By doing so, I mean to critique the assumptions that make this application seem strained, especially the presumption that concepts and practices like governing from a distance, the conduct of conduct, subjectification, and discipline refer to culturally specific discourses that developed only in the course of Western history, that were first institutionalized in Western countries, and that have been introduced to non-Western countries only as the result of colonialism and globalization over the past century.[3] Particularly in the case of China, these assumptions are wrong.

China's long history of statecraft and vast stores of traditional treatises on governing (including those that might be categorized as Confucian, Legalist, or Daoist) contain a multitude of ideas that easily relate to the problematics of governing from a distance, subjectification, population, sovereignty, law, and conducting conduct. Of course there are subtle differences between Chinese and Western traditions of writings on governing and statecraft, but these are not at a level that make comparisons impossible. More important, these ideas have long been institutionalized in the governing of imperial China.[4] To take a single example, consider the examination as a governing technology. Foucault (1979:184–94) rightly devotes an entire subsection of his classic *Discipline and Punish* to examinations. Many of the insights Foucault provides there, such as those about the simultaneously individuating and homogenizing effects of examinations, could be used to illuminate the governing dynamics of exams in both imperial and contemporary China. But who could imagine that examinations in China are a recent, Western import? Examinations have been a significant governing technology in China for well over a millennium, and both the philosophies that justify their use and the governing dynamics they engender (from techniques of teaching and self-discipline to the dynamics of evaluation, cheating, and the prevention of cheating) have become minor traditions in their own right.

In short, I take the focal points of governmentality theory—an interest in the interrelations among the means of conducting conduct at many levels (by governments, corporations, schools, families, teachers and individuals), in mentalities of governing, in practices of discipline, and in processes of subjectification—without suggesting that these techniques, discourses, and practices are necessarily recent imports from the West. Instead I use the theoretical terms of governmentality theory as categories that allow both comparison and contrast between governing processes in China and those elsewhere in the world, as well as between those that are legacies of the preindustrial era and those that have emerged relatively recently.

Michael Herzfeld's (2005:21–32) concept of cultural intimacy is also useful for understanding the interrelationship between cultural dynamics and processes of governing that I propose here. Herzfeld uses this concept to point out both the reliance of states and bureaucrats on the cultural poetics of the populations they govern and the ability of the ideological pronouncements of government to be taken up in a variety of ways by people seemingly located at great removes from the centers of political power. In China, where education is both a metaphor for governing[5] and a tool of governing (Bakken 2000), and where the written word is a sign of political power and artistic devotion and simultaneously the focal point of primary school education, Herzfeld's concept particularly rings true.

The interfaces between state governing and societal traditions of governing are numerous. Governing elites legitimate their policies in the literary and poetic traditions that are taught in schools. The literary content taught in schools is thus a matter of intense debate, manipulated endlessly by state elites, but often at least partially reflective of popular demand. The same logic applies to the teaching of science. As Susan Greenhalgh (2008) eloquently argues, since the end of the cultural revolution, the language of science has become more and more central to the justification of both policy and regime in China. Policies are defended as scientific, and the teaching of both politics and science in schools treats the concept of "science" as a sacred term. Scientistic excesses in policy design[6] emerge as young people in schools learn to value science above other forms of learning. Common people also both use official language to make their own, serious social demands and crack jokes with ironic twists of official phrases. And finally, as Frank Pieke (2004) points out, the government itself is an organization composed of social relationships that may be analyzed as a form of society whose structure is influenced by the wider society in which it is enmeshed.

While Herzfeld's argument directs attention toward the ways in which cultural forms circulate among various state and societal agents, Harri Englund (2002) argues that an anthropological focus on global flows and circulating discourses has unfortunately contributed to a tendency to disconnect culture from place. He writes that "all phenomena in global circulations are at once particular and capable of spreading widely as elements of the globalist imagination" (261). He directs anthropologists to pay attention both to the processes by which particular cultural dynamics are put in place, whether these dynamics are seen as having local or nonlocal origins, and to the process by which once "local" cultural processes spread out from a particular locality.

Accepting Englund's argument leads to the third of this book's key terms, emplacement. Emplacement holds together my other two major concepts—culture and governing—for governing educational desire, especially in China, can be conceived as an attempt to install a particular cultural process in a particular place. Governments at all levels enforce policies within particular geographic regions, and cultural patterns vary across space. If governing actions have any effect on people's subjectivities and if cultural patterns have any effect on governmentalities, then the cultural dynamics of governing must in some way relate to place.

Gilles Deleuze and Felix Guattari's famous opposition of nomadology to state processes of fixed territorial governing seems designed with Chinese history in mind (1987:351–474). Not only was governing in China's long imperial history often undertaken under the shadow of the fear of invasion by "nomadic hordes," but, more important, as Fei Xiaotong

(1992) puts it, it has been self-consciously "from the soil" that Chinese "earthbound" processes of governing have derived. Governing agents in China have long imagined that their subjects were (or at least should be) tied to the land they farmed. The person/place tie became the state's key to controlling and taxing the population. Contemporary China's spatial hierarchy of governing is perhaps the most complex in the world, including six layers—national, provincial, prefectural, county, township, and village. China's household registration system attempts to tie every resident to a single space defined by this hierarchy. It has been retained in an era of growing migration, despite the great administrative difficulties this entails and numerous calls for its abandonment, precisely because the Chinese government cannot imagine how to govern without the ability to assign every resident to his or her place (Fei-ling Wang 2005).

Research Sites and Processes

I organize this book in terms of different perspectives on processes of emplacement, beginning with the "local." I view the local as an artifact of both the processes of my research and the processes of Chinese governing. As an anthropologist, I feel most comfortable in discerning cultural dynamics through personal observation. I undertook research in three different counties in Shandong Province to gain some comparative scope, but the bulk of my research took place in one county, Zouping. In all three of the counties I relied on face-to-face research methods. In each county, I gained an understanding of the local education system by interviewing officials in the county's educational bureaucracy and making day-long visits to as many schools as I could (between ten and twenty-five schools per county). In Zouping, I spent a month at each of three different primary schools, following the day-to-day activities of a sixth-grade class at each school and spending time with the teachers of that class in their group offices. In Zouping, I also conducted a household survey of the students in the sixth-grade classes that I attended, visiting their homes in a wide variety of village and town settings.

These research experiences (completed mostly in 2005 and 2006, with final updates made in 2007 and 2009) built upon nearly two decades of previous research trips to Zouping but differed in character from my earlier research. In previous research I often felt constrained by my identity as a foreign researcher.[7] For a variety of reasons, research in Zouping schools was much more open. In 1999, I volunteered to teach an oral English class to local teachers. This experience enabled me to establish relationships with many teachers and made me aware that by teaching English I had something to offer the local educational community. I continued to teach twice-weekly evening English classes during later research trips to Zouping. In addition, my own identity as an academic was valuable in an educational context. I was viewed both as someone who had succeeded in the pursuit of educational excellence (and thus as a good role model who had mastered the art of studying) and as someone who could provide comparative information on schooling in Western countries.

Sitting through weeks and weeks of sixth-grade classes was sometimes boring but was also a necessary part of the research experience. Not only did it give me a feel for both what was taught in Zouping's schools and how that teaching was conducted, but it also gave the students an opportunity to know me and become comfortable with me. Like the students, I sometimes pined for the bell to ring and sometimes became engrossed in the topic at hand. My level of written Chinese improved during this period, and I enjoyed the Chinese teachers' introductions of the subtleties of certain poems or characters. When I first entered a classroom, the teacher would introduce me to the students and I would take a seat near the back of the class. During my first day of class, the students would be overwhelmed by curiosity, often rushing up to me during class breaks and asking for my autograph. But after a few days they would settle down, and after a week most ignored my presence. Between classes, those sitting near me sometimes included me in their informal chat and games, providing a more child-centered perspective on schooling. I gave a lecture or two to each class I visited, and the students and their parents were mostly delighted with the idea of my coming to their house to do a household interview. The parents were eager for any information they could get on their children's schooling, and the children were proud to show me their homes and families. When conducting household interviews, I had to find my way only to the outskirts of a given village or neighborhood. Once I did so, one or more students would assume the role of local guide, leading me around to the households I had arranged to visit. The students would occasionally attend each other's household interviews, as sometimes did relatives and neighbors of the household I was visiting. Some of the interviews thus transformed into group discussions with up to a dozen participants chiming in. The sense of debate and dialogue that emerged in such cases greatly enriched the research.

I selected the three schools to reflect the diversity of living situations in

Zouping. One school was the central primary school for a relatively poor rural township. The students lived in the twenty-five villages that fed the school. Most rode a bus to and from school each day, with the longest bus rides taking fifty minutes each way. The students' parents all had rights to farmland in their villages. The parents often divided their labor so that one parent farmed the family's allotment of land while another worked off-farm either in one of the many small factories scattered throughout the township or doing business in the local markets. Other households specialized in agriculture, farming the land of several households, raising pigs or chickens or producing more specialized agricultural goods. In a few households both parents worked off-farm while they rented their land rights to neighbors or relatives.

The second school was located in the old part of Zouping city and served the long-term residents of the county seat. The parents worked in the older factories of the county seat (including the beer factory and the mineral water factory), in banks and local businesses, or in branches of the county government. The third school was on the fringes of the county seat. As the county seat has expanded, new villages have been swallowed up every year, and many of the people whose children attended this school had either recently lost their agricultural land or lived in villages that might one day lose their land.[8] This part of the city was also adjacent to the new industrial zone (*kaifa qu*), where dozens of factories had established themselves since 2002. These factories brimmed with migrant workers from both inside the county and farther afield. While most of these workers were too young to have a child in sixth grade at the time of my research, the school was planning for a future increase of migrant worker children, and there were already eight children from migrant worker families in the class that I attended.[9] Some of the newly landless, suburban villagers made their living by running rental houses for the migrant workers. Other suburban village households whose children attended this school had opened small businesses that served the migrant worker population, while still others worked in construction or ran small subcontracting businesses to help build the physical infrastructure of the rapidly expanding county seat.

Organization of the Book

Without confining myself to a relatively small spatial framework, I could not have observed the intensity of the desire for educational attainment in the manner that I did. But the local here cannot be considered merely an artifact of my research. As a site, Zouping County was marked as local by Chinese processes of governing long before I arrived. The educational bureaucracies, schools, teachers, parents, and students all worked for and had their household registrations at levels of government (county, township, and village) that are considered to be local or grassroots (*difang, caogen*) in common Chinese political parlance.

The "local" thus becomes the starting point for my explication of educational desire in this book. That my imagination of the cultural dynamics of governing came together in a particular locality, however, does not imply that I imagined that these dynamics had nothing to do with wider processes. After a description of local processes of governing (chapter 2), the rest of the book progresses to three overlapping, wider perspectives on processes of governing. I call these perspectives "encompassing the local" (chapter 3), "historicizing the local" (chapter 4), and "the universal in the local" (chapter 5).

I derive the concept of encompassing the local from Benedict Anderson's famous book *Imagined Communities* (1991). In it, Anderson describes the contrast between ancient empires and modern nation-states as one between exemplary centers and geographically bounded communities (9–36), a theme that had earlier been explored by anthropologists like Clifford Geertz (1980). An exemplary center governs by setting an example that is to be imitated with greater or lesser adherence depending on a given subject's spatiocultural distance from the center. There are no fixed boundaries but rather a gradual fading of influence as one moves away from the center. In contrast, a modern nation-state encompasses its territory by spreading its government evenly throughout its geographic boundaries.

Anderson's discussion of governing through practices of spatial encompassment has been developed further by James Ferguson and Akhil Gupta (2002), who focus on the popular imagination of the state. They argue that

> the state (conceptually fused with the nation) is located within an ever widening series of circles that begins with family and local community and ends with the system of nation-states. This is a profoundly consequential understanding of scale, one in which the locality is encompassed by the region, the region by the nation-state and the nation-state by the international community. (982)

Ferguson and Gupta's image of concentric circles is quite useful to discussions of governing in China. Not only is the state organized in terms of such concentric circles (village, township, county, and so on), but Chinese concepts of personhood and social belonging have also been theorized within China in terms of such concentric circles. China's most famous anthropologist, Fei Xiaotong (1992:65), used the image of the ripples that form after a stone is thrown into a lake to depict how Chinese people traditionally conceived and created human relationships. He argued that the egocentric networks of relationships thus formed were at the heart of everyday moral reasoning. The overlap here between the structures of contemporary government and cultural models of relatedness, personhood, and moral reasoning suggests a historically deep circulation of governing ideals and practices among governing agents located in many sites of China's governing hierarchy.

Chapter 3 (encompassing the local) examines the manner in which higher levels of government, namely, the national and provincial governments, enact and attempt to enforce policies that structure patterns of educational desire across the territories that they govern. It further examines popular and local government reactions to such policies, the governing dynamics that emerge, and the reasons underlying the relative success and failure of different policies in achieving their stated goals. Unlike Anderson, I do not wish to contrast encompassing and exemplary processes of governing to differentiate the modern from the premodern. In China, there were encompassing processes of governing long before the contemporary period, and exemplary practices of governing still matter. But chapter 3 focuses primarily on encompassing practices in the contemporary period. Past encompassing practices of governing and present exemplary ones are explored in other chapters.

Chapter 3 thus contextualizes educational desire in Zouping primarily vis-à-vis the national Chinese scene. In contrast, chapter 4 (historicizing the local) examines governing practices that traverse the East Asian region. How can it be that strong dynamics of educational desire map so well onto people who were once governed in a "Confucian" fashion?[10] In chapter 4, I examine contemporary governing practices that have clear echoes in the history of the examination systems of late imperial China. The range of practices examined in this chapter include the pedagogical practices of teachers as well as meritocratic ideologies enunciated by states, with examples that can be considered exemplary as well as encompassing. The chapter is explicitly comparative, drawing comparisons between governing practices observed in Zouping and those observed elsewhere in East Asia.

I call the final substantive chapter of this book "The Universal in the Local," after a discussion of "global assemblages" by Stephen Collier and Aihwa Ong (2005) and assemblages of governing by Dean and Hindess (1998). Collier and Ong begin with a formulation from Anthony Giddens:

> Universal refers to phenomena whose significance and validity are not dependent on the 'props' of a 'culture' or a 'society.' They are rather, to repeat Giddens' phrase . . . "based on impersonal principles, which can be set out and developed without regard to context." (10)

Collier and Ong illustrate their conception of the universal with Max Weber's discussion of economic rationalism. On the one hand, Weber traces the growth of economic rationalism from a particular Protestant cultural background. On the other hand, Weberian social scientists describe how quickly it can spread to a wide variety of cultural contexts in which Protestantism does not exist. Universal phenomena "have a distinctive capacity for decontextualization and recontextualization, abstractability and movement, across diverse social and cultural situations and spheres of life" (Collier and Ong 2005:11).

Dipesh Chakrabarty's (2000) interpretation of Marx enriches Collier and Ong's conception of the relationship between the universal and the culturally contextualized. Chakrabarty writes that " 'Abstract labor' gave Marx a way of explaining how the capitalist mode of production managed to extract from peoples and histories that were all different a homogenous and common unit for measuring human activity" (50). But Chakrabarty goes a step further by insisting that the processes of drawing equivalences between various sources of labor always involves the concrete cultural work of translation. The process of decontextualizing and recontextualizing commodity exchange does not just happen but requires considerable effort and attention to local cultural contexts by a host of managers, human resource specialists, and so on.

Though valuable as a starting point, the works of Collier and Ong and Chakrabarty can be read as more "diffusionist" than is the notion of the universal that I wish to develop here. An old debate in anthropology pitted "diffusion" against "independent invention" as forms of explanation for similarities across cultural areas. "Diffusion" implied that a given cultural trait was invented in a single place and gradually diffused to other areas through travel, trade, warfare, marriage, and other forms of human interaction. "Independent invention" argued that peoples in separated cultural territories came up with nearly identical solutions when faced with similar problems. In discussing the universal in the local, I include processes of both independent invention and diffusion. Just as "economic rationality" may have independently developed in different cultural traditions (arguably in Chinese as well as Protestant contexts, if not elsewhere; see, for example, Gates 1996), so has educational desire arisen in other places. In chapter 5, I consider both how the dynamics of educational desire have spread out from their original East Asian contexts and how governing dynamics similar to those in contemporary Zouping have existed in times and places with no direct historical relationship to Zouping.

The three wider perspectives on governing—encompassing the local, historicizing the local, and the universal in the local—are in no sense mutually exclusive. It is possible for a single practice of governing to be simultaneously an encompassing practice of the contemporary Chinese state, historically related to earlier, imperial processes of governing, and a potentially universal, de- and recontextualizable, translatable practice. The different chapters are thus different perspectives on governing practices of emplacement rather than mutually exclusive categories of governing practices.

The Ethical Conundrums of Writing Culture

My focus on the relationships among cultural dynamics, governing practices, and dynamics of emplacement is in part meant to address the reluctance of some anthropologists to seriously grapple with the problem of place-related cultural dynamics. Anthropologists are much more likely to describe governing processes in China as deriving from Western processes such as neoliberalism than as having origins in either Confucian or even Chinese Marxist visions.[11] Educational sociologists likewise posit a singular Western origin for the "world culture" of education (Meyer and Ramirez 2003; Ramirez 2003). Most anthropologists, at least, would probably accept the argument that governing in China is necessarily a mix of the imported and the indigenous, the modern and the traditional, but the terms in which this mix is theorized too often elide the role and importance of indigenous traditions in contemporary dynamics of governing.

In part, the emphasis on the Western and the modern is a reaction to the critiques of the culture concept that compelled Fischer to offer the new

definition of the concept quoted above. Especially important has been
Edward Said's (1978) concept of "orientalism." Debates about orientalism have spread so widely that a tight definition is difficult, but the term
generally suggests the abuse of ascriptions of particular forms of mental,
physical, or social characteristics to groups of people (particularly those
who have experienced colonial domination) for the implicit purpose of
defining oneself in opposing fashion or ostracizing those people. By suggesting that people from Shandong or East Asia are involved in social
dynamics that encourage high levels of educational desire, am I not making an ascription that could be called orientalist? At issue are not so much
my personal intentions as the proclivities of the wider audience among
whom my writings might circulate. Thus, the fact that the stereotype of
Asian Americans as a "model minority" circulates widely in the United
States and links to images of Chinese educational desire makes my topic
even more risky.[12]

To reduce this danger, I have tried to write about the topic in a way
that disrupts the stereotypes. The focus on governing, on specific forms
of conducting conduct and their waxing and waning over time and space,
provides a context for understanding educational desire. That I depict the
social forces that promote the governing of educational desire as universalizable and local in addition to being Chinese and East Asian demonstrates how high levels of educational desire can arise among people who
are not East Asian. I accept the risk that remains because I believe that
a refusal to consider the impact of the emplacement of these governing
dynamics both within China and among East Asian populations is just
as problematic as exploring the issue. To imagine that national traditions
of governing have no effect on national cultural dynamics is to echo the
neoliberal refrains that governing has no impact, that there is no such thing
as "society," and that human action can be explained only in terms of economically rational individuals, or at least that such a state of affairs is the
teleological endpoint of human history. In contrast, in the spirit of Philip
Corrigan and Derek Sayer's (1985) work on nation building as "cultural
revolution," I see state formation and cultural change as interlinked and,
at least in part, as processes that localize culture and generate geographically visible patterns of difference.

Anthropology has much to gain from a renewed interest in national
cultures. Such an interest cannot begin from the nationalist presupposi-
tion that a given national culture is a timeless and natural entity but rather
must focus on the relationships among governing actions and embodied

forms of culture and subjectivity while acknowledging that national governments are often significant actors. Such an interest cannot be exclusive—national governments are just one type of governing agent. Because many other agents attempt to govern educational desire, patterned variation within and across national boundaries is also significant. Furthermore, not only do the governing actions of nonnational-level governing agents sometimes stymie the efforts of national agents, but there are also social forces that no agent controls (though some attempt to harness), theorized in this book as the universalizable aspects of educational desire. Nonetheless, space must exist for analytic attention to cultural variation at the national level. Charges of "orientalism," critiques of the culture concept, and the abuse of nationalist ideologues have wrongly prevented anthropologists from giving this construct the analytic attention it deserves. Especially in the case of China, a country with a long history of statecraft and governing that is in the midst of a powerful project of nation building, the dynamics of a national governing culture require exploration.

The question of why high levels of educational desire have arisen in Zouping, Shandong, China, and East Asia, and the theoretical intersection of the concepts of culture, governing, and emplacement are meant as mutually illuminating reflective foci. Just as I hope to use these three concepts to understand why educational desire is high in Zouping now, so do I wish to use the topic of educational desire to illustrate why the concepts of culture, governing, and emplacement are an important nexus for thinking about social change and continuity in the contemporary world. Let us begin, then, by examining educational desire as it maps into the local context of Zouping.

CHAPTER TWO

Educational Desire in Local Context

Anthropologists have often criticized the concept of modernity and with justice.[1] In contemporary China, ideologies of modernization (*xiandaihua*) have so permeated the social fabric of society that the desirability of "development" is almost universally accepted. The term "backward" (*luohou*) refers to modernity's opposite and is used in both official and nonofficial contexts to denigrate a huge and endlessly shifting variety of behaviors, people, and ethnic/geographic identities. I have contributed to the chorus of anthropological criticism of ideologies of modernity myself (Kipnis 1995) and do not want to rehash at length what are now commonplace arguments. Rather, I wish to begin from an examination of the social circumstances that make this ideology so easy to accept in places like Zouping. As Joel Kahn (2001) notes, modernity is not just a theory of social scientists or an ideology of political elites but also a lived language of experiencing and debating the world for, perhaps, billions of people.

Like many parts of eastern China, Zouping is undergoing a transition from a place in which the majority of people farm the land and live in villages to one in which the majority work off farm and live in towns and cities, from one in which the majority are semiliterate to one in which over fifteen years of schooling has become the norm, from one in which consumption is extremely limited to one in which it is triumphantly promoted and conspicuously displayed, all in the context of an enforced demographic transition, authoritarian nationalism, and the emergence of nationwide forms of intersubjectivity and institution building, to say nothing of the pervasive ideologies of modernity and development themselves. Over the twenty years that I have been conducting research in Zouping, the county seat has grown from a poor and shabby dirt-road town of 25,000 to a city

FIGURE 3. Map of Zouping County, as displayed in a Zouping primary school. The county seat and other urban areas are darkened; buildings in the background are in the county seat. This image demonstrates the pride the school hopes to inculcate in the children with regard to the "modern" buildings rapidly being built there.

of 250,000 complete with public buses, car dealerships, parks, skyscrapers, swimming pools, libraries, and public squares. While urban poverty is still apparent in some areas, much of the new housing is in apartment complexes that include all the amenities—from broadband internet wiring to air conditioning—that one would expect to find in a first world setting. Planning allows for the city to grow further, to a population of 350,000, by the year 2015. Some of the other towns in the county, most notably Weiqiao, Changshan, and Handian, have grown in size, and as of 2008, about half of the population of the county (approximately 725,000) lived in towns and cities rather than villages.[2]

Over this same period, all Zouping villages have gained paved road links to the county seat (not to mention electricity and running water), making many of them simultaneously suburban commuting areas and farming communities. While adobe housing still exists in some villages, the vast majority of village residents now live in brick homes; quite a few village households own cars or small trucks, and motorbikes are commonplace; televisions and mobile phones are nearly universal.

Until 1995, in terms of economic development, Zouping could have been considered a relatively middling rural county in China. In that year, however, a highway constructed from Jinan, the capital of Shandong Province, to the port city of Qingdao provided Zouping with a direct transportation link to the export markets of South Korea and Japan. This access, along with the growth of the Weiqiao textile factory (now called the Weiqiao Textile Group, the largest cloth producer in the world), has spurred extremely rapid economic growth. In 2005 Zouping was for the first time named one of the hundred most economically developed counties in China (there are roughly two thousand rural counties in China). In 2005 the average annual income for a working adult amounted to approximately US$1,250.00.[3]

Between 1955 and 1995 South Korea made the transition from one of the poorest nations in the world to a first world nation. Zouping County, like much of Shandong Province, is on track to make a similar transition between the years 1985 and 2025. In terms of both time and many statistical indicators, it is already more than halfway through that transition. While I do not presume that Shandong will automatically end up with a standard of living similar to that of South Korea, it is certainly a possible future.

While the speed and visibility of changes to Zouping's infrastructure are a matter of pride for some, and evidence of the value, power, and perhaps even inevitability of "modernity" for the majority, it would be foolhardy to imagine a utopia lacking in discontent. Many who feel left behind by recent growth are vocal, and even among the relatively well-off, nostalgia for a more peaceful, simple, and harmonious past is evident. Moreover, the allure of the modern has not led to a full-scale rejection of all that is categorized as tradition. Traditional music, martial arts, and visual arts are all flourishing. It would not be too much to imagine that Zouping could one day culturally resemble the Japan described by Marilyn Ivy (1995), where the very speed of modernization has generated deep-seated anxiety about the dissolution of national and local identities and, hence, a great interest in cultural traditions.

But what I want to emphasize here is that it should not be surprising that a majority of Zouping residents assume that their children's lives will be radically different from their own, that modernity entails material progress, and that to fall behind means impoverishment. In the context of a book about educational desire, perhaps what matters most is how parents imagine the world that their children will come to inhabit. In Zouping, the importance of educational success in such a world can fit with both dreams of modernity and nostalgia for tradition. Children can be taught traditional arts, moralities, and literatures to prepare for modern lives; educational striving is imagined to exist in both the world of the Mandarins and that of internet entrepreneurs.

By saying that it is reasonable for Zouping residents to think with the categories of modernity and tradition, I wish to suggest the importance of simultaneously taking these categories as ideological and thinking through the problem of historical transitions. Such a dual emphasis raises a problem. If tradition and modernity are taken as ideological categories that can be filled with almost any sort of content, what language should be used to discuss the historical continuities and breaks that relate to a transition from an agricultural to an industrial society? The notion of path dependency provides one useful metaphor. It enables us to imagine how the past influences the present even when past social and cultural forms are not simply rejected or reproduced. To move further down the same path is not to run in place. As a theoretical language, however, path dependency also has its dangers. One must always keep in mind the possibility of changing paths. Even more important, one cannot imagine that Zouping is a singular social whole that is being carried down a singular path (Kipnis 2003a). The paths in Zouping's history are multiple and criss-crossing.

This chapter examines the governing of educational desire in Zouping through a combination of historical and ethnographic data. It depicts the expansion of the education system, the growth of educational infrastructure, and the desires for educational attainment that can be seen as both the cause and the result of the expansion. Without community and government desire for educational attainment, the political will to fund it would not have existed; but the expansion itself has made university attendance at least a possibility for the majority of Zouping residents, feeding popular desires for educational success. Throughout this chapter I try to depict how governing agents—in the education bureaucracy, in the schools (including teachers and the students themselves), and in the community at large—act to express, reinforce, create, and fund educational desires. The governing here is not simply a top-down expression of state will, nor can it be said to render state/society dualisms entirely irrelevant. The resulting process of educational development is one of the most important paths of Zouping's recent history.

Educational Development in Zouping

Recent economic growth has enabled a surprising degree of investment in educational success in Zouping, by county, township, and village governments, by local corporations and by parents and families. But economic growth does not explain everything. If having money is a prerequisite to spending it, the availability of funds does not in itself explain the choice to spend on educational services in particular. Consequently, though this section focuses on educational development during the recent period of economic expansion, I wish to begin with a glance at educational development through a wider historical lens, including periods of both economic expansion and desperation.

Stig Thøgersen's (2002) excellent history of twentieth-century educational expansion in Zouping provides an easy starting point. Thøgersen suggests that while educational historians have recognized that educational development does not directly correlate to economic growth, they too often see it as a nation-building fantasy of ambitious elites. Consequently, political ruptures are imagined as more important to educational development than societal continuities. The case of Zouping, however, does not easily fit such an imagination (Thøgersen 2002:6–7).

Along with the rest of China, Zouping has seen a seemingly shocking series of political ruptures in the twentieth century—the end of the imperial examination system and the fall of the Qing dynasty, an embattled period of Nationalist/warlord rule followed by Japanese colonialism, the establishment of the People's Republic of China and Chinese Communist Party (CCP) rule, the cultural revolution and the post-Mao era of opening to the outside world and economic liberalism. Yet, across all of these ruptures, some surprising continuities of educational development stand out. First is the steady spread of basic education—the wiping out of illiteracy and the establishment of universal access to first six and then nine years of compulsory education. This spread occurred gradually over the bulk of the twentieth century. While progress was quickest during the 1950s and 1970s, significant improvements also came about during the rural reconstruction movement of the early 1930s. The institutional basis for the universalization was laid by the Nationalists even earlier. Except for the strife-ridden periods of Japanese occupation and civil war (1937–48), basic education spread throughout the twentieth century (and even the Japanese attempted to expand primary education) (Thøgersen 2002: 240–43). In January 1995, the education system in Zouping was inspected by a team of provincial cadres, and Zouping was declared to have achieved the "two basics": nine years of compulsory education was available for all (of course, that does not mean all attended, as I will describe below), and illiteracy had been wiped out among those under forty-five years of age (Thøgersen 2002:214). This accomplishment was the result of efforts that stretched across most of the twentieth century.

In addition to the two basics, Zouping's residents have "consistently demanded three things for the education system: schools should provide basic academic skills, especially the ability to read and write; they should promote upward social mobility; and they should contribute to the character formation of the students and teach them how to manage social relationships" (Thøgersen 2002:6).

Partially in reaction to this social desire, "revolutionary" changes in government have not always meant drastic changes to what is taught and how the teaching is conducted. During the late Qing dynasty, the Zouping area had a few traditional academies (*shuyuan*) and numerous arrangements for private teaching (*sishu*). These institutions taught literacy through the Confucian classics. With the end of the imperial examination system, the traditional academies and some of the sites of private teaching became primary schools (*xiaoxuetang*) emphasizing basic literacy and computational skills through many of the same texts (Zouping Gazetteer Office 1992:765–81). Teachers in the new schools were recruited from the ranks of the old private teachers and academies. As everywhere, new teachers were themselves taught by old ones, enabling pedagogical continuities. As late as the 1980s, there were teachers who had begun their education in a Confucian private academy (Thøgersen 2002:19). Moreover, until the late twentieth century, the primary site of employment for the relatively highly educated was as teachers; outside of the gradually expanding education system, there were few employment opportunities for the relatively highly educated in Zouping to apply their skills. In the traditional academies, rote memorization—learning through chanting texts aloud and copying them out—was the primary teaching method, and memorization is still heavily used as a pedagogic technique today. The memorizing of Confucian classics has, in fact, been recently reintroduced to the primary school curriculum.

The relationship of educational success to social advancement has also had its ups and downs, but here again some important continuities emerge. During the Qing dynasty, under the old imperial examinations system, dreams of educational success were tightly tied to dreams of becoming an official. From the beginning of CCP rule to the early 1990s, urban, government jobs were assigned to tertiary graduates. In Zouping, especially during the 1970s and 1980s, a tight relationship existed between graduating from a tertiary or specialized secondary educational institution and advancement in the spatial social hierarchy determined by China's household responsibility system. Government jobs, housing in the county seat, free medical care, better schools for one's children, and urban household registration all came together through guaranteed job assignments arranged upon graduation from a tertiary (or specialized secondary) institution. Many of those who were able to move from one of Zouping's villages to the county seat during this period achieved their geographic/social mobility through educational success. Though the job assignment system ended in the early 1990s, and the value of a specialized secondary diploma has eroded, a tertiary diploma still enhances one's chances of securing a government job. Ironically, however, though the desire for educational success seems to have continued to expand, the relative value of a tertiary diploma is perhaps lower than it has ever been—not only because of an inflation in educational credentials, but also because the strong expansion of the Zouping economy has meant that there are now many routes for rural youth to get urban jobs. Moreover, many blue-collar jobs pay even more than the government jobs that used to be the target of desires for social advancement in the late twentieth century. Nevertheless, at least at an imaginary level, the link between educational and career success remains tight.[4]

The official recognition of having achieved the two basics in 1995 has hardly meant the end of the expansion of Zouping's education system. Since 1995, the county education bureau has focused on universalizing three years of preschool and three years of senior middle school education (as of 2005 bringing the total number of years of schooling to a minimum of fifteen for nearly 90 percent of Zouping youth), building spectacular new schools with facilities that rival those of the best private schools in first world nations, increasing teacher training and pay for teachers and centralizing control of the county's education system as a whole.

Let me begin with teachers. The universalization of primary school in Zouping was in part accomplished by relying on villages to finance most of the cost of their own schools. The county government would chip in by supplying some teachers who were on the county payroll. But villages themselves were responsible for both school facilities and the salaries of the remaining teachers. This led to a disparity between state-salaried and "people-sponsored" (*minban*) teachers. Not only were people-sponsored teachers paid less than state-salaried teachers, but they also usually lacked formal credentials and pedagogical training. Villages usually hired their own high school graduates who had failed to test into a tertiary or specialized secondary institution. As the county government grew wealthier, it worked to put a higher proportion of teachers on state salaries. Throughout the reform period, people-sponsored teachers who were judged to be effective were given specialized short courses in pedagogy and promoted, while the rest were retired to make way for the growing numbers of local normal school graduates. In 1978 two-thirds of Zouping primary school teachers and half of the middle school teachers were people sponsored. By 1986, half of all teachers were state sponsored (Thøgersen 2002:219). In the 1990s, the pace of replacing people-sponsored teachers accelerated. A ban on hiring new ones was enacted in 1993, and fewer than 10 percent of all teachers were people sponsored in 1999. By 2003, no people-sponsored teachers were left in Zouping.

Teacher salaries have also continued to rise. When I first visited Zouping in 1988, state-sponsored primary school teachers made roughly 150 yuan per month. In 2006, even new primary school teachers made 1,200 yuan per month, while the most experienced primary teachers made close to 2,000 yuan per month (US$250). In 2006, secondary school teachers were making between 1,700 and 4,000 yuan per month. Since late 2005, all teacher salaries have been paid directly by the county government. In addition, all junior and senior secondary schools and many primary schools in Zouping have built large blocks of modern apartments to sell to their teachers and other employees at subsidized prices. At least since the turn of the century, Zouping has been able to use its relatively high salaries to recruit teachers from poorer parts of the country in a bid to ensure that Zouping has more than its fair share of the best new normal school graduates.[5] Since 2000, the county education bureau has also increased funding opportunities for ongoing teacher training.

The construction of new schools and refurbishment of existing ones has gone hand in hand with centralization of the county education bureau's control through school consolidation. Following national policy guidelines, the county education bureau found the economic logic of large centrally located schools compelling and tied investment in new facilities to the closing of smaller schools. As a consequence, the reduction in the number of schools in Zouping can be taken as a proxy for the improvement in educational infrastructure.[6] At the end of the 1980s, Zouping had over 700 primary schools and 70 junior middle schools distributed in the county seat, 14 smaller towns, and over 600 of the 850 villages in the county's 16 townships (Zouping Gazetteer Office 2004:69). This amounted almost to a primary school in every village and a junior middle school for every 10 primary schools. Only villages within easy walking distance of each other shared a primary school. By 1999, the number of schools had been reduced to 200 complete primaries, 150 partial primaries (schools for grades 1–3), and 30 junior middle schools. In part the reduction of schools reflected a reduction in the student population, brought on by China's birth control policy. During the 1990s, most of the consolidation took place through encouraging wealthier villages to build larger primary schools, which then would school children from the surrounding area. School buses were introduced to carry children from villages that did not have their own primary schools. The fact that the county had by 1995 managed to construct a paved road to every village facilitated the transportation of students. The reduction in the number of junior middle schools has further required turning all junior middle schools outside of the county seat into boarding schools (the senior middle schools were already boarding schools). Junior middle school students generally return home once every two to four weeks, depending on grade level.

In 2000, the scale of consolidation was increased as county and township governments began to take over all the costs of education from the villages. By 2006, the number of schools had been reduced to 63 primary schools (including partial primaries) and 20 junior middle schools. There were plans to close 8 more primary schools in 2007. The junior middle schools were distributed so that each township had only one junior middle school with 5 others (including 2 private junior middle schools) being located in the county seat. These schools taught as many as five hundred students per grade with a total of about fifteen hundred students for the three junior middle grades.

The consolidation of primary schools proceeded most quickly in the poorer, more rural townships. In those places, the county education bureau had the leverage to dictate school funding terms and reduced school numbers to one or two large primary schools per township. These primaries were built from scratch and usually located in the central town of a given township. Such primary schools provide education for students from between twenty and forty villages each. On average, such schools teach fifteen hundred students in six grades. Some of the more wealthy areas of the county retained six or seven primary schools per township, serving approximately five villages each, but only because these townships agreed to fund more of the costs of running the schools themselves; even in these townships, the smaller schools are in process of being phased out.

The model of large, centrally located schools has been applied to the expansion of preschool education as well. Many of the village primary schools had kindergartens attached to them, and during the 1980s and early 1990s the county worked on encouraging at least one noncompulsory year of preschool. But during the mid-1990s the county education bureau decided to work toward universalizing three years of preschool education for children aged 3–6. Because this education is not compulsory, fees are much higher than for public primary schools. For example, in one poorer township in 2005, fees were 60 yuan per month at the public preschool as opposed to 105 yuan per four-month semester in the primary school, and in 2007 school fees for primary schools were waived completely. Fees for some of the private preschools in the county seat can be quite high, surpassing 350 yuan per month in 2006. But despite these costs, parents fear that their children will fall behind if they are not allowed to attend, and preschool enrollment rates increased from 61 percent in 1986 to 94 percent of preschool-aged children in 2006.[7] Especially in the rural townships, preschool education has been expanded by building large preschools in the towns and busing the young children in for the entire day. In Sunzhen township in 2005, for example, there were only three preschools, the largest of which was located in Sunzhen town and enrolled more than nine hundred students from thirty-five villages. The children ate two meals a day there and had a nap at lunchtime. Overall, the number of preschools dropped from 547 in 1999 to 197 in 2003 (Zouping Gazetteer Office 2004:392–93) to 146 in 2005 and has continued to drop since. Moreover, most of the small preschools are located in the county seat and richer villages. The majority of the county's rural population is now served by large preschools similar to the one in Sunzhen.

The trend toward school consolidation was evident in every county I visited in China and is a nationally promoted policy. The county education bureau argues that consolidating schools allows them to provide a much higher standard of education. They give four reasons for this. First, the large schools are able to afford better equipment. Second, the more centralized schools enable the recruitment of better teachers (teachers preferring to live and work in towns rather than villages). Third, the centralization of schooling enables a more standardized approach to teaching. Finally, centralized schooling makes it easier to manage the students.

There is both truth and implied elitism in these claims. In the large schools, teachers specialize more, teaching only one subject to one or two grade levels, which makes them more competent in their subjects and gives them more time to devote to lesson plans. But there is also an elitist presumption that by taking rural children out of their "peasant" homes for the entire day for preschool and primary school students, and placing them in boarding schools for middle school students, the children will be more competitive with urban children on exams and become more "civilized" than they would with a purely village upbringing (see also Murphy 2004). If one accepts that learning to speak more standard Mandarin and learning a standardized curriculum make one more "civilized," then both claims are probably true. But along with the good intentions and educational successes institutionalized in Zouping schools, hints of antirural prejudice emerge. More than once, primary school teachers in rural schools pointed out to me the dirt under their students' fingernails, offering this dirt as proof of a general lack of home hygiene. Principals of rural schools also emphasize the need to standardize (*guifanhua*) student behavior and teach them good habits (*haoxiguan*). For such principals, the civilizing mission in Chinese schools today is a matter of the installation of a national culture that includes speaking standardized Mandarin, writing proper Chinese characters, and practicing good study habits, proper hygiene, proper posture at the desk, and proper forms of politeness in student-teacher and student-student interaction.

Educational Financing and Facilities

That the large consolidated schools provide better facilities is undeniable. Yet uneven financing has led to some inequality in facilities. Over the past decade, township governments have been the primary funders for building primary and junior middle schools in the rural areas of the county. Where these governments have lacked significant revenues from industrial taxes, they have built the schools by borrowing money, and it is difficult to say whether the lending institutions will ever see a return (Kipnis and Li 2010). In the county seat, money for school building has come from the county government, a few large industries (most notably the Weiqiao Textile Group), and, in some cases, borrowing money. But despite the need to borrow money, even in the poorer townships the new primary schools house large computer labs, language labs, halls with movie projectors and stages for showing movies and putting on rituals and performances, musical equipment for a school band, tracks for athletic competitions, basketball, ping-pong and volleyball courts, and computer networks that give every teacher in a given school access to a personal computer and the

FIGURE 4. Traditional Chinese zithers (*guzheng*) in a Zouping primary school. Photograph by the author.

Zouping County education intranet. These facilities were roughly equivalent to those of the good public primary school my own son attended in Canberra, Australia.

In the two large new primary schools in the county seat, facilities were truly spectacular. In addition to the equipment described above for the rural primary schools, there were also separate rooms for Chinese chess, Western chess, and Go (*weiqi*) (one room for each game with 35 wood carved game sets distributed on tables in each room), specialized rooms for art and calligraphy, separate music classrooms with pianos and other instruments, an indoor sports hall complete with such specialized equipment as automatic ping-pong ball servers, rooms with equipment for cooking and woodwork for practical classes (not used at this point), separate science labs for physics and chemistry with all of the equipment necessary to do the electrical and chemical experiments now done only in middle school (just in case Chinese students progress to the point where primary-aged children do what is now expected of junior middle school students), a large cafeteria (presently used only by a minority of students, as most

FIGURE 5. Chemistry lab in a Zouping primary school. Photograph by the author.

county seat students return home for lunch), as well as setups for multi-media equipment in every classroom. Notably, these schools were built with funding by the Weiqiao Textile Group for the children of their workers and for the children of the suburban villagers whose land was taken over by the new factories, that is to say, *not* for the children of Zouping's governing elite. The facilities at these schools rival those at the most elite private schools in the West.

The history of academic senior middle schools in Zouping, like that of the lower-level schools, is marked by an expansion in the availability of places and an increase in the quality of the physical equipment alongside a reduction in the number of schools. Senior middle schools have always been centralized institutions in Zouping, located in the county seat and largest towns and financed primarily by the county government. In 1998 there were five senior middle schools with enough spaces for 5,000 students, slightly less than a quarter of the senior-middle-school-aged population. Another 2,000 attended vocational middle school. But beginning in 1999 the county government began to expand access to senior middle school education rapidly. It first expanded the facilities at two of the existing schools so that by 2003 there were spaces for more than 13,000 students (Zouping Gazetteer Office 2004:394). In 2005, it built a new campus for the number one senior middle school with a capacity for more than 8,000 students. At the same time it closed one of the other academic senior middle schools. As of 2006 there were two elite senior middle schools (the number one middle school and Huang Shan middle school, both located in the county seat) and two other senior middle schools, as well as a vocational school. The number one senior middle school had roughly 7,000 students, the Huang Shan middle school roughly 5,300; the other two academic middle schools had a total of roughly 3,500 students and were operating well below capacity. There were plans to shut them down once the senior-middle-school-aged population had dwindled (because of the birth control policy) to the point that there were enough spaces to satisfy demand at the two elite schools. In addition, the vocational school enrolled roughly 4,000 senior-middle-school-aged students, though it was becoming a last resort, used only by those who had no hope of reaching college. In all, according to cadres in the county education bureau, in 2006 over 90 percent of the Zouping senior-middle-school-aged population was attending some form of senior middle school.

FIGURE 6. Library in a Zouping primary school. Photograph by the author.

TABLE 1. **Structure of Schooling in Zouping, 2006**

School Level	No. of years	Student Age	Compulsory	Fees	No. attending (percent)
Preschool	3	3–5	No	High	90+
Primary	6	6–12	Yes	Low	99
Junior Middle	3	13–15	Yes	Low	95
Senior Middle	3	16–18	No	Moderate-High	90
Tertiary Short-Course	2–3	19–21	No	High	35
Tertiary Undergraduate	4	19–22	No	Extremely High	30
Tertiary Total					65

Note—This is a rough table. Especially at the tertiary level, fees can vary considerably. For senior middle school, fees vary with test scores. Approximately 80 percent of children attended academic senior middle schools. Others attended vocational senior middle school. Fee levels reflect the perception of the majority of people I spoke with, though of course some people had different perceptions. The percentage of children attending tertiary schooling has been increasing rapidly every year. The percentages reported here for tertiary attendance are based on the age cohort that graduated from senior middle school in 2005.

The facilities at the two elite academic middle schools are also impressive. Especially eye-catching is the new number one middle school, which had a campus built from scratch in the new section of town between 2002 and 2005, at a cost of 230 million yuan. Again, much of the money was borrowed, but in this case there is a concrete plan to repay the loan. Money for repayments is being earned through a private junior middle school opened on the site of the old campus (called the "old number one junior middle school," to be discussed below) and by charging high fees to students who come to the new number one senior middle school from outside the county or who are from the county but score below a cutoff on the senior middle school entrance exam. The campus of the number one middle school resembles that of a small university. In addition to an outdoor track and pristine athletics fields, there is a huge indoor athletic complex with an Olympic-size pool, an indoor track, and equipment for gymnastics, basketball, and various other sports. As one would expect, there are high-quality language labs, science labs, computer labs, libraries, art and music buildings, and all manner of specialized equipment. The entire campus is networked, and all classrooms are equipped with multimedia projectors. The greens and gardens between the classrooms are immaculate. The southern part of the campus is the living area for students and includes dormitory space for eight thousand students, as well as cafeterias, stores, clinics for sick students, and pharmacies. Overall, there are only two areas in which conditions are noticeably worse than those at the most elite of Western private schools. First is class size. On average there are close to sixty students per class at Zouping senior middle schools (and almost that many at the junior middle and primary schools). Second, in the dorm rooms students sleep eight to the room. These two conditions undoubtedly reflect concessions to budgetary pressure. But the willingness to economize here and not elsewhere reveals a tendency to consider immersion in relatively large groups a normal circumstance for young people, as well as an emphasis on mass-produced standardization in the educational culture.

The Chinese government, especially the central government, has often been criticized for underspending on education. Such accusations are reproduced both in articles on critical websites within China and by some teachers and parents in Zouping.[8] Certainly, school funding has been mostly a matter for local governments in China, and very often the various levels of government deflect responsibilities to those below them. The burden of funding what the county does not fund is placed on the townships, the burden of funding what the townships do not fund is placed

FIGURE 7. Central office building of the new Number One Senior Middle School. On top of the building is the school's motto, "Be the First to Worry and the Last to be Happy," taken from a famous essay by the Song dynasty scholar Fan Zhongyan. Photograph by the author.

on the villages, and the burden of funding what the villages cannot fund is placed on individual households. How can the truth of this criticism be squared with the history of educational development in Zouping? Two trends stand out. First, though the higher levels of government can be said to have underspent on education, very often rural households and lower levels of government have picked up the slack. Second, over time, as its own tax revenues have increased, the county government (the highest level in Zouping) has picked up more and more of the spending burden.

A few of the discussions I had with parents and teachers can help illustrate these facts. One rural man from a relatively poor township, a fruit and vegetable vendor who was extremely knowledgeable about market prices for all types of food in this area, complained to me about the prices being charged for school lunches at his son's primary school. As these lunches cost about 1.2 yuan per day (depending on how many pieces of steam bread a given student consumed), I initially did not think the school could make much money, but this man went over the costs with me in great detail and concluded that the school was making about 0.1 yuan profit per lunch (per student, per day). Over the course of the year, he figured that he was paying an extra 20 yuan per year for his son's lunches. With approximately eight hundred students attending this school, that amounted to an income of 16,000 yuan for the school. He added that in the past, the schools had charged various fees to parents whenever they needed money, and that in the past such fees would have amounted to much more than 20 yuan a year. He did not consider 20 yuan per year to be excessive but was disappointed by the underhanded way in which the school was making this money. Later the school's principal confirmed this man's allegation. The principal explained that the county had recently taken over paying the salaries for all personnel at the school and that the township government had stretched its budget to build the school and purchase all of the equipment, but that neither the county nor the township gave the school an adequate budget for operating expenses, of which electricity and other utilities were the most expensive. In the past he would have levied the parents a water and electricity fee, but as a ban on charging school fees had been enacted, he had no choice but to try and make it up through the school lunches.

The rapidly evolving practices of school financing in places like Zouping can also be seen in the funding of teacher salaries. A junior middle teacher from another relatively poor township described how until 2005, she had been paid less than half of the salary of similarly ranked teachers in the county seat. Then, the county government announced that it would fund teacher salaries from the county coffers rather than requiring each township to pay (and separately set) its own salaries. In 2006 she made slightly more than her colleagues in the county seat as the county has decided to offer slightly higher salaries to the teachers who teach in the more rural schools. She added, however, that her colleagues in the neighboring county were paid not even half of what she made and that their salaries were still paid by the township governments. The consolidation of primary schools also illustrates the gradual centralization of school funding in Zouping. In the 1980s, when most villages had their own primary schools, primary school funding came primarily from the villages themselves. Richer villages naturally had better schools than poorer ones. The early stages of consolidation were achieved by the county and township governments by offering richer villages a deal in which they could retain a school in their village if they agreed to accept students from many surrounding villages and to pay for the upkeep of the school building only. The final phases of school consolidation have been achieved by removing both the primary schools themselves and the burden for funding them from the villages altogether.

The continued willingness of rural households to spend on education is perhaps best illustrated by the attitudes of Zouping parents toward university tuition. University tuition in China has skyrocketed over the late 1990s and early twenty-first century, in 2006 reaching a point where most Zouping households with a child in college were paying between 11,000 and 15,000 yuan per year for tuition, room, and board. This amount is more than the average annual income of a working adult in Zouping (roughly 10,000 yuan). Despite this fact, Zouping education cadres insisted to me that every Zouping child who had succeeded on the university entrance exams was now attending university. Though some poorer students may have limited themselves to less expensive universities and courses, like agriculture, forestry, and education, all had, by one way or another, managed to pay the tuition. I was initially quite skeptical of this claim but became more convinced as I conducted household interviews in rural townships. All the parents I spoke with said that they would attempt to find a way to pay for their child to attend college if he or she were able to succeed on the university entrance exam. I further found that university education had replaced house building as the most important large-ticket expenditure for many rural families. During the 1980s, providing a house for a son was a financial prerequisite for the son's marriage. Zouping brides rarely consented to a marriage to a rural man whose family could not build the new couple an independent house (Kipnis 1997:84–90). Now, however, the hope of most parents is that their son will not live in the village after he grows up. Rather, the hope is that university education will enable him to find a job, housing, and bride in an urban setting. I visited many rural households with a child in college who were living in dilapidated old houses that seemed well below their means. When I asked if they were building a new house, the parents of these households replied that their strategy was to save everything for their children's education and that they would build a small new house (for their old age) once their children had completed college.

Some parents need to borrow from relatives to finance their children's education, but, fortunately for these parents, many consider financing the education of a niece or nephew an honorable and worthwhile investment. One man bragged to me how he was financing the education of two of his nephews (he had two younger sisters, each of whom had a son). He ran a successful pig-raising business in which his own adult son also worked. He said, "My son didn't get the chance to go to college and now has a good job with me. I am very proud to be involved in the education of my nephews [*waisheng*].[9] If they can get a good job in the city it will be good for the entire family." The county education officials had similarly argued that financing the university education of an impoverished but talented student was considered so glorious that there was always someone willing to give support.

In short, the previous underspending on education by higher levels of government should not be taken either as a permanent situation or as an indication of an overall lack of willingness to invest in education. One way or another, spending on education in Zouping has been high and steadily expanding over the past decades. A lack of centrally funded educational budgets has, however, led to inequalities of educational access in the recent past, and I can only applaud the recent trend toward more centralized educational funding in Zouping. This trend may well be national in scope, as will be discussed further in the next chapter.

Educational Glory

The willingness to help pay the university tuition of impoverished but talented students is just one indication of the glory attached to educational success in Zouping. Village gossip spreads news about the educational successes and failures of village children, to the delight and chagrin of their parents. I was often surprised at the ability of parents to tell me which children in their villages and extended families were attending or had attended college as well as which colleges they had attended. Such knowledge was most obvious amongst relatively well-educated villagers. But I met several adults who themselves had only a primary school education and were still well versed in such matters.

Zouping students who are admitted to famous universities or win scholarships are the focus of considerable media attention. Stories about them complete with pictures of family members and interviews are broadcasted on the news programs of local (county and prefectural) television stations and written up in local newspapers. Such students also have their pictures displayed prominently in the government display cases located at the center of the busiest shopping district in the county seat. They are also glorified by their high schools, who write of the accomplishments of their best students in all of their own promotional materials. While I was conducting interviews in one of the poorest villages in Zouping, two illiterate grandparents told me the name of a Zouping graduate from another part of the county who had won admission to Qinghua University—the most famous university for sciences in China.

Senior middle school teachers are likewise glorified if they are particularly successful in getting their students to do well on the university entrance exams. Usually senior middle school teachers are assigned to follow a particular class during its three-year journey through senior middle school. Class groupings of students stay together for the full three years, and a particular math teacher, for example, might teach mathematics in grades ten, eleven, and twelve to two or three classes of sixty students. In this manner a teacher's effectiveness is fully on display. If most members of that class do well on the mathematics section of the university entrance exam, then that math teacher will be rewarded. If a given teacher has an exceptional proportion of his or her students reach college, then his or her name, picture, and accomplishments will likewise be publicized on television, in newspapers, and in the government display cases in the center of town.

Such forms of lionizing educational success have a relatively long history in Zouping and are memorialized as official history. The two most famous and celebrated historical figures in Zouping are Fan Zhongyan, a Song dynasty scholar official whose statue stands prominently in one of Zouping's first parks, and Liang Shuming, a famous scholar and 1930s rural reformer whose grave forms a monument in the Yellow Mountain

Reserve in the middle of the city. A quotation from Fan, "Worry before anyone else worries; be happy after everyone else is happy," forms the official motto of the number one senior middle school. High school students interpreted these words for me as suggesting that one must place the affairs of the nation before one's own happiness and, in joking tones, that happiness will come only to those who first worry about their studies. Liang actually placed educational development at the center of his rural reform program, founded the number one senior middle school, and educated many of the generation of Zouping rural teachers who were active through the 1970s (Thøgersen 2002:1–4).

Yet the worship of educational success is neither a timeless quantity nor without opposition. Many have argued that Maoism was inherently anti-intellectual and that Maoist governance in the villages promoted an anti-intellectual culture and anti-intellectual leaders (e.g., Edward Friedman et al. 1991). After my first field trip to Zouping in the late 1980s, I described an anti-intellectual "peasant subculture" among some Zouping villagers (Kipnis 1995). Such villagers tended to scoff at the value of book learning and take pride in their village identities, which in some sense were related to school failure as the successful minority would end up moving out of the villages. But at that time there was both a thriving agricultural and village enterprise economy (at least in some parts of the county) and a much less well-established school system. During the 1980s, only a minority of students made it to senior middle school, and many were not even able to attend junior middle school. The success of some village economies and the difficulty of leaving the village through educational success forced and allowed many young people and their families to imagine intergenerational futures in the villages. In more recent visits to Zouping, however, I found little evidence of such an imagination, at least among the parents of primary school students. Among these parents, as described in the introduction, the dream of having their child attend college was universal. In 2005, the only time I heard anti-intellectual sentiments expressed was when speaking to people who had dropped out of junior middle school, and even among them it seemed muted. While dreams of intellectual success and anti-intellectualism may necessarily be paired cultural phenomena, in Zouping the former has gained steadily at the expense of the latter over the past two decades.[10]

This change in popular attitudes is perhaps best reflected in the evolution of the terms of address used for adult strangers. In Zouping, Shandong Province, and many other parts of China, "teacher" (*laoshi*) has become the preferred form of address for people one does not recognize, especially when asking for assistance from a stranger on the street or in a store. During the 1980s, the term "master" (*shifu*) had replaced "comrade" (*tongzhi*) for this purpose. This shift indicated a move away from the centrality of pursuing a communist future as a basis for social solidarity. Yet "master" still retained a certain working-class value structure as the term denotes a person with practical skills, such as a skilled worker in a factory, a plumber or electrician, or a martial arts instructor. But during the first years of the twenty-first century, "master's" connotations of a person without formal educational credentials have become a liability. "Teacher" implies not only that the person one is addressing is a kindhearted superior who is obliged to help (as does the term master) but also that this person has graduated from a tertiary institution. Now "master" is used only if the person one is addressing obviously embodies a working-class persona. One could argue that the entire social history of communist China is summed up by the comrade, master, teacher series (see Gold 1985; Kipnis 1997:159–60; Vogel 1965). But here it should suffice to note how this change in terms of address indicates a respect for educational success that, though not necessarily universal, has been popularly accepted as a general principle for public social interaction.

Educational Intensity

The glory attaching to educational success in Zouping feeds the intensity of the competition at Zouping schools. Since 1999, the number of students who have been able to attend college in Zouping, Shandong Province, and China as a whole has increased dramatically. This enlargement of the pool of students who have at least a moderate chance of reaching university has increased both the absolute number and the percentage of young people who participate vigorously in the intense culture of academic competition at Zouping's middle schools. In 1979 approximately 100 senior middle school graduates from Zouping made it into some form of tertiary education. In 1989, nearly 300 senior middle school graduates did so. In 1999 there were roughly 1,600 graduates from academic middle schools, and about 30 percent of these (470) did well enough on the university entrance exam to gain admittance to a regular university (*benke*), while another 45 percent (719) did well enough to enter a tertiary short course (*zhuanke*). In 2004, out of 5,000 students who graduated from academic middle schools, nearly 40 percent (1,977) did well enough on the university entrance exam to enter a regular university, and another 45 percent (2,502) did well enough to gain admittance to a tertiary short course. In short, not only has academic senior middle school become relatively easy to attend (with over 80 percent of a given year's age cohort choosing to attend), but university enrollments have expanded at an even more rapid pace, allowing an even higher percentage of senior middle school graduates to gain admittance to a tertiary institution.

That a higher percentage of students have gained admittance to tertiary institutions, however, has not meant a reduction in the intensity of study discipline at Zouping middle schools. In fact, the intensity of the discipline seems only to have increased over the past decade. This intensity allows Zouping to outpace most other places in the province in university admittance. In 2005, Zouping was the top county in Binzhou Prefecture in terms of the percentage of the age cohort that gained admittance to a tertiary institution. The intensity is the result of purposeful governing strategies on the part of the educational bureaucracy, and this success allows Zouping's number one middle school to attract full fee-paying students from outside the county. The income from these students has been used to repay the loans taken out to build the new campus of the number one senior middle school.

All of Zouping senior middle schools and all of the junior middle schools located in the rural townships are boarding schools. In 2005, students at senior middle schools were allowed to visit home on one Sunday a month only, and even this privilege was curtailed for twelfth-grade students during the last four months before exams. At junior middle schools, ninth-grade students were allowed to return home one Sunday a month, eighth-grade students one Sunday every three weeks, and seventh-grade students two Sundays per month. The boarding school environment allows the educational authorities to subject the students to boot-camp-like schedules. At senior middle schools, students were awoken at 6:00 a.m. and scheduled into classes, study halls, and other mandatory activities until lights out after 10:00 p.m. For junior middle schools, the schedules were much the same, with the exception that lights out comes one hour earlier. In 1999, these schedules were followed for six days a week, as students were allowed to return home on Sundays every week, but by 2005 the schedules were enacted for seven-day weeks, with students returning home only as described above. Below is the summer season schedule for one junior middle school in 2005.

6:00 a.m.: out of bed; 10 minutes for dressing and toilet

6:10–6:30: morning chore; all students assigned a communal cleaning chore, such as cleaning particular halls or bathrooms; students from a single dorm room share a chore

6:30–7:00: breakfast

7:00–7:05: prepare for class; students must be seated at their desks and quiet, focusing their minds on the upcoming morning read

7:05–7:30: morning reading period; students memorize (by chanting aloud) a text assigned by either their Chinese or their English teacher

7:40–8:25: class period 1; students generally stay in the same classroom all day, while the teachers rotate in and out; students talk freely to each other during the ten minutes between classes; one minute before the next period is to begin, a bell rings and students return to their desks and become quiet

8:35–9:20: class period 2

9:20–9:50: between class exercise; students go down to the schoolyard, line up in evenly spaced rows and columns, and do exercises, in unison, to a broadcasted recording that is the same every day; in 1999, these were military drills, but in 2006 they switched to an aerobics dance routine that was done to an up-tempo version of the American folksong "Oh, Susanna"

9:50–10:35: class period 3

10:45–11:30: class period 4

11:30–12:15: lunch

12:15–13:40: rest; many Zouping residents customarily take a short nap after lunch during the summer; students must be on their beds and quiet, but they can read instead of sleeping if they wish

13:50–14:00: prepare for class, at desks and quiet, focusing mind on upcoming class

14:00–14:45: class period 5

14:45–15:00: eye exercises; the intensity of study at Chinese schools leads to problems with nearsightedness for a large number of students; the national educational bureaucracy has designed an eye exercise routine to help with this problem; the routine involves massaging the areas around the eyes while the eyes are closed; the students do these exercises at their desks; as with the morning exercises, these exercises are done in unison, to a pre-recorded broadcast that is the same every day

15:00–15:45: class period 6

15:55–16:40: class period 7

16:40–17:20: activity period; some form of sport, music, or artistic activity done under the supervision and direction of teachers

17:20–18:00: dinner

18:10–18:30: evening discussion; students return to desks and meet with their head teacher and discuss either a news story or issues arising in school life; often this "discussion" is little more than a series of announcements by the teacher or a lecture on how the students should focus and study harder

18:30–19:15: study hall 1; students do homework quietly at their desks

19:25–20:10: study hall 2

20:20–21:15: study hall 3

21:40: lights out

The senior middle school schedule is much the same except that there is a fourth study hall in the evening (and a correspondingly later lights out), and the afternoon "activity period" is often also replaced by a study hall. During the winter, there is no noontime rest, but time is allotted for an equivalent amount of rest by changing the wake-up and lights-out times and adjusting the rest of the schedule accordingly.

The boot-camp-like study discipline at these schools makes them attractive to some parents in China's larger urban areas. Urban high schools in large cities are almost always day schools and are unable to match the discipline of the boarding schools that exist in almost every county seat. Consequently, just as some Western parents send their children to Catholic schools or military academies for the discipline, Chinese urban parents concerned with study discipline sometimes pay hefty out-of-district fees to send their children out of the city to attend public boarding high schools in county seats like Zouping. While there are also Zouping students who move to larger cities to attend private schools, more out-of-district students come to Zouping to attend middle school than the other way around, reversing the stereotype of rural schools as schools that no urban Chinese parent would want his or her child to attend.

I often made myself available to students at middle schools to either practice their oral English or ask questions about Australian life. On such occasions I was usually introduced as a professor from Australia interested in Zouping's schools. I was surprised to find that being a "professor" often became more of a focal part of my identity than being a white foreigner. Seeing me as embodying educational success, students were as inclined to ask me for study tips as they were to ask me about life or schools in Australia. One of the more common questions was: "Faced with the dilemma of either getting enough sleep or cutting back on sleep to quietly do extra study during rest periods, which strategy was most likely to lead to better exam results in both the long and the short term?" Thus I discovered that many students continued to study after lights out with flashlights. Though the schools officially discourage the practice, some teachers push their students to do so before key exams. Moreover, every Zouping middle school student I met complained about being tired from the overload of study. Clearly this is a system that pushes students to the edge of what is humanly possible. And the pushing lasts for a full six years in Zouping and even longer in some of the other rural counties I visited in Shandong, where boarding schools began in grade four of primary school rather than in junior middle school.

The pressures for exam success are felt by the teachers as much as the students. The county administers standardized tests twice a year in every subject in every grade so that it can compare both teachers and schools as a whole. To make sure that classes are comparable, in junior middle school they are rearranged each year so that each class has an equal number of students who did well and did poorly on the previous year's tests. Teachers and schools are compared not just on average test scores but also on the rates at which they have allowed "late-developing" students (*houjin-sheng*) to catch up with the rest of the class and the rate at which they have enabled the already successful students to continue to succeed. In senior middle schools, classes of students stay together for three years but are composed of equal numbers of students with relatively high and low scores on the senior middle school entrance exam. Teachers are compared every semester, but bonuses are based on the results in the university entrance exams after three years of teaching a given subject to a particular class. All Zouping teachers have computers that are linked to the county-wide educational intranet. Successful teachers are also offered incentives to put their lesson plans on the intranet, and less successful teachers are encouraged to model their lesson plans after the successful ones. Like their students, teachers are expected to work seven days a week for much of the year. At two of the senior middle schools that I visited, the principal had installed electronic card swipe systems in all teachers' offices, so that the principal could monitor the amount of time teachers spent in their offices. Key teachers at another school were required to carry mobile phones and leave them on twenty-four hours a day, seven days a week, so that the principal could call them in for a meeting or consult with them at any time. The secondary schools have sold many of their teachers large and well-appointed apartments at subsidized prices, but because they are located on campus, some teachers now see these apartments in part as a means of keeping them permanently available.

The pressure is even felt at the primary school level. At primary schools both in and out of Zouping, I often heard principals complain about the average age of their teachers. As teachers retired at the age of 60 for men and 55 for women,[11] I had trouble understanding this complaint. Weren't experienced teachers considered an important resource? One primary school principal explained that the ages between 30 and 40 were the best for teachers. By 30 they had plenty of experience and after 40 their energy levels began to decline. Only those under 40 were thought of as having the energy to constantly upgrade their curriculum and teaching techniques to keep up with the demands of the exam system.

Entrance exams have been a key feature of the Zouping education system during the entire post-Mao period. While the most important of these remains the university entrance exam, other exams have also been important. Before the county had enough junior middle school places to universalize junior middle school education, there was a standardized junior middle school entrance exam. During the early 1990s, after there were enough overall junior middle school places for all students, this exam was still used to select students for the best junior middle schools. But by 1997, this exam was dropped and students were assigned junior middle school places according to school districts. The county's two private junior middle schools, however, still administer their own standardized entrance exams. Of these, it is the old number one junior middle school whose exam routine is most noteworthy. As described above, this school was formed when the new campus of the number one senior middle school was built. The county took over the old campus and started a private tuition fee-charging public junior middle school there. To attract students, this school maintained a close relationship with the new number one senior middle school and offered students a fifty-point bonus on the entrance exam for that school. But the leadership of the junior middle school was also worried that the fifty-point bonus might make its students complacent. To prevent such a situation, the school instituted a sliding tuition rate based on (initially) the school's own entrance exam and then on the countywide standardized exams that are conducted each semester. In any given semester, of the roughly 560 students at a given grade level, the 50 top-scoring students will pay no tuition, students 51–100 will pay 40 percent of the full tuition, students 101–150 will pay 60 percent, and students 151–200 pay 80 percent. This information is posted publicly on school bulletin boards and reprinted in newspaper ads.[12]

As can be seen from the exam policies of the old number one junior middle school, the senior middle school entrance exam is still a very serious endeavor. At the end of junior middle school, all students take a standardized exam that determines whether or not they are offered a place in one of the two elite academic senior middle schools. Students who pass the cutoff score on this exam are then assigned a place at one of these two schools. The other students may either pay an extra fee (called a "school support fee" [*zanzhufei*], a onetime fee of 12,000 yuan in 2005–7) to attend one of the elite schools (if their scores were reasonably close to the cutoff) or choose among the remaining two academic senior middle schools and the vocational senior middle school. Of the Zouping county students attending the two elite middle schools in 2006, roughly half of them gained entrance without paying the school support fee.

During the late 1990s, some junior middle schools were outperforming others on the senior middle school entrance exam, and the county education bureau feared that some schools were likely to become despondent: sites of high dropout rates and few hopes of attending a good senior middle school, let alone a university. To remedy this situation, the county education bureau shifted from an exam system to an exam and quota system. Every junior middle school was assigned a quota of places (now roughly equivalent to 30 percent of the graduating class) at the elite senior middle schools. The standardized senior middle school entrance exam was then used to select which students at a given school received that school's quota places (for more detail, see Kipnis 2001b). In effect, despite taking a countywide exam, students were mostly competing only with students from their own junior middle school. A number of places, however, were reserved for the top-testing students in the county who did not secure one of their school's quota places. In this way, the county maintained an incentive for schools as a whole to outperform schools from other districts, while at the same time ensuring that no school fell so far behind that its students would feel that there was nothing to be gained by studying hard for exams. As county education officials explained to me, for a competition to have the effect of pushing everyone to the limits of their endurance, it must be a competition among relative equals. No one can be allowed to get too far ahead or behind.

As of 2006, the primary school level was the only place in the Zouping education system where some attempt had been made to limit the intensity of educational competition. Standardized tests were still administered twice a year, and as in the junior middle schools, classes were not streamed so that teachers could be compared on student test results. Teachers did take this competition seriously and pushed their students hard during class time, but at least there were some limits on homework amounts and school hours. In 2006, at rural Zouping primary schools, students spent seven hours and forty-five minutes a day in class (including ten minutes between classes, but not counting the long lunch break). At the Sunzhen Primary school, for example, students began their morning reading period at 7:45 a.m., finished their last morning class at 12:00 noon, resumed classes at 1:00 p.m. and left the school at 4:30 p.m. At my son's Australian primary school, by comparison, students spent five and one-half hours per day at school (from 9:00 a.m. to 3:00 p.m. with a thirty-minute lunch break). However, unlike students at the secondary schools, Zouping primary students did not attend school on weekends and completed, on average, less than an hour of homework per night, even in sixth grade (the final and most pressured of the primary grades). In previous years, when entrance to junior middle school was based on competitive exams, many rural primary schools in Zouping extended the school day further and gave larger amounts of homework (see Kipnis 2001b).

At primary and secondary schools, classes compete in a wide range of other activities in addition to exams. Class sizes are quite large (averaging close to sixty students per class at all levels), and classes stay together for at least an entire academic year, while teachers of various subjects rotate in and out of the classrooms. Classes compete with each other in all manner of athletic, musical, artistic, school spirit, hygiene, and community service activities. Winners in such competitions are announced at Monday morning flag-raising ceremonies.

In this way the schools consciously promote classes of students to form collective identities. If you ask a Zouping primary student which grade level she or he is attending, the response will almost always include both the grade level and the class, as in "I'm in sixth-grade class number three." The formation of student collectivities also offers students opportunities to govern themselves and each other. Each class at all levels has a student head (*banzhang*) who acts as a liaison between the students and teachers and who is supposed to exhibit model behavior and encourage classmates to do the same. One senior middle school class head told me, "Of course it is hard to tell others what to do as they will resent you, but at the very least, in a situation where many people are breaking rules, you can be the last student to break the rule instead of the first." Extra student leaders can be appointed by the head teacher for a given class for special events like athletic meets.

In sum, education in Zouping is an intense and intensely competitive experience. Middle school students are pressed to the limits of human endurance for the digestion of information. Students' lives are arranged

FIGURE 8. Flag-raising ceremony at a rural Zouping primary school. Photograph by the author.

so that they can do little else than study, and participation in competitive activities is introduced from a very early age. Exams themselves often have large financial consequences for the families of students wishing to continue their education. This exam-related intensity both reflects and magnifies the glorification of educational success.

Family Portraits

What, then, is it like to be a student, teacher, or parent of a student in such an educational system? There are a great variety of ways of inhabiting the system, and the following portraits were selected to show how a variety of people handle the pressure the system generates.

A Motivated English Teacher and His Son

Married to a factory worker and with one son, Teacher Wang lived in a nice three-bedroom apartment at the senior middle school where he taught English. When I first met Teacher Wang in 1995, what struck me was his ambition. Even though he was in his late thirties and already in a secure job, he devoted all his free time to improving his own already excellent English skills. In addition, he took great pride in improving the test skills of his students. In 1999, he told me that he lived for seeing his students make it into top universities and described how the average score of his students on the university entrance exam English section was higher than that of any other English teacher in Zouping. In autumn of 1999, Teacher Wang's own son was in the fifth grade of primary school. In addition to being a good student, the boy was an excellent basketball player. He was extremely quick and agile and had excellent ball skills, though he was not too tall. He played basketball every day on the high school courts next to his apartment building, and unlike many Zouping parents, Teacher Wang was supportive of his son's athletic ambitions.

In spring 2005, I spent a fair amount of time with Teacher Wang and his family again. Teacher Wang was still hard-working but less enthusiastic. He had been appointed to the position of head teacher, made over 3,000 yuan a month, and had become one of many Zouping residents who owned their own car. But he found his duties overwhelming. The principal would call him on his mobile phone even in the middle of the night, and he had to spend time in his key-card-regulated office seven days a week. He had recently been headhunted to teach English at a private school in the city of Qingdao. They offered him over 5,000 yuan per month, but what really tempted Teacher Wang was the thought that his duties might not be so onerous. In the end, because his wife would not have a job in Qingdao and his son would need to find a new school, as well as implicit threats by his present school that they could cause trouble with his household registration and apartment, he elected to turn down the Qingdao offer. His son was then in the tenth grade but no longer had time for basketball. The son explained to me that in sixth grade the coaches at one of the province's specialized sports academies had shown some interest, but in the end they had concluded that he would not be tall enough. In junior middle school, in grades seven and eight, he had found the time to play maybe twice a week, but even then the pressure to spend most of his time studying was intense. In ninth grade, with the senior middle school entrance exam approaching, he could not even play once a week. He did well enough on that exam to enter one of the elite senior middle schools without paying the school support fee, but during the first year of senior middle school (tenth grade) had time to play basketball for only forty minutes on every third

Sunday. He doubted that he would be able to do even this in the second and third years of senior middle school. Though he found his studies tiring, he said that he enjoyed studying literature especially and hoped to pursue that at college.

In 2009, I again spent time with the family. In July of that year the son had done very well (625 points) on the university entrance exam. He was admitted to the English department of Beijing Agricultural University, realizing his own dream of going to college in Beijing and his parents' dream of admittance to a good university. After two years of no basketball, he began playing daily again in July, the morning after finishing the university entrance exam. After arriving at Beijing Agricultural University in September, the school basketball coach spotted him playing with friends and invited him to join the university team.

An Ambitious but Disadvantaged Migrant Family

Mr. Zhang first traveled to Zouping from the relatively impoverished southwestern corner of Shandong as a migrant construction worker in the late 1990s. He and his wife had wanted a son, so despite the birth control policy they had had four children between 1984 and 1999. The first three were daughters and the fourth was a son. He was happy with his four children, but the family had paid heavy fines for all the birth control violations. These fines had left him in debt to relatives until 2002. By 2001 his elder two daughters had graduated from junior middle school. He knew of the factory work available for young women at the Weiqiao textile factory in Zouping, so he moved here with his two teenaged daughters. In 2003 he brought over his other two children (a daughter then in third grade and a son in preschool) and his wife. Though his elder daughters, with full-time jobs in the textile factory, were able to have their household registrations moved to Zouping, he and his wife, both of whom worked casual jobs, were not. Consequently, until 2006, when policies regarding school fees for migrant worker children changed, Mr. Zhang had to pay extra fees for his younger two children to attend Zouping schools. Still, he thought it was worth it because the schools in Zouping seemed better than those in his home county. They rented four shabby rooms in a suburban village house near the factory. The elder daughters could earn 1,200 yuan a month each working fifty-plus-hour weeks in the textile factory while Mr. Zhang and his wife earned roughly 800 yuan each a month as day laborers in various jobs. In 2006, Mr. Zhang's third daughter attended one of the sixth-grade classes that I observed. Though her test scores were below average, she was cheerful in school and had a positive attitude toward her studies. She regularly remained in the classroom after school for extra tutoring from her math teacher. My own prejudices led me to expect that Mr. Zhang would not have high ambitions for his third daughter. He and his wife had attended less than three years of primary school themselves, and I suspected that his desire for a son and the availability of jobs for young women at the textile factory meant that he would rather save his money for his son's education than encourage his third daughter to pursue her studies. But I was wrong. Mr. Zhang told me that if either his son or his third daughter could make it to college, it would be the most glorious thing that he could imagine. He explained that with the elder two daughters there was simply no chance to attend senior middle school. In that part of Shandong in that period, only the best of the best students could attend senior middle school without paying hefty fees. Now, he said, the family's economic situation was better, and he would have his third daughter attend an academic senior middle school no matter what. He was also hopeful that her test scores would improve. She was behind when she first entered Zouping schools and had been improving ever since, he added. His son was now in the first grade, and the parents' ambitions for him were just as high.

An Educationally Successful Rural Household

The Fengs lived in a slightly shabby house in a village about twenty minutes to the north of the county seat. Their house, however, did not reflect the family's economic condition, as the parents were saving all their money for their children's education. The mother farmed the family's allotment of land, earning roughly 10,000 yuan a year from corn, wheat, and cotton, while the father drove a small truck, buying, hauling, and selling produce at markets in roughly a two-hundred-kilometer radius. He said he could make 1,500 yuan a month in this fashion if he worked every day. The father had graduated from primary school, while the mother had finished only three years of schooling. Both parents, however, said that they would have wanted to go further with their schooling if it hadn't been for the poverty of their families at that time. Though the couple could not really understand their children's homework, they pressed their children to study hard and rarely asked them to do chores for fear that it would interfere with their homework. The couple had an elder daughter in her second year of college and a son in one of the sixth-grade classes that I followed. The daughter had always been a good student and had managed to gain admittance to the number one senior middle school and then a regional normal university. The couple paid roughly 12,000 yuan a year for her room, board, and tuition there, even though the daughter skimped on meals so as not to cost her parents too much money. The son had been only an average student during his first three years, but the elder daughter had been tutoring him over the summers, and now he was roughly tenth out of fifty-eight students in his class. The parents were considering having the son take the entrance exam for the old number one junior middle school at the end of the year. "I don't think that we would send him there unless he did well enough to earn a partial scholarship, but it can't hurt to try," said the mother. "If not, he can go to the township junior middle school like his sister." The couple planned to build a small new house for their own retirement after both of their children had attended college.

An Educationally Less Successful Rural Household

The Lins lived in a neat brick house in a village about fifteen kilometers north of the county seat. They let Mr. Lin's brother farm their land so that both parents could concentrate on work in nearby cornstarch and machine tool factories. Each parent could earn about 1,000 yuan per month working six shifts a week. Mr. Lin had graduated from junior middle school but said he didn't learn much there, while Mrs. Lin graduated from primary school. The Lins had two daughters, a nineteen-year-old who worked and lived in the textile factory in the county seat and a twelve-year-old whose sixth-grade class I attended. The younger daughter had a slight speech impediment, was very shy, and was near the bottom of her class in test scores. The older daughter had left school after junior middle school. "She didn't do well on the senior middle school entrance exam and wanted to start earning money, so we let her go to Weiqiao [textile factory]," Mrs. Lin explained. "Like all parents, we really hope [our younger daughter] can go to college. She isn't doing too well now, but maybe she will improve at junior middle school," Mrs. Lin added. Mr. Lin explained further how all the parents' time was taken up by factory work: "Now there is a lot of work available, so it is our job to earn as much money as possible while our bodies can take it. Then we will have enough money for her tuition if she can make it to college as well as for medical expenses in our old age.

We don't have time to pay attention to our daughter's schoolwork and wouldn't know how to help her if we did. Can you give her any tips for improving her studying?"

Two Junior Middle School Dropouts

During my 2005 and 2006 visits to Zouping, I met several young people who had recently dropped out of junior middle school, usually in eighth grade. A teacher at one of the rural junior middle schools told me that nearly 10 percent of students dropped out of her school, though the county education officials assured me that over the entire county, the average was less than 5 percent. I formally interviewed eight such young people and spoke with the families of many more. Not in a single case were tuition costs the primary cause of leaving school. Rather, these students were not doing well at school and did not enjoy or simply could not stand the exam-oriented pressure. One eighteen-year-old young woman, now a hair-dresser in the county seat, explained: "School just isn't for everyone. All the teachers care about are your test scores, and if you don't test well you aren't important. All day long it is just study, study, study; can you imagine living in a boarding school like that when you aren't a good student?" A twenty-year-old young man, now working as a waiter at a restaurant in the county seat, told me: "My parents really wanted me to go to college, but I just couldn't do well at school. I couldn't understand what the teachers were saying and I didn't like to study. In seventh grade there was one test after another. If I wasn't the worst-scoring student in the class, I would be the second or third worst. I couldn't see the point of simply memorizing books, that's not what life is about. Who wants to be a bookworm [literally book-idiot, *shudaizi*]? I told my parents that studying was just a waste of time for me, as my grades would never improve; they weren't happy, but what could they do? Maybe someday I will go to vocational school and become a chef. I've heard that they will let you in now even without a junior middle school graduation certificate."

Conclusion

Dropouts are no doubt an inevitable consequence of any system of compulsory schooling, especially one with the competitive intensity of this one. Their inclusion in this introduction thus serves to balance what might seem to some as too monolithic a portrait of educational intensity in Zouping and to represent some of the county's diversity. Nevertheless, depicting them departs from my primary purpose. That 5 or 10 percent of the junior middle school population leaves school early does not surprise me as much as the fact that more that ninety percent completes it and that almost all those who complete junior middle school go on to noncompulsory academic senior middle schools, many of them paying handsomely for the privilege. When you consider the level of effort and discipline required of middle school students, such figures become exceptional. Put another way, comparing Zouping schools to the middle schools in Canberra, Australia, where I live, it would be fair to say that 80 percent of the middle school population in Zouping is studying with an intensity that is matched by at best a fraction of one percent of the Canberra middle school population.[13] The intensity of study in Zouping is a collective social fact (as is that of Canberra); it is more than a matter of what percentage of individualized decision makers choose or do not choose to attend school.

Viewed locally, the governing that is involved in this intensity cannot be said to have arisen through the efforts of any single governing agent. Certainly it has been cultivated in various ways by the county education bureau and educational administrators at various levels. Such administrators pursue exam success for the particular schools or districts for which they are responsible by investing money in schools and education, squeezing enterprises, parents, and villages to do the same, and by setting standardized exams, systems for evaluating teachers, and rules for resource allocation that encourage exam success. They also glorify educational success in the local media. But these activities do not occur in a vacuum. They are in various ways enveloped by the educational, social, and economic policies of yet higher layers of bureaucracy in the national and provincial governments and supported by the actions of the hundreds of thousands of students, teachers, and parents in the county. The system could not have come together in the way it has without the financial support of parents (for primary and junior middle school fees historically and university tuition today), without the willingness of parents to push their children to study and send them to boarding schools and universities, without the efforts of teachers to stretch the limits of their endurance to work hard in classrooms, and, most important, without the efforts of the majority of students themselves. None of these actors may be viewed as self-determining; yet all exercise agency in their pursuits of educational glory. Like many collective "fevers," the intensity of education desire in Zouping arises from the interactions and mutual influence of thousands of actors and governing actions.

As with any collective fever, Zouping's pursuit of educational glory has its temporal and geographic limits, but delimiting these is no simple matter. The remaining chapters of this book examine the way that this fever is simultaneously a national, East Asian, and global phenomenon. To conclude this chapter, let me focus on some of the ways in which this fever might or might not be considered local.

According to the county education bureau, on an overall ranking of educational performance based on a variety of measures that included student test results in all grades, teacher education levels, school facilities, dropout rates, and more, in 2005 Zouping rated fifth out of 141 rural counties and urban districts in Shandong Province. Thus Zouping is clearly an above-average county in its pursuit of educational excellence. Zouping's success in this matter certainly reflects the particular efforts of local teachers and officials, perhaps going as far back as Liang Shuming's Rural Reconstruction Institute of the 1930s. Recent economic development has also enabled the county government and individual households to invest more in the pursuit of educational glory than most other rural counties could have.

Shandong as a whole has followed what in China is known as the "state corporatist" model of economic development as opposed to the "entrepreneurial household" model (seen primarily in southern China). This form of development places a greater portion of revenues and prestigious jobs under the control of government or quasi-government institutions. Private firms that grow as household businesses keep important positions within the family, while Chinese government agencies and enterprises, as well as the businesses that are linked to them, are more likely to adhere to hiring rules that emphasize educational credentials and examinations. Consequently, competition in the education system may be keener in the parts of China where the state corporatist model of development has prevailed.[14]

The historical intersection of Zouping's economic expansion and rapid urbanization with the nationwide expansion of university places has allowed the majority of parents the dream of having a child attend college, a dream that may not have been possible at another historical moment. That the majority of these parents themselves never had the opportunity to attend college does little to inhibit these desires. In contrast to wealthy Anglo nations like Australia, the United Kingdom, and the United States, there does not appear to be a working class antischool culture that underprivileged parents consciously or unconsciously pass on to their children (Kipnis 2001a). Rather, rapid development has left undereducated Zouping parents with the feeling that times are changing and that their own lack of experience in higher education is irrelevant to the possibilities for their children.

But if Zouping is in some ways exceptional, it should not be considered an anomaly. In both of the other counties that I visited, teachers and principals described an educational desire that was every bit as intense as that in Zouping. The push for better facilities, enabled by school consolidation and resulting in boarding schools, has occurred in varying degrees all over rural China. Throughout China, the household registration policy, which attaches all forms of state welfare to the jurisdiction of an individual's household registration, has created a hierarchy of places with differing levels of welfare benefits, educational opportunities, and access to healthcare and employment. Educational achievement has been a way of moving up this geographic hierarchy since it was established in the late 1950s.[15] In the western Shandong County that I researched, which is considerably poorer than Zouping, many students began boarding at their schools in the fourth year of primary school, and the type of study schedule that begins in junior middle school for Zouping student was eased in over the three years of upper primary school. Sociologists completing surveys on education in Shandong told me that the desire for children to attend college is almost universal throughout the province, though it may be higher in Shandong generally than in other provinces.[16] Newspaper articles report that because of this desire, few vocational middle schools are being built, even though employment rates for vocational middle school graduates are higher than those of university graduates.[17] Reports from rural Jiangsu Province resemble very much the situation I have described for Zouping (Xin San Pian Keti Zu 2003). Finally, I collected school schedules from primary and middle schools in a rural Anhui County that resemble quite closely those described above. The governing of educational intensity in Zouping is fairly representative of what happens in the economically more developed counties in eastern and central China, where perhaps 100 million people live. Zouping's experience is also indicative of the direction that many other economically middling counties in these areas would like to head if they had the money. It is probably less representative of poorer rural areas and of large urban areas, though there are plenty of reports of intense educational competition in these places as well.[18]

In short, the origins of Zouping's educational intensity are partially local and partially exogenous. While Zouping may not be representative of all of contemporary China, it provides a portrait of a type of educational intensity that in varying degrees exists in many Chinese contexts. How national policies have nurtured these desires is the focus of the next chapter.

CHAPTER THREE

Encompassing Educational Desire: National Policy in Zouping County

The governing decisions of Zouping officials, teachers, parents, and students depicted in the previous chapter were encompassed, in various ways, by policy-making actors in the higher levels of the Chinese state, particularly those in the provincial and national governments. By saying that Zouping governing practice was encompassed, I do not mean to imply that local policy and the governing actions of parents, teachers, and students were simply dictated by higher levels of government. Rather, this encompassment involved the continual reformation of a wider context within which local governing took place. The reformation of the wider context itself was a matter of give-and-take among various levels of governing.

This reformation continually occurs at the level of both policy formation and policy implementation. At the level of policy formation, local "experiments," sometimes initiated by the center and sometimes by the localities themselves, are often undertaken in China, temporarily resulting in considerable variation in policy among China's localities. The power dynamics behind the judgment of the relative success of such experiments are beyond the scope of this book. Suffice it to say that when an experiment is deemed successful by the nation's leaders, the central government attempts to impose it on the nation as a whole. But even in this case, the dynamics of policy implementation can result in considerable local variation, ranging from attempts at strictly and relatively universally enforced laws and regulations to relatively softer methods of encouragement, such as the promulgations of "models" in one locale, which other locales are encouraged to emulate.[1] More important for this book, even when the center does its utmost to enforce uniform policies on the nation as a whole, room for local agency, by local officials, parents, children, and teachers, remains. This space for agency exists because of the contradictions among various national policies, the inevitable ambiguity in the wording of particular laws and regulations, and the fact that any human agent, if willing to face the consequences, can resist, subvert, or even openly defy the wishes of a more powerful actor. Nevertheless, policies implemented by the center can be influential.

This chapter examines national and provincial policies that have formed part of the wider context within which educational desire has been governed in Zouping. While any sort of policy, from economic reform to international relations, may have an influence on educational desire, this chapter focuses only on those policies that take the manipulation of educational desire as their goal. Some of these policies have been designed to enhance educational desire, some to curb or redirect this desire, while others take this desire as a social fact that may be manipulated in the pursuit of other policy goals. While all the policies described in this chapter have had significant societal effects, rarely have they unproblematically produced the results their designers envisioned. Especially where policies appear to have been unsuccessful, I examine the implementation dynamics that have led to policy failure in Zouping. Given the extent of educational desire depicted in the previous chapter, it is clear that polices to enhance educational desire have been more successful than those designed to curb it.

Enhancing Educational Desire

The starting point for any discussion of educational desire in contemporary China must be the birth control policy and the relationship between population quantity and quality it imagined and produced. From its conception in the late 1970s, this policy considered the "quantity" and "quality" of the Chinese population to be related in inverse fashion. An increase in the quality of the Chinese population could occur only by limiting its quantity, the policy's designers emphasized again and again. This expectation reflected both the calculations of a planned economy, in which providing jobs and education for a large population was more difficult than for a small population, and the international research that had demonstrated that children in families with only one or two siblings receive more parental attention, education, and resources than do children of large families

(Fong 2004b; Greenhalgh and Winckler 2005). Indeed, from the vantage of this book, the birth control policy appears as a bit of successful reverse social engineering. Where Western researchers found that the emotional and economic costs of successfully raising a highly educated child contributed to a reduction in birthrates and in the number of children desired, Chinese demographers reasoned that forcing a reduction in the birthrate might lead to an increased amount of parental investment in each child. If one accepts that life expectancy and years of education are measures of the "quality" of a population, then, in macro terms, the birth control policy has had some of the effects that its designers envisioned. The only children of Chinese urban families are, by and large, healthy and highly educated.

In Shandong, as in most of the country, the birth control policy was designed in 1980 and initially implemented in 1981. As Greenhalgh (1990, 1993) describes in Shaanxi Province, fierce resistance by rural residents led to an evolution of the policy, in rural regions, from a strict one-child policy to, by the mid-1980s, a policy that allows rural households to have a second child if the first child is a girl. While permission for a first child is given to almost any couple who have legally married, permission for a second child (when the first is a girl) is dependent upon a number of factors, including the size of the official "quota" for live births in a given county or district. In Zouping, rural mothers who give birth to a daughter in their early twenties have had to wait about seven years before receiving permission to give birth to a second child. Mothers who had their first daughter relatively late in life are often allowed to have a second child after a shorter wait, as the "quality" aspect of the birth control policy encourages mothers to give birth at a relatively young age, before the chance of congenital disease increases. Birth control violators are heavily fined; in 2006 I heard of fines as high as 60,000 yuan, roughly six times the annual income of a Zouping farmer at that time.

The demographic effects in Zouping of what has now been close to three decades of the birth control policy have been dramatic. Not only have birthrates drastically reduced, but the policy has also led to a standardization of sibling set structures and a highly visible series of demographic "shadows," in which echoes of historical events, such as the near cessation of fertility during the Great Leap Famine (1960–62), can be seen in the birthrates both one and two generations later, where generations are defined by the minimum legal marriage age, which determines the date of the majority of marriages in rural China and the allocation of a quota for the couple's first child. While social and economic forces other than the policy itself have contributed to the declining birthrate, the policy is the only explanation for the sibling set structures and the demographic shadows.

For those who comply with the birth control policy, only a few sibling set structures are possible: for urban residents, an only son or an only daughter; for rural residents, an only son or daughter (though the latter is relatively rare) or an elder daughter with a younger sibling who is roughly eight years younger (allowing seven years for the arrival of the quota and one for conception and pregnancy). From the vantage point of rural Zouping children, this results in two common sibling roles for boys and three for girls. A boy can be either an only child or a younger brother with a sister approximately eight years older. A rural girl will almost always have another sibling. She can be an older sister with a brother approximately eight years younger, an older sister with a sister eight years younger, or a younger sister with a sister approximately eight years older.

Of course not all families follow the birth control policy. I have conducted household surveys in Zouping several times during the twenty years that I have been undertaking research there, and on each occasion I found that roughly 5 percent of the households had violated the birth control policy. This was also the case during the survey undertaken for this project, in 2005 and 2006. On both this survey and previous ones, I found almost no violations of the birth control policy among officially registered urban residents, about 5 percent among rural residents living in villages, and higher rates of violation among migrant workers living in the county seat, as well as "suburban villagers"—county seat residents who used to be rural dwellers on the outskirts of the county seat, but whose land was swallowed up by the expanding city and who had been given various forms of compensation for this land, including urban housing but not official urban residency. Nevertheless, a 95 percent compliance rate is quite high. Furthermore, over 85 percent of the households I surveyed had one of the standardized sibling set structures described above. Clearly, in demographic terms, the birth control policy in Zouping has been highly influential.[2]

For my purposes, more important than the demographics is how the birth control policy has affected parental desires. At least since the late 1980s, most families in this area have expressed a desire for one son and one daughter as an ideal family form (Kipnis 1997:138–41).[3] Thus, while many families need to curtail their reproductive desires because of the policy, stopping after one son and no daughter, or two daughters and no son, there is little evidence of desire for many children. As the birth control policy's advocates predicted, the experience of fewer children has heightened parental ambition for those children they do have, in rural and urban households alike. Everywhere I went in Zouping, and Shandong more generally, whether speaking to officials, teachers, or parents, I heard the saying "Hoping one's son becomes a dragon and one's daughter a phoenix" (*wang zi cheng long, wang nü cheng fei*),[4] or more tellingly, discussions of this hope as a psychological state (*wangzi chenglongde xinli*). This state was continually described both as the cause of educational desire and as a result of the birth control policy.

Becoming a dragon or phoenix involved more than just economic security, though this was clearly part of the package. When I argued with rural parents over the economic value of university degrees, pointing out that many technical diplomas led to careers that seemed much more lucrative than those attached to liberal arts degrees, parents would counter that even if technical degrees secured a reasonable career, they would never allow one's child "to become a dragon" (i.e., a real high-level leader, whether in government or business) and thus were not as desirable.

From the point of view of teachers and principals, the birth control policy has resulted not just in high levels of parental ambition but also, in a more negative vein, in excessive fears that their child might be injured. This fear, I should note, must be contextualized by the fact that medical costs are high relative to income in China, that at the time of my research medical insurance was rare, and that the financial consequences of hospitalization would have been devastating for almost any family. In a slightly exaggerated tone, a kindergarten teacher once told me:

> We live in constant fear of the children having an accident. If one of the little darlings does so much as skin a knee or get stung by a bee, then someone from the family will be in here haranguing us for hours. The [paternal] grandparents are the worst. Grandma or grandpa often picks up the children before lunch or after school, and the first thing they do is to inspect the child from head to toe and look for the slightest bump or scratch. They are even more careful than when picking through produce at the market! It wasn't like that before the birth control policy.

At three of the urban primary schools that I visited, scattered across Shandong, the children were completely prohibited from chasing after one another on school grounds during class breaks, lunch, or after school. A physical education teacher at one of the schools explained that they cannot take the chance of having an injury on school grounds or the parents

FIGURE 9. Senior middle school class does between-class exercises. Photograph by the author.

will make big trouble. When I pointed out that the result of this restriction was that the children ran around outside the school on the streets where there was much more traffic and danger, the teacher replied that what happened outside of school grounds after school hours was not their concern. Several high school principals told me that part of the reason for the constant surveillance of the students at their boarding schools was to minimize the chances of injury. One high school principal said, "Facing the parents of an injured child is the thing I fear the most." Another told me, "I like it when the students do military drills during PE class. Not only do the students learn to cohere in a group, but it is also much safer than games like soccer or basketball."

In July of 2008, a debate broke out in the editorial pages of the *Qingdao Morning News* over whether schools should be legally liable for any accidents that occur on their grounds. The debate arose in reaction to a case where parents had sued a school because their son had broken his ankle while playing basketball with schoolmates. Most parents who had letters published supported the notion that schools must take responsibility for any sort of accident.[5]

As the example of paternal grandparents who pick up their grandchildren from kindergarten demonstrates, the birth control policy influences more than just the parent-child relationship. Parents often use other kin relationships to further their ambitions for their children. Grandparents are usually happy to help with child care, enabling the parents to work longer hours, often for the purpose of saving money for their children's education. Parents born before the implementation of the birth control policy often come from large sibling sets, and these relatives can be useful for the children's education. As described in the previous chapter, parents of university-bound children sometimes borrow money from their own siblings to cover tuition. In addition, especially in rural areas, where most parents have limited education, parents use their own more highly educated siblings as role models. When these relatives visit over spring festival, they are treated as honored guests, paraded before the children, and asked to provide advice on study techniques. In this manner the parents try to prevent their children from thinking that they cannot test into college just because the parents did not.

Rural parents with a firstborn daughter and a second child often encourage the older daughter to serve as both a model and an educator for her younger sibling. One mother told me that she herself had not done well in school, but that was because of the poverty of her family at that time. With seven brothers and sisters, all of her parents' efforts were devoted to providing enough food. This mother then described how she had told her daughter to serve as an example for the daughter's younger brother, so that he would know that people in their family had the ability to make it into college. The elder daughter had, in fact, managed to secure entrance to a teacher's college and had spent the summer holiday after her freshman year tutoring her younger brother. As a result, the younger brother moved from the middle to the top of the class in mathematics during the sixth grade.

In sum, the effects of the birth control policy on educational desire and practice have been multiple. The policy has increased the amount of energy and money that parents, and other relatives, have to invest in children. It has also led to increased parental anxiety over the safety of their only children and, in rural Zouping, to a frequent imbrication of the roles of "elder sister" and "tutor."

Perhaps the other major way in which the central government has attempted to enhance educational desire is in the area of school funding. As depicted in the previous chapter, valid criticisms exist of the extent to which the central government has placed responsibility for school funding on cash-strapped localities and poor households. But the paths of school funding in China are murky indeed, and it is clear that some of the policies and practices the central government has devised to encourage the funding of schools and the payment of teacher salaries have been influential in many places if not universally effective.

Over the past two decades, higher levels of government have often issued various forms of unfunded mandates to local governments, especially in the area of education. Village, township, and county governments have all been pressured to build new schools (and consolidate schools in the process), hire more teachers, replace "people-sponsored" teachers with ones on the local government payroll, and so on. How seriously local governments take this pressure depends on a number of factors, including the importance of appearing to fulfill these mandates in Party processes of evaluating and promoting local cadres, the availability of local tax revenues to fulfill these mandates, and the ability to find alternative funding methods, such as levying irregular taxes on the local population[6] or taking out questionable loans from local banks or enterprises upon whom political pressure has been brought to bear.

One of the central problems of township-level government during the late 1990s and early twenty-first century was the accumulation of debt by township governments. Leading cadres often need to have significant governing accomplishments (*zhengji*) to get promoted, and at various points in the 1990s and 2000s, the construction of impressive schools has been considered such an accomplishment. For better or worse, successful leaders have often funded their accomplishments by accumulating debts, leaving the debts behind them as a problem for their successors when they get promoted to a new post in a different place. A survey of twenty township governments across ten different provinces in 2004, after many rounds of reform directed at clearing up the debts of rural governments had already been enacted, found that sixteen of the twenty had accumulated debts averaging 10 million yuan. None of these townships had any prospects of raising the funds to cover the debts and just assumed that higher levels of government would have to cover them at some stage. The single largest cause of these debts, accounting for 17 percent of the total, was for educational facilities (Zhao 2007:36–44). The amount of money spent on schools in townships like these is thus much higher than the figure that shows up in official budget reports. And county level governments have borrowed much larger amounts than the townships. Unfunded mandates have thus resulted in the construction of a considerable number of schools, though who will in the end pay for these facilities remains uncertain.[7]

In Zouping, too, large amounts of money have been borrowed for the construction of schools. The new number one senior middle school alone required a loan of more than 200 million yuan. For now, Zouping County is rich enough to make the payments on its loans. Whether that will remain the case for the life of such loans is yet to be seen.

Moderating Educational Desire

If some of the central government's policies were designed to enhance the desire of parents to invest in the education of their children, especially the birth control policy, other, later policies have been implemented in the hope of moderating or redirecting this desire. In the perception of many educational leaders, the psychology of hoping that one's child becomes a dragon has led to both a degree of competitiveness in the education system that is positively harmful to human development and a bias toward academic over vocational forms of education. Education reformers have attempted to address the first of these problems through "education for quality" (*suzhi jiaoyu*) policies and the latter through various campaigns to promote vocational education. Both of these policies have met with limited success to date.

The "education for quality" movement has from the outset been linked to the conception of human quality that was developed in the formation of the birth control policy. During the early 1980s, birth control policy propaganda switched the Chinese translation of the term "population quality" from *renkou zhiliang* to *renkou suzhi*. While the reasons behind this shift are enigmatic, the term *suzhi* implies a type of quality that entails the potential for yet further development, making the term suitable for people who are imagined as being worthy of "human resource investment"; *zhiliang,* in contrast, implies a more finished form of quality.[8] The term *suzhi* quickly became associated with the type of individually embodied human quality that birth control advocates assumed would be raised by limiting population quantity, and raising the *suzhi* of the population has become a priority for leaders at all levels of government. Partially as a result of these trends, the term *suzhi* often takes on hierarchical overtones. In collective terms, entire nations or ethnic groups may be ranked according to their overall *suzhi.* Individually, the privileges of certain people are justified by their high *suzhi,* while others, including rural migrants, litterbugs, the short, the nearsighted, and the poorly dressed are mocked for their supposed lack of *suzhi.*

In 1985, the CCP central committee declared that "raising the *suzhi* of the people of the nation was the basic goal of education system reform" (Guojia Jiaoyu Weiyuanhui 1992:182). In 1986, the new compulsory education law declared that education must focus on improving the *suzhi* of the people. Chinese education reformers soon found a way to use this language for their own ends.

During the 1980s, these educators began to criticize the focus of many schools on university entrance exam success rates rather than on education in a broader sense. They argued that this obsession led teachers to ignore students with little potential to excel in exams, to direct their curriculum toward exam success, and to emphasize excessive amounts of homework, drilling, and memorization as opposed to creative and analytic reasoning in their teaching methods (see, for example, Liu Linping et al. 1997). They derisively called this type of education "education for the purpose of testing on to the next level" (*shengxue jiaoyu*) and later "education for the purpose of passing exams" (*yingshi jiaoyu*). They took inspiration from North American ideals of "competence education," which emphasize that students should learn "competencies" rather than exam-taking skills. In 1988 they coined the term "*suzhi* education" (education for the purpose of improving the quality of the people, or "education for quality") to describe the type of education that they advocated. They thus attempted to gain momentum for their reforms by naming them with the term mandated by Chinese education law.

At a rhetorical level, the strategy of the education-for-quality advocates paid off. The term was increasingly used in both official contexts and academic articles on education reform throughout the 1990s (see Kipnis 2006b for further detail). In 1999 the phrase officially entered the nation's education policy. But this rhetorical success did not necessarily translate into practice. On the one hand, once education for quality had been written into law, education reformers of all stripes simply began calling the types of education reforms that they advocated "education for quality." The originally broad meaning of the term became even broader. As one popular saying goes, "Education for quality is an empty frame, anything can be stuck inside it" (*Suzhi jiaoyu shi yi ge kuang, shenme dou wang limian fang*). Exactly what type of education will enhance the quality of the people is still open to debate. On the other hand, the societal forces that led to such an emphasis on exams in the Chinese education system are multiple and powerful and have been difficult to pin down and overcome through the implementation of this policy.

A closer examination of the complaints behind this education reform movement and the resulting reforms in Zouping County reveals much about the dynamics of policy implementation. From the start the ambiguity inherent in this policy was apparent as some Zouping educators refused to consider an emphasis on exams and "education for quality" contradictory. They felt that raising the quality of Zouping students would be helped not by reducing the emphasis on exams but by changing the content and structure of the exams as well as the ways they were used in evaluating teachers.

During the 1990s, as "education for quality" moved from the status of experimental policy to a goal formally enshrined in the education law, five major changes were introduced by the Zouping Education Bureau. First, the county switched from an examination system to an exam plus quota system for determining entry to senior middle schools. As described in the previous chapter, part of the reason for this reform was to ensure that students at even the poorest junior middle schools had a chance of going to the elite senior middle school. However, the reform was also a response to demands from above in the name of "education for quality." Under the quota policy, the senior middle school entrance exam determined which students at a given junior middle school received the quota-determined places to attend senior middle school. The reform thus reduced competition between schools but not between students. Students, but not principals and school administrators, had reason to take a competitive attitude toward the exams. The quotas also gave the county education bureau considerable leverage over junior middle school principals. If the principals did not implement the other "education for quality" reforms that the bureau desired, the bureau could threaten the school with a quota reduction.

In name, at least, these quotas have remained in effect, and for a time they did give the education bureau a fair amount of leverage. However, as senior middle school places gradually expanded after 2000, the importance of these quotas diminished. The new (above-quota) senior middle school spaces were allotted on the basis of the exams, and by 2004, all junior middle schools were doing so well on the exam that their students' exam scores were earning them at least the number of places guaranteed to them by their quota. Competition among schools reemerged, and both the desire and the ability of the county education bureau to pressure principals not to react to this competition by increasing demands on students and teachers diminished.

Second, steps were taken to train the "higher-level cognitive abilities" of students. One of the primary themes in the literature on "education for quality" is the case for replacing a memorization-based education system with one that teaches creativity and reasoning (Cui 1999; Kipnis 2001b). During the late 1990s, Chinese TV shows on education bemoaned the inability of the Chinese education system to produce creative entrepreneurs like Bill Gates. One Shandong parent I interviewed reproduced an argument I had heard on such a TV show:

> Bill Gates didn't even go to college. When he was young he spent all of his free time experimenting with computers. He didn't have to spend all of his time memorizing useless information in the preparation for university entrance exams. In China, even primary school children are forced to memorize many things. How can China possibly produce a Bill Gates?

In reaction to such arguments, during the late 1990s, in Zouping and elsewhere, many schools began holding special "creativity" (*chuangxin*) classes as part of the regular school curriculum for primary-age students. Scores of articles in education journals suggested activities for such classes, such as posing questions with no definitive answer and then encouraging children to come up with as many different answers as they can think of. Other articles simply advocated more free time for children, so that they could think up their own playtime activities. Often, authors of newspaper and academic articles drew contrasts with Western countries, where children were said never to have to memorize anything and to have many more hours of playtime (Liu Linping et al. 1997). These arguments further led to a nationwide campaign to reduce the homework burden (*jianfu*) of Chinese students (Woronov 2008). In addition to mandating "creativity" classes, the senior middle school entrance exams, as well as other standardized exams set by the county education bureau, gave greater emphasis to "lively" (*huo*) questions that required more than simply regurgitating previously memorized material. Through the introduction of interscholastic competitions in areas like science projects, math Olympics, and creative writing, the education bureau also hoped to develop the higher-level cognitive abilities of Zouping students. Whether any of these measures actually increases creativity is difficult to determine, though it is clear that many of them have not been implemented in the manner that some education-for-quality advocates imagined. Though the interscholastic competitions have lasted, the fate of other measures to improve creativity has been mixed.

Third, the curriculum at all levels was broadened to place more emphasis on subjects not crucial to the key entrance exams for senior middle school and college. This has meant requiring all students to take classes in physical education, art, and music as well as newer subjects like computing, oral English, and varied science lab work. Since the late 1990s, the sayings "all-around development" (*quanmian fazhan*) and "implementing a well-rounded curriculum" (*kaiquan kecheng*) have been a staple of official education-for-quality rhetoric. The ability of primary schools especially to follow the expanded curriculum has been facilitated by the school consolidation movement. Unlike smaller village schools, the new larger schools all have the facilities and teachers to teach these subjects. At the senior middle school level, facilities exist for education in areas like physical education, art, music, and science lab, but their use is often restricted to students specializing in those areas.[9] As education officials explained, senior middle school is not part of compulsory education in China and thus, strictly speaking, is not subject to the education-for-quality laws and regulations. At the primary and junior middle school levels, however, the expanded curriculum has been successfully implemented.

Fourth, in reaction to the burden reduction campaigns, attempts were made to reduce school hours and amounts of homework. The reductions in time devoted to schoolwork were supposed to enable the students to unleash their creativity. While nothing was done to change the exhausting days at the senior middle schools, for roughly two years an attempt was made to ban evening study halls for junior middle school students. This ban failed as the quota system eroded and the rural junior middle schools resisted its implementation. More successful has been the limitation of homework times and school hours for primary school students. Many primary schools reduced their school hours to six for a short period, though by 2003, primary schools began to follow the seven-hour-and-forty-five-minute days described in the previous chapter. But bans on Saturday classes for primary school students introduced in 1999 have remained. Homework regulations for primary school students—no homework in first grade, thirty minutes in grades two and three, forty-five minutes in grade four, and one hour in grades five and six—have also remained in effect in Zouping, at least through the end of 2006. In 1999, these regulations were also resisted by some of the smaller rural primary schools (see Kipnis 2001b for details), but by 2005, with the consolidation of schools effecting the closure of most village schools, all of the schools I visited seemed to adhere to the primary school homework regulations.

Though in Zouping primary schools at least have seen some limits enforced on competitive intensity, such was not the case in all the Shandong counties that I visited. In at least two other counties, Saturday classes and evening study hall classes were in place for upper primary (grades 4–6) students.

Finally, the education-for-quality movement has resulted in some reforms in teaching methods. County education officials have made some effort to pressure teachers into paying more attention to students who do not do well on exams. In performance evaluations, teachers are given extra credit for raising the test scores of so-called late-developing students. In 2006, at one primary school, math and Chinese language teachers were given a 200 yuan bonus for each student in the bottom third of their class whose year-end test scores improved by ten points or more. In several primary schools, I witnessed teachers giving personalized tutorials to such students, sometimes with positive results. Yet despite these efforts, or in some cases because of them, students who do not do well on their exams often feel extremely pressured to improve and somewhat despondent if they cannot. One such student, in the first year of junior middle school, told me that despite extra tutorials in math, her test scores were still not improving. She said, "Even though the teacher gives me extra help, I still feel he doesn't like me and I don't like him either. What can I do?"

Emulating Models, or, Authoritarianism versus Democracy in the Classroom

In 2000, several literature and social science teachers told me that they were making efforts to include more classroom discussion in their courses as a result of the "education for quality" reforms. While some studies have suggested that rural Chinese classrooms are generally moving in a democratic direction by encouraging more discussion (e.g., Sargent 2009), the more time I spent in classrooms, in 2005 and 2006 as well as earlier, the more convinced I was that there were many limits to this reform. The entire structure of the curriculum simply makes it difficult. In primary school and even junior and senior middle school literature classes, students focus their time on what is called "close reading" (*jingdu*) rather than "extensive reading" (*fandu*). Close reading involves completely memorizing a two- to four-page text so that one may accurately answer test questions about the vocabulary used in the text, its content, and implied meanings. Extensive reading involves reading longer texts, such as novels or monographs, without the pressure of needing to memorize or even completely understand every small detail of the text. In classroom discussion of closely read texts, the teacher usually asks students questions for which there is one correct answer that the teacher knows and that might later appear on a standardized test, rather than wide-ranging questions to provoke discussions of issues, questions for which there may be no correct answer.

Many schools, teachers, and parents consider extensive reading a type of relaxing hobby rather than a proper form of studying. In one of the households that I visited, the father, who himself had a primary school education, told me of a cousin who had become an academic after having a postdoctoral fellowship in chemistry. Not uncommonly, he envisioned the postdoc as a degree one studied for after succeeding in yet another round of entrance exams. He said:

> I have a cousin who studied as a postdoc, can you imagine how many exams he had to pass? First he had to pass the exam into junior middle school, as in those days not everyone was allowed into that level of schooling. Then there were exams into senior middle school, college, and for his masters, doctorate, and postdoc. He told me that the secret of passing exams is never to read anything other than what the teacher assigns in class. Reading books outside of class [*kewaishu*] is a waste of time. People who want to be educated should avoid extensive reading.

Even the "creativity" classes could be more about memorization than anything else. In 2000, at one primary school in the Zouping county seat, the principal explained to me how she was implementing an education-for-quality program by moving away from a memorization- and test-based curriculum and toward a curriculum where creativity was emphasized. While this was to be done in all classes, she explained, the creative aspects of the curriculum were to be reinforced in special twice-a-week creativity classes. She then invited me to sit in on a fourth-grade creativity class. In this class, the teacher first read from a book of Tang dynasty poems. The students then chanted the poems in unison after the teacher. Next individual students were invited to stand up and repeat the poems aloud for the entire class. The teacher corrected the students' pronunciation of standard Mandarin and gave suggestions about how to read with more emotion. Over the course of a forty-minute class, three poems were recited in this manner. Absolutely no time was spent in discussing the meaning of the poems, though the teacher did write a few of the less common characters on the chalkboard and briefly discussed their meanings and usage.

After the class I asked the teacher whether the students ever wrote their own poems, either in class or for homework. She explained that as this was a creativity class, there was no homework. But, I objected, given that this was a creativity class, shouldn't the students be creating something of their own instead of just memorizing Tang dynasty poems? She replied that she thought of the class as a "quality-raising" (*suzhi*) one and added that the parents felt that nothing raised the students' quality like Tang poems. Later, when I asked one of the students' mothers why the students were memorizing poems in a class that was supposed to be devoted to creativity, she chided me for taking the word creativity too literally. First of all, she said, students enjoy Tang poems much more than some of the other texts that they have to memorize, so this class satisfied the education-for-quality principle of making education enjoyable. Second, even if students did not understand the poems now, they would appreciate them after they grew up. It was later in life that the poems would make the students more creative. Finally, she argued that in contrast to the politically oriented, official history the students had to memorize in other parts of the curriculum, Tang dynasty poems were truly something that would improve the students' quality. By 2005, creativity classes had been abandoned throughout Zouping, though time on the curriculum for memorizing Tang poems still existed.[10]

The mother of the student in the creativity class raises another important impediment to the implementation of liberal, "education for quality" teaching reforms: the place of authoritarian modes of communist governing in the public education system. Indeed it is in the area of "political quality" that the inherent ambiguity of the term "quality" exhibits its greatest productive tension. Some Chinese thinkers link the education-for-quality reforms to a discourse of political liberalism. Jie Sizhong (2004), for example, argues that a "*suzhi* crisis" of the Chinese nation is preventing the political maturation of China and the emergence of a liberal political system. To allow liberalism to emerge, Jie suggests that the *suzhi* of the Chinese people must be raised by cultivating the following qualities: an independent personality, a strong self-consciousness, a liberation of individuating characteristics, self-actualization, self-respect, a spirit of tolerance, a spirit of freedom, the spirit of equality, the spirit of democracy, the spirit of law, human rights consciousness, and a consciousness of citizenship. Jie (2004:139–80) urges the government to adopt policies that will develop these qualities, especially in the realm of "education for quality."

Moreover, in the eyes of some educational sociologists, both in and out of China, the exam-oriented education that the education-for-quality reformers targeted is inherently authoritarian. Børge Bakken (2000), for example, argues that through its implementation of enforced regimes of imitation and rote memorization, socialist governance in both the Maoist and the post-Mao eras produced close associations between notions of education, order, and discipline. He theorizes the role of "exemplary models" in Chinese education and governing and demonstrates its importance in many aspects of life: the government labels certain villages, cadres, and families as models; handwriting and calligraphy students learn handwriting and calligraphy by copying written characters; teachers are called upon to put themselves forward as models (*wei ren shibiao*); the exam-oriented education system emphasizes memorization. In contrast to liberal desires for citizens who will think independently and be tolerant of difference and entrepreneurial, Bakken describes a process of governing whose the purpose appears to be to produce a citizenry that will follow the models the government puts forth unthinkingly. LeVine and White (1986) take this argument further by suggesting that authoritarian education practices are typical of agrarian societies and that the evolution away from such systems of education commonly occurs in the process of industrialization. In short, many authors link the memorization-based education system targeted by the education-for-quality reforms to authoritarian government.

Such links, however, have not prevented others from promoting "authoritarian" education as a form of education for quality. Officials concerned with political education have demanded that one of the qualities that *suzhi* education policies are to cultivate be a high level of "ideological *suzhi*" (*zhengzhi sixiang suzhi*). Depending on who is describing ideological *suzhi*, this category is constituted by items as diverse as loyalty to the CCP, love of country, respect for the law, the ability to resist bourgeois liberalization, a democratic spirit, a Marxist worldview, an atheistic worldview, and so on. Some of these items are similar to those on Jie's list of the qualities needed for producing a modern, liberal, democratic citizenry. But others are clearly not. For example, some advocates of education for quality emphasize that students must be taught to recognize the need to maintain Communist Party leadership. One method for accomplishing this goal is to teach a version of history in which the only possible conclusion is that without the actions of the CCP there would be no new China (Cui

1999:118). A second is to promote love for the nation, love for the Party, and love for socialism through a primary school curriculum that emphasizes the evils of imperialism, the accomplishments of socialism, the beautiful places in China, and the symbols of the nation and the Party (Cui 1999:134–35).

The contradictory mix of liberalism and authoritarianism promoted in the name of "education for quality" influences discussions not only of what to teach but also of how to teach. On the one hand, as suggested above, much of this literature emphasizes open-ended discussions, child-centered classrooms, and other nonauthoritarian classroom practices. However, those who write about teaching political education deflect these suggestions with reminders that with regard to political attitudes teachers must keep "one hand hard and another hand soft" (Cui 1999:116–17). Such authors warn that when discussing issues like whether a Marxist materialist worldview is superior to a religious worldview (one that includes beliefs in gods or spirits), the teacher must ensure that all classroom discussion ends with a pure affirmation of the former (Cui 1999:133).

An explicit contradiction between the "authoritarian" and the "liberal" aspects of education for quality became apparent to me when I was touring schools in Shandong in 2000. Most of the schools had their hallway walls covered with black-and-white portraits of Marx, Engels, Lenin, Stalin, Mao Zedong, Deng Xiaoping, and Jiang Zemin, as well as various famous scientists and Chinese patriots. These schools seemed incredibly dreary to me as an Australian parent used to seeing bright school hallways filled with colorful student artwork. But I understood the portraits as an instantiation of Bakken's theory of the use of exemplary models—children are to be exposed to larger-than-life heroes. Everyday student artwork is too flawed to be displayed in the same space as the images of such perfect beings. The display of such portraits is also explicitly advocated in the literature on inculcating high ideological *suzhi* (Cui 1999:139–40).

One experimental junior high school I visited, however, did have the walls covered with student artwork, essays, and projects (Kipnis 2001b). Not a single portrait of a socialist leader or famous scientist was to be seen. The principal of this school explained to me that she was following the *suzhi*-raising education principles of encouraging student initiative, taking a student-oriented approach to education, and demonstrating to the students that their efforts and initiatives mattered in shaping the world. In one of the few cases of teaching independent organizational skills in China that I have ever heard of, this principal also had her students plan and run their own athletic meets, school plays, and social clubs. When I described the hallway decorations of the experimental junior high school to the principal of another school, he wondered how students could learn the proper respect for the Party and develop a high degree of political *suzhi* in such an environment. He argued that the portraits of socialist leaders and scientists on the walls show students who they should respect.[11]

That these opposing viewpoints were expressed only when I forced the contradiction into the open demonstrates the sensitivity of the issue. There are very few explicit debates in the "education for quality" literature, especially in regard to political education. When discussing this topic, some authors include contradictory examples, suggesting that "faith" (*xinren*) in the Party and independent thinking are easily integrated "qualities" (*suzhi*) that can and should be taught at the same time (e.g., Guan 2003). Others demonstrate their liberal thinking not by explicitly declaring their objections to teaching "faith" in the Party but by refusing to mention this "faith" in their lists of qualities that should be taught. The Shandong Province research group on education for quality, for example, uses the category of "moral *suzhi*" rather than ideological *suzhi*[12] and makes no mention of either faith in the Party or love for socialism as qualities to be inculcated (Shandong Yanjiu Ketizu 1998). Finally, some others demonstrate their authoritarianism by emphasizing faith in the Party and love for socialism as the most important qualities to be taught (e.g., Ma 2001; Xiong and He 2002). But no one explicitly writes that faith in the Party or socialism and independent thinking are contradictory. To do so would be to exceed the limits of what is permissible to express in public in contemporary China.

That no one dares to express this contradiction, however, should not fool us into thinking that Chinese governing is a single noncontradictory blend of authoritarian and liberal techniques. Rather, as implied by the different decorative choices of the two principals, as well as the different emphases of various authors on the topic of political education, sometimes the application of one technique excludes the application of another, and a choice must be made. That individual teachers can be painfully aware of this contradiction was made clear to me by a senior middle school political education teacher whose class I attended in 2005.

The lesson I witnessed was part of the mandatory curriculum and had been taught as long as the teacher could remember. It concerned an analysis of the "contradictions" involved in the transformation of an egg into a chicken.[13] It compared the role of the internal factors (a fertilized

chicken egg) with that of external factors (a conducive environment, particularly an appropriate temperature). While conceding that both factors
must be present for the transformation to occur, the lesson concluded that
the internal factors are the basis for the transformation and, thus, more
important. Both the teacher and the textbook finally applied these terms
to other contemporary and historical political problems, such as the internal contradictions and external environment of economic development
in China. Though the teacher spoke eloquently and did his best to apply
the "education for quality" principles of involving the students in discussion rather than simply lecturing, none of the students appeared to have
grasped the logic of the discussion. No one could come up with a correct
answer to any of the teacher's questions, and getting the students to volunteer any sort of answer was like pulling teeth. I, too, had difficulty grasp-
ing why the internal and external "factors" (*neiyin* and *waiyin*) should be
called "contradictions" (*maodun*) and why, even if one conceded that the
internal factor was more important in the case of the chicken and the egg,
it should always be the case that the internal contradiction is most basic.

After the class the teacher sighed and told me that teaching ideology
and politics is always difficult. The content is abstract and serious (*yansu*),
he said, and it is always difficult to spur on classroom discussion. I commis-
erated with him and shared the difficulties I encountered when teaching
unmotivated undergraduate students in the United States. I then asked
why he did not use the education-for-quality technique of encouraging the
students to discuss the lesson in a more free-form style. Could he not just
put them into small groups and let them decide what was a contradiction
and how the internal and external factors related to one another?

He replied by acknowledging that such an approach would perhaps
work in other classes but quickly added that it was really out of the question for an ideology and politics class. He pointed out that this particular
lesson came from some of Mao Zedong's most important essays.[14] But, I
asked, had not the Party already admitted that Mao had made errors in
the past? He replied that this was the case but that these errors were not
taught to middle school students. More important, the Party line on this
aspect of Mao Zedong thought was clear, the lesson was both absolutely
correct and a treasure of the Chinese people.[15] Besides, on the standardized exam there would be only one possible correct answer on this topic
and it would do the students no good to pretend otherwise.

The next time we met, the teacher deepened his analysis. He told me
that the students' intellectual *suzhi* could be raised much more quickly if

it were possible to approach thought and politics as items for real, open debate. Unfortunately, he said, this approach would not improve their political *suzhi*. So, he joked, the Chinese student could be thought of as a hatching chicken produced by the internal contradiction between intellectual and political *suzhi* and the external contradiction produced by too many students wanting to attend college and the resultant competition in the university entrance exams.

This example shows how authoritarian and liberal teaching techniques are not simply blended into a single smooth system of governing but exist in mutual contradiction with one another in a context where some people might attempt to choose or champion one of them over another. This is true despite the facts that Chinese educators label all of these techniques with the singular title "education for quality," that the Chinese state declares its education system to be entirely "socialist," and that some academics describe the Chinese education system as thoroughly "neoliberal" (e.g., Anagnost 2004).

Education for Quality Redux: Burden Reduction and Privatization in the Post-2008 Reforms

Attempts at implementing education-for-quality reforms are ongoing. In February 2008, as I was first writing this chapter, Qi Tao, the young, ambitious head of the Shandong provincial bureau of education, assisted and influenced by an equally ambitious and strong-willed deputy, Zhang Zhiyong, announced that he was redoubling his efforts to implement education for quality. Though many educators felt that campaigns for "education for quality" had become a spent force, Zhang and Qi promised that, this time, things would be different. They gave several reasons for their optimism. First of all, underlying societal conditions had changed. Compulsory education now reached all Shandong children, and university education would soon become a reality for more than half. More important, this time reforms would be implemented in a mandated, uniform manner across all school districts in the province. No one would gain or lose an advantage on the university entrance exam. Significantly, this round of reforms was to be applied to the senior middle schools as well as to the junior middle and primary schools.

Several concrete measures were announced. Time at school was to be reduced, with mandatory classes forbidden during holiday periods and on weekends. The reforms were announced just as schools were going on winter vacation, and their immediate implementation meant that no students in Shandong, not even the graduating students of senior middle school, who were in the midst of cramming for the university entrance exam, were to begin classes before the tenth day of the lunar new year. A principal in the city of Zibo had an official sanction put on his record and was publicly shamed for violating this rule. In addition to enforcing holidays, all schools were forbidden to hold classes on either Saturday or Sunday.[16] While students might study, it was expected that they would do so on their own volition rather than in uniformly organized study halls. According to Qi Tao, one of the biggest problems with rural boarding schools was that students lose the ability to regulate themselves and their time, as every waking minute is scheduled for them. He expected these reforms to increase the students' ability to make responsible choices on their own. Instead of classes and study halls, on weekends boarding schools were supposed to offer voluntary activities (that did not involve exam preparation) from which the students could choose. Second, even senior middle schools were to have a balanced and varied curriculum. Principals of schools that allowed physical education, art, and music classes to be sacrificed for extra exam study, or had students specialize too early (in literature for humanities students and science for science students), were to be punished. Finally, the financial links between exam success and teacher bonuses or student scholarships were to be ended. It was no longer permissible to give bonuses to those senior middle school teachers who had exam success or reduce tuition at private schools for students who did well on exams.[17]

While I cannot ascertain the fate of all of these policies, in July of 2008, when I made a late research visit to Shandong, the campaign to limit homework periods was continuing at full pace. A deputy head of the provincial government (*fu shengzhang*) promised not to rest until all education-for-quality goals were fully implemented. Twenty-five more principals had been punished, with three more being expelled from their posts. As the results from the 2008 university and senior middle school entrance exams were calculated and communicated to individual students, schools were prohibited from publicizing the exam successes of their students, either individually or in the form of statistical summations.[18] Parents of Zouping primary school students told me they no longer received the year-end exam results of their children in the form of a numeric score and class rank (like 68/100 points, 23 out of 58 in class, for each subject); rather, they received a simple and much less exact A, B, or C overall ranking. Exam scores were still to be reported to parents, but only at the beginning of the next school year when arranging classes, so that children could enjoy a "pleasant summer vacation." Education officials in two different counties told me that, at least for the period of this policy campaign, they did not dare to violate directives from the provincial education bureau. But they also doubted how long the campaign could last and added that Zhang Zhiyong was rapidly accumulating political enemies. Moreover, in large urban areas anyway, the ban on evening and weekend study halls in public schools had led to a rapid vamping-up of private, after-school study classes (*buxi ban*). While public school teachers were prohibited from working in such schools themselves, many were suggesting specific private study classes for their students, with the result that almost all of their students attended. If such private courses multiply, then the effect of many of the "burden reduction" measures will be limited. Moreover, a form of inequality will emerge in which poorer students and those who live too far from urban centers to have access to private classes will be disadvantaged (see Kipnis 2001b).

In September 2009, during my last field trip before completing this manuscript, a twofold reaction to the reforms seemed to be emerging in Zouping. On the one hand, a large private tutoring and after-school class business sector had emerged. The sector especially targeted primary school students on weekends and both primary and middle school students during vacation periods. On the other hand, the high schools and junior high schools and their students had devised methods to maintain their high exam scores by selectively following the provincial government's directions. Both reactions deserve further comment.

In the high schools and junior high schools, "mandatory" weekend and evening study halls had been banned, but there were still "voluntary" ones. The classrooms were left open during the evenings and weekends, and bells denoting the start and end of each study hall still rang, though teachers were not permitted to supervise or even attend these study halls. When I visited one high school during the evening, the classrooms were still full of students quietly studying. According to the students and teachers I spoke to, over 85 percent of senior middle school students still attended these "voluntary" study halls. Teachers suggested that at least 5 percent of the students instead worked with private tutors, while 10 percent went off to "play." A senior middle student told me: "Ten percent of the students always neglected their studies. When there were mandatory study halls, they just daydreamed and copied homework from their friends. Now these students are free to skip class altogether, but other than that, little has changed." This statement raises an important point about how Zouping students had always governed themselves. Even with mandatory study halls, the students had to produce the self-discipline to concentrate on their homework. The new regime, rather than producing new forms of self-discipline, as Qi and Zhang suggested, simply allowed existing forms of self-discipline to reproduce themselves in new ways.[19]

For the private tutoring business, however, the change has been revolutionary. This sector has forced itself into all of the crannies that the reforms have opened, as well as expanding its original business of providing after-school classes to primary-aged children. The ban on vacation classes has resulted in large summer and winter vacation study classes offered to students at all levels. There is a fair amount of diversity in these courses, with a few providers offering athletic, musical, or artistic activities in addition to exam topics, but these courses are both far smaller than the courses in exam-related topics and often directed at students who intend to take the specialized exams in arts, music, and physical education.[20] For senior middle school students who did not do well on the university entrance exam and wish to retake the final year of senior middle school and retake the exam (*fudu sheng*), new forms of "private" academies have also sprung up. These courses used to be run, at fairly high tuition rates, by the public senior middle schools. As such classes have been declared illegal for public schools to run, the county education bureau has simply arranged for them to be run "privately"—in buildings removed from school grounds, but at more or less the same cost and with teachers who are seconded from the public schools at their usual pay. A large private tutoring sector has also arisen for those students who can afford it. One high school student told me: "Since the teachers no longer attend study halls, if you have questions about your homework, you must either hire a private tutor or rely on your friends. When I had trouble with physics, my parents were happy to arrange a private tutor for me." Indeed, in addition to entrepreneurs in the private education sector, the primary beneficiaries of the reforms have been middle school teachers, who now have their weekends and evenings free. There has also been an expansion, perhaps unrelated to the recent reforms, in the after-school and weekend courses that have long been directed at primary school students. As with the vacation courses, these are offered in a wide variety of exam-related and non-exam-related areas, with exam-related topics, especially English, predominating.

Further evaluating the success of this last rounds of reforms is beyond the scope of this book, but both the design of the reforms and the problems encountered while implementing them are indicative of the social forces that make "education for quality" difficult. Parents' desire for the educational success of their children, a fire fanned by the birth control policy, is not easily reduced. Even if in the near future the majority of senior middle school graduates are able to attend college, there will still remain an educational hierarchy in which some university degrees are considered better than others. Without public exams, it is difficult to imagine a method of selecting those admitted to the best schools that can garner legitimacy. The interests of localities in securing high rates of educational promotion for their students remain. In China, as in many places, there are tensions between local governments and the offices of more central government departments, like the provincial education bureau.[21] When the interests of these governing agents diverge, often the distribution of financial responsibilities determines how compromises work out. This latest round of reforms has not been matched with a shift of fiscal responsibilities from the counties to the provinces. Where county governments, like Zouping, have borrowed hundreds of millions of yuan to build new schools, and the repayment of these loans is dependent on strategies that maximize test competitiveness, local governments may be reluctant to cooperate with the provincial education bureau. In addition, the political need for "correct" answers—in history and literature classes as well as politics and society classes—further inhibits certain forms of curriculum reform. Even the language that directs middle school administrators to implement the latest round of reforms reflects the link between authoritarian dictate and education: administrators are told to carefully "study" (xuexi, i.e., memorize, regurgitate, and implement without variation) the official documents on "education for quality." Furthermore, as will be further explored in the next chapter, respect for the classics of Chinese culture, by parents and educators alike, often translates itself into a curriculum focused on memorizing those works. The emphasis on memorization leads to exams, which demonstrate publicly the success of efforts at memorization. This preference is expressed in another popular saying: "Education for quality is flashy, but exam-oriented education is solid" (Suzhi jiaoyu honghong lielie, Yingshi jiaoyu zhazha shishi). Finally, the authoritarian aspects of China's policy implementation process have led to a particularly sneaky form of resistance by those lower down in the governing hierarchy: while the policy is implemented in word, the words of the policy are twisted to match the desires of those implementing the policy rather than those who designed it.[22]

Promoting Vocational Education against the Grain of Educational Desire

Another aspect of parents' desire for their children's academic success is their preference for an academic over a vocational university. Throughout Shandong, parents and students treat vocational education as a last resort. All counties in Shandong have both vocational and academic high schools; moreover, students in vocational senior middle schools can go on to various forms of tertiary education in technical education and eventually even nontechnical university education. But because only academic high schools offer a direct chance to participate in the university entrance exams, the most direct and prestigious route into the university, parents and students select vocational high schools only when there is no chance of admission to an academic senior middle school.

In Zouping, during the twenty-first century, roughly 80 percent of junior middle school graduates go to academic senior middle school. This is despite the fact that many of these students have had to pay large, one-time fees to gain admittance to academic senior middle school, because their test scores were not high enough. Of the remaining 20 percent, some choose to go to vocational high school and others simply drop out of the system. In 1999 and 2000, the reputation of the vocational high school was so low that more students abandoned education altogether than continued there, though by 2005 efforts to improve vocational education had met with some success, with 15 percent of junior middle school graduates choosing to attend (75 percent of the total who did not attend academic senior middle school). Even the principal of Zouping's vocational high school said that no student whose test scores were high enough to be admitted to one of the top two academic middle schools had ever chosen to go to vocational senior middle school instead.

The recruitment methods utilized by vocational schools both in Zouping and two other Shandong counties further illustrate this parental reluctance. These schools had programs that seemed attractive to me, including preparatory courses for tertiary vocational degrees in subjects like nursing, chemistry, information technology, and electronics; specialized secondary-level diplomas in (depending on the school) kindergarten teaching, accounting, and auto mechanics; and sometimes specialized training courses arranged with factories for work with the high-tech machines that are used in white goods and automobile manufacturing. But despite such programs, recruitment is difficult. During the first semester of each academic year, teachers and administrators from the vocational schools visit every junior middle school in their counties to promote their programs. At the beginning of the second semester, they obtain a list from the junior middle schools of the bottom 20 percent of students in each graduating class. Teachers and administrators split into groups and visit the homes of these students on weekends when they have a Sunday off from junior middle school. Even though they are dealing with students who have a very limited chance of succeeding on the test into academic senior middle school, first visits are usually met with parental silence, so repeat visits are necessary. During a typical visit the representatives of the vocational schools explain the employment opportunities of their recent graduates (at this point often quite spectacular), as well the comparatively limited fees that their schools charge. Though parents and students rarely voice their intentions at such meetings, coming as they do before the senior middle school entrance exam at the end of the spring semester, the vocational school teachers are at least able to plant the seeds of alternatives to academic senior middle school in the heads of these families. After the great majority of such students reproduce their typically poor exam results on the senior middle school entrance exam, a number of them agree to apply to the vocational school programs. In one county vocational school, the principal told me that without such aggressive recruiting techniques, he was certain that his school would be shut down. "We had spaces for 280 new students last year, but only 260 applied. If we hadn't recruited so aggressively, we might have only had 50. Prejudices against vocational schools are strong and the psychology of hoping one's child becomes a dragon is strong."

These aggressive recruitment techniques reflect nationwide policies to promote vocational education. In 2005 the State Council issued a decision that declared that by 2010, half of all senior middle school places and half of all tertiary places should be devoted to vocational education. China has been suffering from a shortage of technical workers in a variety of fields (as well as a glut of university graduates), and policy makers hope that by directing more students toward vocational education, labor markets will become more balanced. The State Council decision also indicated that provincial and local governments should make efforts to ensure that a wide variety of necessary courses are on offer and to work closely with employers in the areas of curriculum design, arranging practicum, and securing employment for their students. Schools were directed to keep careful track of the employment records of their students and not only to help students find their first jobs but also to be available to help students find new jobs if they lost their first jobs. Finally the decision stipulated that rural districts that had universalized nine years of education should be spending at least 30 percent of their education budget on vocational education.[23] In August 2006, the Ministry of Education reiterated the 2005 decision and announced the successes that had resulted from it, stating that the central government had allocated over one billion yuan directly toward building vocational schools and an additional 1.8 billion toward those schools through programs directed at poverty alleviation in the western provinces. As a result fifteen hundred vocational schools had received funds from the central government.[24]

These decisions and actions of the central government led the Shandong provincial government to issue a series of decisions and notices to the localities that echoed the demands of the central government. Counties and prefectures were directed to ensure that they spent 30 percent of their education budgets on vocational education, to expand vocational educational opportunities, and to pay close attention to the employment prospects of their students. As the situation in Zouping indicates, this has led to some improvement in the state of vocational education, though it seems unlikely that 50 percent of secondary education will be vocational anywhere in Shandong by 2010.

In some locales, impressive new vocational facilities have been developed. In July of 2006, in Qihe County of Dezhou Prefecture, a specialized vocational education center was formed by combining existing vocational secondary and tertiary schools. The new center received 7 million yuan from the central government to purchase new equipment and 5 million from the provincial government to upgrade dormitories and classrooms. When I visited in late 2007, the school seemed quite impressive. Students were studying courses that varied from auto mechanics, to the computerized control of specialized spot-welding robots used in a range of factories, to electronics, computers, nursing, and veterinary science. There were more than four thousand students on campus (including both secondary and tertiary students, up from two thousand on the old campuses less than five years ago), a relatively large figure for a county-run vocational school, but still considerably smaller than the eleven thousand academic senior middle school students in the same county. Most impressive, however, was the series of agreements that the center had arranged with more than one hundred employers from all over the country. Famous manufacturers including Haier in Qingdao, Fushikang in Beijing, Hangzhou and Yantai, Jinan Heavy Machinery, and 160 less famous but still good employers had signed agreements that bound them to offering the school's graduates a certain number of jobs per year in exchange for rights to recruit students from the school. According to school officials, in 2007 over 98 percent of graduates had either signed contracts for jobs within one month of graduating or gone on to a higher-level technical course. Eighty-five percent of those who took employment directly after graduating were satisfied enough with their positions four months later that they were not looking for another job. Most of them were already signed onto relatively secure three-year contracts, and starting salaries for graduates averaged 1,200 yuan per month. Moreover, the factories in the major urban centers of Shandong (Qingdao, Jinan, and Yantai) offered urban household registrations to workers who remained with the companies for three years or more. Employment and household registration in a large city are considered desirable by the vast majority of rural students, and many vocational schools seemed to offer an easy road to such positions.

While these employment statistics might seem exaggerated, they fit a broader picture for which I saw evidence all over Shandong. Every vocational school teacher I spoke with said that their graduates found jobs quite easily. They often added that factories were currently desperate for skilled labor and would seek out schools in the hope of securing employment agreements. In contrast, university teachers often discussed the difficulties their graduates had in finding employment. Average salaries for liberal arts university graduates were less than the 1,200 yuan a month promised to new skilled laborers, and unemployment rates were much higher. One newspaper article said that 4.13 million young people graduated from Chinese universities in 2006 and that more than 30 percent of them were still unemployed nine months after graduation (French 2007).[25]

Recent reforms meant to boost vocational education in Shandong and the country at large seem to have met with both success and failure. On the one hand, the relatively rosy employment picture for skilled workers in Shandong has enabled these schools to practically guarantee their graduates jobs. Enrollment figures for these schools are up considerably from the year 2000, and facilities and funding for some of these schools have increased. On the other hand, despite their recently impressive employment records, parents and students are still treating these schools as last resorts. The schools are able to recruit only from the pool of students whose academic skills were such that they could not gain entrance to an academic senior secondary school. Even the officials at the Qihe vocational center described above admitted that this was the case. Perhaps if the current rates of employability for vocational school graduates and lack of employability for university graduates continue, parental attitudes will gradually shift or at least diversify. But how long this might take is anyone's guess.

Manipulating Educational Desire

The current glut of university graduates in China is itself a rather recent phenomenon, related to the rapid expansion of university places beginning in the late 1990s. This expansion resulted from policies initiated by Zhu Rongji, then finance minister. According to both popular legend, as described to me by several Chinese academics, and Western scholarly investigations (Bai 2006), Zhu's reasons for expanding university enrollments were primarily economic and had little to do with education per se.

In the second half of 1997, during the aftermath of the Asian financial crisis, China's economic growth had slowed rapidly. The government responded with various measures to stimulate the consumption of houses and cars and otherwise increase consumer spending, but the public was in a cautious mood. Growth remained sluggish, unemployment was growing, and despite the high levels of savings available, consumers were holding onto their money. By 1998, the official unemployment rate had reached 9 percent, and 3 million secondary school graduates were about to enter the job market. At that time there were tertiary places for less than 10 percent of secondary school graduates (Bai 2006:129). Then, Tang Ming, chief economist of the Asian Development Bank Mission in China, came up with a proposal to expand university enrollments. He argued that no matter how tight Chinese parents were with their money in other respects, they would spend their savings to have a chance to send their children to college. By expanding the number of university places, funding this expansion by charging higher tuition rates and expanding the physical plant of China's universities, the policy would expand consumer spending and thus internal demand (*nei xu*), spur the construction industry and increase employment, and divert more secondary students from the job market. In addition, university expansion would create jobs for tertiary teachers, textbook writers and publishers, cafeteria workers, and so on. Many scholars supported Tang's argument and added that increasing the nation's average educational level would also meet goals of improving population quality (*suzhi*).

The implementation of Tang's ideas expanded the country's tertiary education system in several ways, all of which involved raising tuition rates.

First, all the state-run universities were allowed to raise their tuition. Second, these universities were able to offer extra places for local students who did not need dorm places and did not test high enough on the university entrance exam to secure a first-tier place. Tuition for these extra places could be even higher than the rates for the rapidly rising standard tuitions. Students who took these places were called day students (*zoudu sheng*). Third, universities were allowed to use their facilities to offer additional courses for diplomas that did not carry the university's name. These became semiprivate institutions, and they charged a wide variety of tuition fees. Finally a range of more vocationally oriented tertiary institutions (*da zhuan*), with courses in topics like accounting, teacher education, forestry, nursing, and so on, were also encouraged to expand.

In Shandong, at least by 2005, these four types of university places were clearly differentiated on the form for applying to university. The minimum university entrance exam scores followed three tiers for liberal arts and professional colleges, with vocational tertiary schools placed in a completely separate category. Though there was considerable variation within each tier, the minimum score for admittance to the standard university places was highest, scores for day students were in the middle, and scores for semiprivate places were lowest of all.[26] Only students with urban household registrations were eligible to apply for many of the day student places, and many courses gave point bonuses to local students with urban household registrations.

Overall, the policy has worked more or less exactly as Tang Ming imagined. Nationally, by 2004 there were places for over 19 percent of the age cohort that were entering college that year, in comparison to 9 percent in 1998 (Bai 2006:129). In Shandong, the number of new tertiary places rose from 62,994 in 1998 to 400,573 in 2005 (Shandong Sheng Tongji Ju 2006:468). Roughly half of the 400,000 places in 2005 were for regular four-year university courses, the highest percentage ever (Shandong Sheng Tongji Ju 2006:474). Because of the shadow effects of the birth control policy, the age cohorts born between 1986 and 1991 are quite large, and the 400,000 university places accommodated only about 25 percent of the age cohort entering university in 2005. But this is still a large percentage compared to the 6 percent in 1998. And by the time this book is published, the size of the age cohort will decline rapidly while the number of tertiary places will continue to expand. In 2011, there will be tertiary places for more than 50 percent of the age cohort (Shandong Sheng Tongji Ju 2006:54).

Tuition rates have also shot upward. By 2005, tuition rates averaged over 10,000 yuan a year among the Zouping parents with a child in college whom I surveyed. This amount was roughly equivalent to the annual income of local farmers or factory and service workers. When dorm fees and food costs are added in, average annual costs exceeded 13,000 yuan. Often, these fees hit marginal students the hardest, as the top tier of state-run universities charge relatively low tuition rates (for example, 6,000 yuan for the sociology department at Shandong University in 2006), while the other tiers charge more. As described in the previous chapter, Tang Ming's predictions about the spending habits of Chinese parents were on target. Zouping parents will save for decades to send their children to college, scrimping on almost all other forms of consumption. Wealthier Zouping entrepreneurs will also sponsor the pursuit of higher education by the children of their relatives. Offering a chance to spend on university tuition has proven a most effective way of getting Zouping residents to part with their money.

The expansion of university places, in turn, has helped expand the range of educational desire in Zouping. Since the mid-1990s, the desire to attend some sort of tertiary institution has spread from an elite to the masses. For most of the current generation of Zouping youth, this desire would have to be considered a realistic rather than just a pipe dream. However, even with mass tertiary education, places at the top universities remain limited. Consequently, at least to date, the competitiveness of the system as a whole has not diminished.

Conclusions

Policymakers in the Chinese national government have often tried to manipulate educational desire. While the birth control advocates hoped to increase the quality of the Chinese population by increasing the desire of parents to educate all their children, education policy reformers have tried to direct this desire away from a narrow emphasis on attending college and scoring highly on competitive exams. In the late 1990s, state economic managers saw the potential for economic growth in educational desire and successfully milked it for all it was worth. In the process, they helped to expand the reach of this educational desire to an ever-widening proportion of the national population.

Though policymakers have attempted to manipulate educational desire in various ways, it is apparent that not all these attempts have been equally successful. In general, it has been much easier to bolster this desire than tame it, much more profitable to bet on its expansion than to invest in its redirection. Thus, the processes of policy encompassment described in this chapter cannot be seen as all-powerful. Policymakers bump up against all manner of other agents, and they are always more likely to succeed when they work with rather than against the agencies of those whose behavior they would like to influence. If governing agents other than central policymakers have been involved in the generation of educational desire, then exactly who are these other agents and how were the dynamics associated with them generated historically? Through what kinds of governing practices do they work? These are the questions for the next chapter.

CHAPTER FOUR

Historicizing Educational Desire: Governing in the East Asian Tradition

Educational desire is a cultural phenomenon that has its roots in the governing practices of imperial China. Let us call these legacies "the imperial governing complex."[1] This complex is not a social whole in any functional sense of the term but rather a plethora of potentially interacting and overlapping social practices and imaginaries whose congruences have often been consciously noted by the philosophers, educators, artists, and governing agents who enact them. The geographic scope of their influence extends to populations descended from polities where governing officials were pressured to read the Confucian canon and were often selected through an examination system that focused on selected texts of this canon, that is, the region commonly called East Asia. The range of these practices and imaginaries is large. They reach from ideals of self-cultivation to teaching techniques; from aesthetic judgments about the beauty and emotional resonances of calligraphy, artwork, poetry, prose, and, indeed, all forms of cultural expression to the procedures by which social hierarchies are constituted and the moral logics by which they are justified and legitimated; and, above all, from teaching or education in a narrow formal sense to governing—the conduct of human conduct—in the broadest sense of the term. The methods of transmission of these various practices, ideals, and imaginaries have included pedagogy, by which I mean both the explicit content of what is taught and the methods by which those contents are taught; the social and political practices of constituting and legitimating hierarchies; and stories, artworks, and essays about dreams of personal, social, and national utopias.[2] While aspects of the complex have evolved (drastically, some might argue) in relation to postimperial projects of industrialization and nation building, the links to the imperial period remain visible in the consciousness of many Chinese thinkers.

This chapter examines how legacies of the imperial governing complex have been enacted in Zouping (and China more generally) during the twenty-first century. It explores these legacies both inside and outside of the education system proper and ends with brief comparisons with other East Asian countries. To introduce the cultural logics of this complex, I begin with four broad themes: exemplarity, examinations, holistic hierarchy, and nation building. I take the first of these themes from Børge Bakken's (2000) excellent book, *The Exemplary Society*. As described in the previous chapter, exemplary governing involves models of various types—essays, artworks, people, and behaviors—that can be put forth as ideals that everyone should attempt to imitate. These models are used when children first learn to write Chinese characters and when they learn to compose essays, but also in almost every other realm of governing. There are model workers, husbands, mothers-in-law, students, teachers, corporations, villages, towns, birth control advocates, and so on. Metaphorical expressions often link the logics of modeling in one of these realms, such as calligraphy, to others. The word "study" (*xue*), for example, often means to imitate a model in a process of internalization—mental or bodily memorization. Just as one "studies" writing by tracing model characters, so does one "study" how to be a person (*zuoren*) by imitating the behaviors and dispositions of one's teacher. Bakken (2000) argues that for many Chinese, imitation is the conceptual heart of social order (127) and, consequently, that education (*jiaoyu*) is as much a way to rule as a way to teach (96). Once the masses have been properly taught, they will be loyal subjects, the ancient ruling logic goes, while more modern concerns suggest that once the masses have been properly taught, the nation will be strong again.

But teaching through exemplarity can lend support to authoritarian leadership by eliminating the justification for questioning the ways of the teacher. If the student is to learn by imitating the teacher/leader, then debate and questioning become irrelevant. Chinese education reformers eager to critique what they see as latent authoritarianism in Chinese pedagogy have often noted this parallel. For example, in a newspaper editorial in the influential national newspaper *Southern Weekend* (*Nanfang Zhoumo*), Mo Gong (2005) argued:

Our schools put forth all sorts of authoritative models: thought models, political models, model schools, model academics, model teachers, and so on. These
authorities cannot be doubted, cannot be criticized, and cannot be analyzed;
they can only be followed. This sort of education is far removed from the type
of citizenship education that a modern society should promote. It is a feudal
legacy. (27)

Such views, however, are not universally held, and it does not seem entirely accidental to me that the first "Confucian Institute" to be set up at
a Chinese university was established at the "People's University" (*Renmin
Daxue*), the official CCP school in Beijing. While the official line at the
school is to treat Confucian works as a form of philosophy that may be
interpreted critically, some at the institute believe that Confucian writings
should be approached as sacred classics that may be interpreted but not
criticized (Billioud and Thoraval 2007:9). This particular view of Confucian texts is very similar to that taken by Party ideologues toward the
official writings put forth by former Party leaders.

Overlapping but also in tension with these logics of exemplarity are the
cultures of examination that so dominate education in China today. On
the one hand, success in examinations is very much a matter of skill at rote
memorization or the imitation of models. The more one can memorize
and the more quickly and accurately one can access what has been memorized, the better one is likely to do in exams. On the other hand, the selection of leaders and the creation of social hierarchies through examinations
are procedures designed to avoid the types of personal loyalties that can
arise in teacher-student relationships or in any other process of "studying"
a particular person. Tensions arise between hierarchies generated through
impersonal procedures like exams and those that are based in personal
loyalties. Examinations reflect an impersonal, meritocratic imagination.
The most capable, as determined by the examination, should rule. Without examinations, wider Chinese publics often assume that nepotism or
corruption of some form played a role in the selection process, delegiti-
mizing the hierarchies thereby formed. Thus examinations are trumpeted
as an alternative to democracy. The government argues that increasing
the education levels of cadres alone will be enough to reduce corruption.
With the CCP's hostility toward liberal procedures like elections, a free
press, and an independent judiciary as checks on cadre power, examinations have come to play a crucial ideological role in the CCP's claims to be
able to fight corruption.

The authoritarian aspects of CCP governing implicitly interweave logics of exemplarity and meritocratic examination with those of holistic hierarchy. Any system of governing in complex societies generates hierarchies of authority, but these systems become more authoritarian when the checks and limits on the power of those in positions of higher authority are negligible. Ideologies of absolute hierarchy, where the highly positioned are considered superior in every way to those below them, legitimate such hierarchies. In contemporary China, the notion of *suzhi* (human quality) is often used to legitimate hierarchy in such a fashion. While it can refer to limited and specific qualities, *suzhi* is often used to imply that each individual or group of people embodies a specific overall level of quality that is simultaneously reflected in physical attributes (such as height, beauty, athleticism, and accurate vision), mental attributes (test scores, verbal and written agility, artistic expression, mathematical reasoning, and overall intelligence), and moral attributes (the ability to resist corrupting influences). When such a form of quality is asserted to exist, it is easy to assume that those selected because of their success in a particular examination are not just better test takers than the rest of the candidates but also more intelligent in every way and morally superior as well. Such visions of hierarchy mesh well with ideals of exemplarity in which leaders are supposed to be moral exemplars. They also provide opportunities for dissent in which the disaffected can challenge the legitimacy of rulers by pointing out seemingly minor flaws (in areas like handwriting or historical knowledge), which can then be taken as evidence of a low level of overall quality. To differentiate this conception of human quality from more mundane conceptions, I call it Quality with a capital Q. To distinguish this form of hierarchy from more liberal structures of inequality, I call it holistic hierarchy.

The final theme is that of nation building. The old imperial examination system was always thought of as a way of building a common culture among the ruling class. All Mandarins memorized ("studied") the same Confucian classics in preparation for the exams. But now that education is universal, the process has been extended from the elite to the masses. As the number of people literate in Chinese characters and able to understand standard spoken Mandarin exceeds one billion, the central Chinese government has self-consciously viewed the curriculum more and more as a tool to build a unified, patriotic, and Party-loving national culture. Rural children all over the country are targeted to have their classroom habits "regularized" (*guifanhua*),[3] while a standardized manner of approaching math problems, artistic creation, physical exercise, chores, handwriting, and test taking is imposed on all. A unified set of patriotic themes is likewise force-fed to children in literature, history, social science, and thought and morality classes. Even though some of this standardization takes place at the provincial rather than the national level, allowing for some relatively localized content to enter the curriculum (but remember that all provinces are larger than the average country in Europe and four are more populous than Germany), all provinces must have their curriculums approved by the national education bureau, resulting in large degrees of similarity. The fact that all of this content is assessed through standardized exams only increases the degree of unity in what is studied and learned across the country, and even the forms of cynicism that high school students develop in reaction to this onslaught are shared by previously well-separated locales. The "great arch" of nation building that Phillip Corrigan and Derek Sayer (1985) saw as a "cultural revolution" in Europe is progressing rapidly in post-cultural-revolution China.

While I will point out the overlaps among these themes wherever possible, I must caution again against reading the imperial governing complex as a structural functional whole. The overlaps are the result of the conscious and unconscious manipulation of cultural forms by both the governing agents who enact aspects of the complex and their critics, but they are not functionally necessary. In any given instance some of the elements may not appear, and it is entirely possible for one aspect to exist in isolation from the others. In the rest of this chapter I first explore these themes as they became manifest in Zouping and then unravel the complex by exploring how it varies across East Asia.

Exemplary Governing in Contemporary Zouping

Let me begin with the campaign of the city of Zouping to become a "public health" exemplar in 2005. On August 31 of that year, Zouping's mayor (*xianzhang*) went on the local television station to give a speech about Zouping's drive to be named a public health city (*weisheng chengshi*) by a provincial inspection team. He said that the drive would require significant sacrifices by Zouping residents over the upcoming months but that the honor would bring glory to the city as a whole and demonstrate the high level of Quality of Zouping people to the entire nation. Off the record, other local officials told me that being a named a public health model would be considered a political accomplishment for Zouping's leading cadres, helping their careers, and would also enable Zouping to escape the financial supervision of the prefectural government, making it in many respects the administrative equivalent of a prefectural-level city rather than a county-level city. In early September, road crews began tearing up most of Zouping's sidewalks and a few main streets in order to lay new water pipes and build sidewalks of greater width in preparation for the upcoming inspection. The city became a dusty or muddy mess (depending on the weather) as sections of almost all the previous paved streets filled with dirt. On September 20, the primary school where I was conducting research began preparing for the inspection. In addition to the usual weekly cleanup period, during lunch and after school students and teachers alike scrubbed windows, dusted bookshelves, mopped floors, and cleaned toilets. Every corner was inspected for dirt again and again, and the placement of chairs and desks was measured with rulers so that all furniture was perfectly aligned. This cleaning was done several times a week until the formal inspection finally took place on October 18. On September 22, all the school's teachers further began spending their nonclassroom time preparing for a public health "examination." A dozen pages of multiple choice questions about how to treat and prevent the spread of various common and not so common illnesses, how to keep a clean house, how to handle and prepare food, and how to clean one's body were distributed to the teachers so that they could read over them and memorize the correct answers. A few days later, the teachers began going over the questions with the students. Classes usually devoted to English, Chinese, physical education, and thought and morality were sacrificed so that students could review the questions until all could produce the correct answers. I was told that all employees of state-related work units, including schools, factories, government offices, and banks, would have to take the test, as well as all schoolchildren who were in the fifth year of primary school or higher. In late September the test was administered, though no feedback on the results reached the teachers or students. By October 11, the sidewalks and streets had all been repaved and Zouping was beginning to sparkle. Streets and buildings were cleaner than they had ever been. Many small street vendors had had their licenses temporarily revoked, and flower displays had been set up at all the large intersections. On October 18, the police stopped traffic to let busloads of inspection-conducting officials from the provincial capital, Jinan, tour the city. The caravan stopped wherever the inspection leaders demanded, appearing to examine the city with great care. At the end of the month Zouping was officially declared a public health city.

The campaign to become a public health exemplar brings together aspects of all four themes described above. First, the exercise was one of achieving the status of an exemplary model as determined by officials from a higher level of the government. As is common in China, this modeling is tiered. By winning the title, Zouping became a public health model for other county-level cities in Shandong, but not higher-level places. Second, exemplarity in one respect (public health) is considered a sign of an overall superiority that brings glory to the city in all respects and is linked to the possibility of a rise in the national urban administrative hierarchy (at least in terms of financial supervision), in this case from a county- to a prefectural-level city. Third, an exam is used as part of the process, and the line between education in schools and other aspects of governing is crossed in multiple senses. Schools are part but not the whole of the exercise, and exams are part but not all of the procedure. Fourth, the approach to preparing for the exam is to memorize the correct answers to pregiven questions. This in no sense is considered "cheating" but rather is seen as respecting the demands of higher-ups. No time is given to debating or discussing whether one particular method of self-care or disease prevention might be better than another or to suggesting alternative procedures. The whole exercise might be seen as one of respectfully imitating the correct model of public health knowledge passed down by the exemplary authorities, in an attempt to move up the scale of overall exemplarity ahead of one's neighbors. Finally, the exercise promulgates unitary public health standards, for both knowledge and infrastructure, across the province and the nation. The public health campaign is part of the overall national drive toward modernization and standardization.

Calligraphy and Character(s)

Exploring these themes at the more concrete level of pedagogic practices in schools requires a brief introduction to the practical and aesthetic demands of Chinese character writing. As practices, Chinese writing and calligraphy link education to wider realms of governing. Many sinologists have noted that calligraphic inscription is a significant act of power in Chinese politics (Jenner 1992; Kraus 1991; Yen 2005). In imperial China, writing was the method through which emperors issued their edicts. In contemporary China, leading cadres are often asked to write a few characters on ritual occasions, such as the opening of a new park or building, and their calligraphy is often seen as a sign of their overall personal mental/moral/physical Quality. As William Jenner (1992) puts it: "In China power does not speak—it writes" (184). From an anthropological perspective, Yuehping Yen (2005) has carefully described how popular Chinese ideas about Chinese characters and calligraphy lead to a myriad of practices that bridge the realms of self-discipline, self-cultivation, the imagination of political and religious power, and imaginations of personhood. Adam Chau (2008) depicts how publicly written official characters are meant to subject the common people who read them through a manipulation of their emotions.

Scholars often debate whether Chinese writing is ideographic/pictographic[4] or phonetic. Some poets, linguists, philosophers, and even anthropologists have seized upon the ideographic/pictographic aspects of certain Chinese characters to make more general arguments about Chinese or Asian thought or to refute universal theories of the relationship between orality and literacy. But others have emphasized the fact that 90 percent of Chinese characters do contain phonetic elements in order to dispute such arguments based on the idiosyncratic nature of Chinese writing.[5] While agreeing with the careful linguistic analyses of this latter group of scholars, my argument here more closely resembles those of the former. The poetic, imaginative, and political importance of the ideographic/pictographic aspects of Chinese characters is crucial to understanding popular linguistic ideologies and practices. In art classes children practice calligraphy (with ink and brush as opposed to the pens used in handwriting classes), are taught that calligraphy is an artform, and are shown the importance of calligraphic inscription in traditional Chinese painting. (Traditional painting combines four artistic elements: the painting itself, lines of poetry, the calligraphy in which the poetic lines are written, and the seal, which involves carving characters in stone). In literature classes, students are taught, for example, the artistic/poetic importance of the pictographic moon element in many of the characters that appear in the classic Li Bai poem "Night Thoughts" (*Jing Ye Si*).

静夜思	**Night Thoughts**[6]
床前明月光	Before the bed, bright moonlight
疑是地上霜	I took it for frost on the ground.
举头望明月	Raised my head to gaze upon the bright moon.
底头思故乡	Bowed my head and thought of home.

The pictographic element for moon, 月, appears in many of the characters of the poem. Because the moon can be seen from everywhere, gazing at the moon is a metaphor for thinking of loved ones when separated by great distances. During the annual mid-autumn festival, separated friends and family members gaze at the full moon and imagine how their loved ones are also simultaneously gazing at the same moon.

In practical terms, the number of Chinese characters and the number of elements in them (over two hundred, which must be produced in a variety of shapes and sizes to fit their position within the overall character) make learning to write characters a much more difficult task than learning Western alphabetic writing. Children spend significant time practicing writing characters in the early primary years. This practice begins with detailed attention to posture at the writing desk and the way in which the child holds the pen. All children must learn how to write with their right hand, and left-handed writers of Chinese characters (almost uniformly Westerners who learned Chinese as young adults) are considered curiosities. Even in sixth grade, time was often devoted to handwriting practice. At three of the roughly twenty primary schools I observed around Shandong, sixth-grade students spent twenty minutes a day (a short period just after lunch) practicing handwriting; at most others they spent two or three twenty-minute periods a week practicing handwriting, while at a few they were assumed to have mastered handwriting by that time. But at one of the latter schools I discovered at least two (male) students with significant handwriting problems, indicating that more practice would have been beneficial.[7] Children learn to write by first tracing model characters and then writing them freehand in boxes of uniform size. Boxes for writing characters are often subdivided into quadrants, so that the relative size and position of each of the elements that make up the character, as well as its overall shape, may be better ascertained. Children also learn to write English letters in a precise and uniform way, and most sixth-grade students could easily outdo me in this regard. Embarrassingly enough, I often had my English handwriting corrected when writing on the board in front of primary school classes.

The difficulty of learning to write, the artistic/poetic resonances of handwriting, and the popular imagination of characters as primarily an ideographic/pictographic form of writing all contribute to the popular and institutionalized links between the evaluation of a child's handwriting and the evaluation of his or her overall Quality. Because Chinese writing is imagined as ideographic, just by learning characters one is imagined to

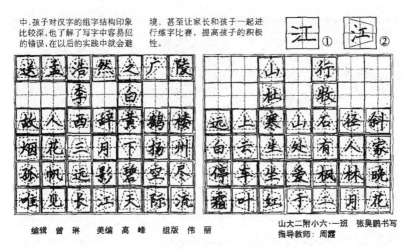

FIGURE 10. Character-writing practice page showing desired shape of characters. Photograph by the author.

embody Chinese history, thought, and philosophy (Yen 2005). A thorough knowledge of Chinese characters thus seems naturally to reflect wider forms of intelligence. The discipline required to learn to write characters is further taken as a sign of the degree of self-control a child has developed with regard to all aspects of his or her personality. Though Western experience would suggest that computers and printers might make handwriting less central, and even some Chinese commentators worry that computers will thus lead to the demise of Chinese culture (e.g., Zeng 2005), the importance of handwriting remained firmly institutionalized at the time of my research. On the university and senior middle entrance exams (as well as all lower-level tests and exams), essay questions were required to be handwritten. Teachers stressed that students with bad handwriting would naturally make a bad impression on the examiners. Many employers also require job applicants to submit handwritten resumes or write something by hand during the job application process so that the applicants' handwriting may be assessed. Many dimensions of the language ideology embedded in these practices may be seen in the complexity of the connotations of the word *wenhua,* which can mean "culture," the number of years of schooling one has completed, but also, and most literally, the transformations in one's personhood that occur through the process of mastering written Chinese language.[8]

Many Chinese artists have experimented with ways of making original

FIGURE 11. Primary school bulletin board with the couplet "Write your characters well one stroke at a time; act as a true person for a lifetime." Photograph by the author.

statements through calligraphy about both the importance of writing to Chinese culture and the pain of learning to write as a primary school student. Most famously, Xu Bing has created calligraphic installations of immense scale that are filled with false characters. Because Chinese is an old language with thousands and thousands of obscure characters that very few people recognize, and because Xu Bing does a beautiful job of combining seemingly plausible calligraphic elements into his false characters, educated native Chinese speakers can spend hours at one of his displays carefully examining the seemingly correct, obscure characters and trying to guess what they might mean from their pictographic elements. Xu Bing was educated during the period when the People's Republic of China introduced "simplified" Chinese characters and thus had to learn how to write many characters twice. In an interview interpreted by Perry Link he said:

At the time of the simplified movement in China, I was in the first and second year of elementary school. Chinese people need to spend a lot of time to memorize over 4000 characters. For example, in one semester we learned a lot of characters, a lot of new words, but the next semester the teacher will say that the government published a new way to write certain characters, so you need to learn more. So maybe the next semester the teacher will say again that the government has published another 100 new words. Some new words from last semester won't work anymore, so you need to forget them and go back to the old writing system. That really confused us about the culture. Historically, the Chinese people think that the word really is important, like it was made by the sky [heaven] or by nature. But during this time, we were really confused about culture. So my generation of Chinese artists or Chinese people always has an awkward relationship with the book, with culture, and with language. (Cited in Silbergeld and Ching 2006:114)

In another artistic project, a slightly younger generation of artists used an image of absolutely terrible handwriting with the words "A heavenly space for bad kids" (坏孩子的天空) to introduce their collection of irreverent and nonconventional art. Here I find it telling that bad handwriting, rather than, say, a picture of a truculent teenager with numerous facial piercings, is used to introduce the notion of adolescent rebellion.[9] In one sixth-grade literature class I saw a teacher single out a boy who had turned

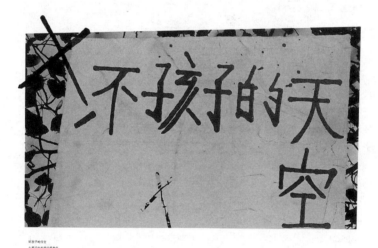

naughty kids

the chinese new generation

born after 1970

FIGURE 12. Cover of art exhibition catalog. Reproduced with the permission of the publisher *Timezone 8*. Photograph by the author.

FIGURE 13. Handwriting of a talented student, as displayed on a primary school wall. Photograph by the author.

in an essay written in bad handwriting and make him stand while she discussed, for close to five minutes, the particular handwriting mistakes he had made in his essay, how these mistakes demonstrated both a general disrespect for the teacher and the ingrained laziness in his character, and how important good handwriting was for future exam success. Later in the same class, the teacher singled out a girl with a beautifully written essay and told the class that the other students should use her essay as a model for future assignments.

Newspaper articles often comment upon the lowly place of boys in primary schools and often link this to their poor handwriting and the extent to which female teachers especially dislike fidgety students with poor handwriting (see, for example, Gao 2005). In fact, being peaceful and quiet (and therefore able to sit still when writing as well as to study for long periods) is considered a positive trait for girls in urban Zouping, and I met several girls and two female teachers whose name (*mingzi*) was the single character *jing,* meaning quiet. Regular newspaper advertisements for drugs to cure hyperactivity (*duodongzheng*) clearly target boys.[10] While being quiet and peaceful is idealized for girls more than boys, and while girls are stereotyped as having better handwriting than boys, many boys nevertheless do have excellent handwriting. And regardless of gender, well-written essays or even pages of handwriting exercises with beautiful handwriting are conspicuously displayed in the halls of primary schools.

The Imperial Governing Complex in School Life

Not only is handwriting a basic skill important to essay writing and art, it is also both a metonym and a metaphor for proper studying in general. Just as one learns good handwriting by copying and imitating model characters, so does one learn good essay writing and historical facts by copying model essays and learn the proper ways of comporting oneself as a person by studying (imitating) model characters.

In the previous chapter I described some of the emphasis on memorizing Tang dynasty poems and Confucian classics in primary school. These works are memorized partially during periods in which classes as a whole rhythmically and repeatedly read (chant) a given text aloud, and partially through homework assignments. Here consider the justifications for such practices given in the preface and epilogue of the 216-page textbook of classic writings that upper primary students in Zouping memorize. The writings include a selection of poems (mostly from the Tang and Song dynasties), nearly the entirety of the Analects of Confucius (*Lunyu*), and selected portions of the writings of Mencius, the Doctrine of the Golden Mean (*Zhong Yong*), the writings of Zhuangzi, the writings of Laozi, the Book of Changes (*Yijing*), the Book of Songs (*Shijing*), and a short essay by Fan Zhongyan, a scholar official who is held up as a historical model in Zouping and whose statue occupies a prime location in one of the city's prettiest parks.[11] The preface to the textbook argues that because primary school children are in the "golden period of memory expansion" (*jiyili fazhande huangjin shiqi*), memorizing beautiful classics will have a subtle but powerful influence on their personalities, causing them to have a lofty intelligence and laying the basis for an exemplary character (Zouping

Ertong Jingdian Daodu Xiehui 2004:iii). In the postscript, the editors describe an experiment undertaken in 1998 by psychologists from the Hong Kong International Education Foundation and the Shanghai East China Normal University to test the effects of twenty minutes a day of memorizing classics on Shanghai primary school children, in grades one through three. Children were divided into participating and nonparticipating groups, with the nonparticipating children spending the twenty minutes doing other school-related activities. After one year of the experiment, the students who had spent twenty minutes a day memorizing classics could write and recognize more characters than the nonparticipating children and had better memories and concentration skills. Moreover, 90 percent of the parents and teachers of those students believed that the moral behavior of these children had improved significantly. They claimed that the children were more confident and polite in interacting with adults, harmonized their behavior more with other people (as a result of the practice of chanting in unison), and had learned some proper manners from the content of what was memorized. It was also anticipated that knowledge of the memorized classics would reap further benefits when the children were old enough to both quote lines from the model writings they had memorized and replicate their style when writing essays of their own (Zouping Ertong Jingdian Daodu Xiehui 2004:217–26). Regardless of what one makes of the scientific veracity of such arguments and experiments, the justificatory logics behind the memorization are clear. Memorizing classics results in holistic improvement in children's overall Quality, and the memory of how to write individual characters is one of the central aspects of this overall improvement.[12]

On September 28, 2009, the 2,560th birthday of Confucius, primary school children throughout Shandong performed chantings of sections of the Analects. In his birth city of Qufu, a thousand children participated in the chanting, while a total of ten thousand participated in other rituals (*Qilu Wanbao* Editorial Staff 2009). Zouping primary schools held their own performances to mark the occasion. At one school, I witnessed the entire student body reciting sections of the Analects while a group of sixteen girls performed a stylized dance with oversized book covers (representing the Analects) as props.

Part of the moral training from the memorization of model essays is thought to result from the emotional embodiment of the content of the essays. When reading essays aloud or reciting them, whether individually or as members of groups, students are constantly encouraged to put more feeling into their readings (*ganqing touru*). As many of the essays can be quite maudlin, depicting, for example, the sacrifices parents that make for their children or that solders and Party members make for the nation, there is plenty of room for emotive display through facial expression and tone of voice. Emotive investment forces the students to involve their entire bodies in the readings and adopt a particular moral/emotive stance toward the world. This bodily investment makes the experience of reading aloud more memorable and thus is also a study aid that raises class averages on end-of-semester tests.

Teachers often ask the class to evaluate the extent to which a given student has brought out the emotional resonances of an essay, and students can be quite precise about which words and passages were recited with the correct emotions and which could be improved. The following passage from a sixth-grade literature textbook makes these connections explicit to students and illustrates the connections among memorizing exemplary essays, nation building, and moral evaluation.

Reading is a process through which the reader and the author exchange thoughts and feelings. Consequently, when reading an essay, not only do you need to understand what the author is saying, you also have to experience the emotive world contained amongst the characters.

When you read, put your heart into the essay, put your body and mind into it, this is the way to experience the emotive world. For example, when you read the essay "Establishing the Nation Ceremony" [*Kaiguo Dadian*], imagine that you were actually at the scene, with the three hundred thousand other people who participated in the ceremony. In this manner, when you read, "Chairman Mao declared: 'The central government of the People's Republic of China is today established,'" feelings of pride and excitement will rise up and you will really understand why the author excitedly exclaims, "Such a solemn declaration, such a sublime sound . . ." When you read, "The newly designed national flag—the five-starred red flag—rose into the sky. Three hundred thousand people together removed their hats and respectfully stood, raised their heads and gazed at the new red national flag," you will experience the five-starred, red flag rising, sense that from this point, the Chinese people have really stood up, and feelings of endless love for the new China will rapidly rise. When you read the description of the review of the troops, just like the author you will feel deep admiration for those who have sacrificed to protect China.

Reading aloud with feeling is an important method of experiencing the emotive world of the essay. By reading aloud with feeling you can both express the emotions that you are feeling and can more deeply understand the essay's emotive world. (Renmin Jiaoyu Chubanshe Xiaoxue Yuwen Shi 2005:42)

The performative/exemplary aspects of proper emotional investment are brought out further when teachers read essays in front of the class. Many times I witnessed performances by literature teachers that were worthy of Oscars. But lest we imagine that it is only Zouping or Shandong teachers that perform in this fashion, consider a depiction by anthropologist Terry Woronov (2003) of her initial visit to a fourth-grade literature class in Beijing:

> After some introductory remarks about the content of the material, [Teacher Liu] stood up straight and very formally in the front of the room, held her copy of the textbook in one hand at arm's length in front of her, and began to read the text aloud. To my astonishment, her reading looked and sounded to me like an aria from a Peking Opera: pitched high enough to sound almost falsetto, with huge dynamic range, her free hand gesturing broadly as she spoke. I looked around the classroom, expecting the children to burst our laughing at what seemed to me to be an excessively dramatic reading of a textbook, but instead they were watching Teacher Liu with rapt attention, eyes shining, leaning forward in excitement. When she finished reading, Teacher Liu dropped her arms, returned to a less formal stance and regular speaking tone, and asked the students: "Class, did you like that story?" The children roared back: "Yes! We liked it!" "Was it beautiful? (*Haobuhao ting?*) "Yes!" they yelled, "It was beautiful!" (Chap. 5, p. 1)

Woronov moves from this depiction to make arguments related to some of the language ideologies described above:

> At the heart of literacy pedagogy in Beijing there is an ideology of transformation: that learning to write, read, and speak standard language in the correct ways transforms children. . . . Language thus produces the writing (and reading and speaking) subject, rather than the other way around. (Chap. 5, p. 4)

By such performances, teachers serve as exemplars for the rest of the class. Calligraphic inscriptions of the saying 为人师表 *weiren shibiao* (act as a person of exemplary virtue, be exemplary enough in one's actions to merit the title teacher) were on display in many of the Zouping schools I visited to remind teachers of their responsibilities as example setters.

Often, this saying was inscribed above large mirrors in the hallways so that teachers could check their dress and appearance and see whether these were properly exemplary. But it was not teachers and school administrators alone who thought that teachers taught by being exemplary. The popular importance of this view was brought home to me by the opinions of Zouping parents about class size. As described in chapter 2, classes in Zouping could often be quite large—50–60 students per class in primary school and as high as 70 per class in some secondary schools. Such class sizes were in part a reaction to economic/demographic constraints—the school age population was about to decline (because of the birth control policy), and the education bureau considered it wasteful to build new classrooms and hire new teachers when student numbers would only be so high for a few more years. What was surprising to me was that parents never complained to me about class sizes. When I asked, parents often took just the opposite point of view: it was good that their child was in a classroom with so many other students, because large class size was evidence that other parents had maneuvered to have their children put in that class and, thus, that the teacher of that class was excellent. Crucial to this viewpoint is the assumption that teachers teach more by setting an example than by giving individual attention to students; consequently, the "quality" of the teacher was much more important than the number of students in a given class. Dramatic readings with all the emotional resonances in the right places were one way that literature teachers acted out this exemplary role.

Parents and students also sometimes strove to be exemplars. One evening, when visiting a friend who worked at a bank, I saw a set of handwriting practice books on the living room coffee table. At first I thought that they belonged to his son, but when I inquired he replied: "Those are mine. Now that my son is in the first year of junior middle school, I feel it important to set an example. I never watch TV anymore. When I am home in the evenings, I practice my calligraphy." On another occasion, I asked the head student (*banzhang*) of a junior middle school class what she did to deserve her position. She replied: "You have to lead by being the first person to do certain things (like entering the classroom or volunteering to help the teacher) and the last to do others (like pushing in line at lunch). You have to act a bit like a model [*mofan*]."

The nation-building aspects of the Chinese curriculum begin with the basic habits that are enforced on both teachers and students. Teachers are required to dress appropriately, to stand with good posture at the front of the class, and, to the extent of their abilities, to speak standard Mandarin.

A television show aired in 2004 depicted American teachers sitting on their desks, in a seemingly informal posture, chatting with the students of the class. Several Zouping teachers asked me, "Do Western teachers really do that?" and "What type of example does that set for the students?" By 2005, almost all the teachers I met spoke excellent standard Mandarin, while a minority of older teachers in rural primary schools spoke their Mandarin with a local accent. The percentage of teachers able to speak standard Mandarin has increased rapidly over the past two decades, and county education officials told me that by 2015 all Zouping teachers would be able to speak accentless, standard Mandarin. In all schools I visited there were billboards posted on the wall announcing the importance of speaking standard Mandarin, and the teachers I saw always did so to the best of their ability when in the classroom, though they often spoke in local dialect when in their offices.

Students learn a basic set of classroom interaction rituals in the first years of primary school. Students arrive at their desks a few minutes before a class begins. A warning bell tells them when they need to become quiet, and the teacher usually enters the classroom after the warning bell. When the teacher enters, the head student (*banzhang*) stands and says, "Begin class" (*shangke*), and the rest of the students stand. In unison they chant, "Hello, Teacher" (*laoshi hao*). The teacher responds with a variant of "Hello students, be seated," and the class begins. At the end of the class, the teacher signals the head student again, who leads the rest of the students in again rising and saying in unison, "Goodbye, Teacher." When students wish to speak, they raise their hands while seated, and if the teacher requests that a student speak, he or she stands and speaks loudly in clear, standard Mandarin. After finishing speaking, the student will remain standing for any discussion of his or her response until the teacher tells the student to sit down. If a student has poor posture at his or her desk, or does not speak clearly when the teacher calls out his or her name, the teacher will criticize the student. When students perform in front of the class, the class always offers applause before moving on to evaluation and criticism of the performance. I have seen close variants of these rituals performed in every classroom I have ever visited in China.

Principals at the majority of rural primary schools that I visited in Shandong, including Zouping, told me that the cultivation of good habits (*peiyang hao xiguan*) was at the center of their pedagogic strategies. They stressed that rural students in particular needed attention paid to their habits, as their parents were not likely to be able to teach these them-

FIGURE 14. Second-grade students sitting with proper posture. Note that the students were distracted as I unexpectedly entered the room on a onetime visit to this school. Photograph by the author.

selves. Good habits include the classroom behaviors described above, the use of proper terms of address when speaking to adults, a proper approach to homework and study that includes setting aside a regular time each day to complete the homework; in the absence of formal homework assignments, independently undertaking a review of materials covered in previous classes and a preparation of materials for upcoming classes; proper attention to detail in completing assignments, including punctuation, presentation, and completeness; and proper personal hygiene. Good habits were thought of as the basis for future success in secondary school. Principals learned which good habits to inculcate in children by reading nationally circulating education journals and from memos passed down through the education bureaucracy. In 2009, at a primary school full of the children of migrant laborers, the principal told me of the importance of teaching first- and second-grade students how to sit properly at the desk: "If you have proper posture at your desk, you give full attention to the task at hand and learn quickly. If I can standardize [*guifanhua*] their posture, even migrant worker children can succeed."

The Zouping education bureaucracy itself works to standardize approaches to teaching across the county. In line with exemplary understandings of "standards," anything that differs from the standard is understood to be inferior to it, generally the consequence of poverty and the resultant underinvestment and backwardness. In this broader context of rapid modernization and exemplary norms, "standard" (*biaozhun*) facilities are in fact excellent facilities. In addition, by requiring all students across the county at every grade level to take standardized tests in all subjects twice a year, and requiring (almost) all classes to be composed of an equal number of students who did well and poorly on the previous year's tests, the Zouping education bureau can easily determine if certain teachers are outperforming others (at least in terms of exam scores). The bureau uses this knowledge to promote standardized approaches to teaching across the county. In addition to the tests, the county education bureau has set up a Zouping education computer intranet through which teachers can share lesson plans and teaching tips. Every school in Zouping has now been wired into the intranet, and all Zouping teachers have access to a computer that is linked to the intranet. When a given teacher is particularly successful in terms of exam scores, then he or she will be encouraged to post teaching tips on the intranet. Members of the education bureau will also visit that teacher's classes and post their own spins on what those teachers are doing well. Teachers whose students produce good test results and who impress members of the bureaucracy are given bonuses and held up as exemplary models for the rest of the teachers. Teachers whose students produce poor test results will be pressured to study the teaching methods and lesson plans of the more successful teachers. Consequently, not only are teachers teaching the same curriculum from the same textbooks in pursuit of the highest scores on the same standardized test, they are also being pressured to adopt exactly the same methods of teaching this standardized package.

Finally, no discussion of nation building could be complete without attention to the heavy dose of nationalism and pro-Party propaganda that suffuses the curriculum, particularly in subjects like history, government, literature, and thought and morality classes. In the 2005–6 sixth-grade literature textbook used in Zouping primary schools, for example, six of the twenty-seven lessons to be memorized were about the sacrifices and accomplishments of CCP members during various twentieth-century wars. Another five of the essays were about topics that I would classify as soft nationalism—depictions of the beauty of various places in the beloved country. The remainder of the essays or poems included traditional

Chinese stories and translations of essays by foreign authors. While none of these latter essays could be considered explicitly nationalistic or pro-Party, they all contained a moral message of some form or another by, for example, depicting family members sacrificing for one another or efforts to promote the ecological balance of the planet. There were no essays that adopted explicitly sarcastic or ironic stances. The explicitly pro-Party parts of the book utilize this didactic structure to promote an unquestioning view of the moral superiority of the Party. As many researchers writing about moral education in China have argued, the CCP promotes a form of moral education in which morality, politics, and ideology are intertwined and in which morality is often defined in terms of correct ideology and politics (see, for example, Nie 2008).

Pro-Party pedagogy, however, does not directly lead to the production of nonquestioning, pro-Party subjects. Study after study has shown that secondary and tertiary students do not generally accept the view that the CCP is a beneficent organization or that patriotism necessarily involves loving the Party (Nie 2008; Rosen 1989, 1994). This failure occurs for many reasons. First, the curriculum itself becomes more contradictory as students progress through secondary school, advocating, for example, both the rule of law and a degree of respect for Party leadership that places high leaders above the law. Second, secondary teachers themselves explain to the students that some specific arguments or historical narratives may be wrong, and some teachers even admit that they themselves disagree with the textbook, or they say that students can believe what they want in private but must repeat the official lessons in any exam-related context (Kipnis n.d.; Nie 2008:79). Third, the atomizing, competitive pursuit of exam success as the overwhelming imperative of secondary schools contradicts lessons about self-sacrifice for the collective good. Finally, students' experiences outside of the classroom contradict what they are taught inside it. Nevertheless, this teaching does have nation-producing effects. For example, across the country, secondary and tertiary students uniformly know about the student movements in the name of science and democracy that occurred in Beijing and around the country in 1919 but are largely ignorant of the massive pro-democracy movement that took place in Beijing and around the country in 1989, as all information about this movement has been blocked out of the public sphere in general and the history curriculum in particular. Around the nation, primary school students, at least, are often impressed by narratives of bravery by CCP members, and patriotism is generally embraced as an ideal by all, even when narratives of Party members as model patriots are questioned. As Véronique Benei

(2008) argues, nationalism (though perhaps not love of the Party) is the product of embodied emotion as much as of intellectual knowledge. When Zouping primary school students endure the weather together through four seasons of outdoor Monday morning flag-raising ceremonies, or share dreams of travel to the national capital while suffering through their classes, patriotism takes root. And even when official pedagogic narratives produce nothing but cynicism, it is a form of cynicism that is widely shared throughout the nation. Jokes made about curricular items in a high school in, say, northeast China will very likely be understood and appreciated by students in the southwest.[13] In Michael Herzfeld's terms (2005) such jokes may be seen as part of the "cultural intimacy" that is important to nationalisms everywhere: "If the nation is credibly represented as a family, people are loyal to it because they know that families are flawed—that is part of love—and so they rally to the defense of its compromising but warmly familiar intimacy" (cited in Fong 2004a:644).

Perhaps partially in reaction to the pro-Party slanting of social sciences and the humanities, at the secondary school level the sciences are generally held in higher esteem. In eleventh grade, students must choose whether they will take the science or humanities version of the university entrance exam (with the exception of a minority of students who specialize in art, music, physical education, and so on), a choice that entirely determines which classes they will take for the last two years of secondary school. While there are many individual exceptions, it is generally believed that the smarter students gravitate toward the sciences. Throughout Shandong, the percentage of students who enroll for the sciences exam is much higher at schools designated for academic excellence than at average schools. But it would be wrong to understand the science curriculum as culture-free or even ideology-free. Throughout China, teachers and textbooks preach that science is the form of endeavor that ultimately can make the biggest contribution to China's modernization and greatness. Scientific weakness is taught as the cause of China's military and economic decline during the late nineteenth and early twentieth century. Scientists, both foreign and Chinese, are held up as exemplary models, and pictures of famous scientists are displayed alongside those of Marx, Engels, and Mao Zedong in many of Zouping's primary school classrooms. In one of the many lessons that are devoted to issues of national defense, Zouping's sixth-grade students learn of the glorious political decisions and scientific work that led to China's successful testing of atomic weapons.[14] When bright secondary students gravitate toward the sciences, they are reacting to a scientistic ideology that is institutionalized throughout the education system. Moreover, the specific bits of scientific knowledge that they learn are uniform across the country.

Beyond the primary schools, in the privately run weekend programs for primary school students that mushroomed in the county seat in 2008 and 2009, parents and their children pursued the cultivation of their own cultural capital more than the construction of the nation. Yet these activities still reflected the ideological character of the official discourse concerned with building the nation through improving the Quality of the population. The most popular of these activities either were directly related to exam success (as in the case of English lessons) or were promoted explicitly as having the potential to raise students' Quality. Almost all such activities related to imaginings of an upper-class habitus in either Western terms (as with ballet and piano lessons) or Chinese ones (calligraphy, art, and traditional upper-class instruments like the *gu zheng*). The upper-class status imagined here was holistic in that it combined economic and cultural capital, worldly power and cultivated, embodied talent.

To sum up the discussion of the imperial governing complex in Zouping schools, consider one day in a sixth-grade class during the autumn of 2005, when the campaign to become a public health city was under way.

> **7:20 a.m.**: I arrive in the classroom to find two girl students already there cleaning chalkboards and dusting windowsills. Over the next five minutes the class fills up, and by 7:28 all fifty-eight students have arrived. A bell rings, the students sit at their desks, get out their books of classic readings to memorize, and begin reading aloud the poem "Wu Yi" (Without Clothes).

In general school attendance was outstanding in Zouping. While sickness naturally occurs, parents consider missing school potentially disastrous for their child's future and go to great lengths both to prevent illness and to keep their children in school whenever possible. As described above, girls are usually the head students in primary school and take the lead in helping the teacher with extra chores.

> **7:30–7:50**: morning reading period. At 7:30 a second bell rings and the children chant aloud "Without Clothes" in unison while Teacher Zhang (the head teacher and literature teacher for this homeroom) walks in and out. They chant the six-line poem over and over for fifteen minutes until Teacher Zhang asks them to switch to two other poems, which they memorized earlier in the year.

They chant these in unison without looking at their textbooks. At 7:50 a second bell rings and the students stop chanting and begin talking among themselves and running around the class.

Morning recitations naturally enact the exemplary pedagogy described in this chapter.

8:00–8:40: period 1, literature. At 7:58 the warning bell rings and the students return to their desks and quiet. Teacher Zhang arrives and the students stand and greet her. She returns the greeting and asks them to sit down. These rituals occur at the beginning and end of each class period, so I will not mention them in the rest of this summary. The class formally begins before the 8:00 bell rings. The lesson focuses on the four-page textbook reading "Couplets in Prison," which discusses how some communist revolutionaries maintain their spirits while in jail by writing poetic couplets. The teacher first asks the students questions about the text, such as "What did so and so say when . . . ?" which are correctly answered by literally reading a line or two from the text. After twenty minutes of this sort of didactic exchange, the students break up into small groups to analyze the couplets that the protagonists of the story write. For the final five minutes each small group reports back to the class as a whole. For homework they are to work on memorizing the text.

Here again, exemplary teaching techniques are used in relation to close reading and exam preparation. Analyzing the meaning of the couplets allows some discussion.

8:50–9:30: period 2, math. Math Teacher Liu leads the students through an example word problem that requires the students to multiply fractions. She then gives the students ten minutes to complete five more problems on their own. Next she asks the students to raise their hands and volunteer answers and explain their reasoning. One student who gives the wrong answer is required to remain standing while two other students discuss what is wrong with his approach and eventually come up with the correct answer. The students are finally given more problems that they work on until the end of the period. Their homework is to finish those problems.

Math education is perhaps fairly similar the world over (Meyer and Ramirez 2003). The practice of standing after a wrong answer reflects the standardized classroom behavior described above. The emphasis on explaining one's mathematical reasoning does go beyond rote learning. Nonetheless, at least at the primary school level, math everywhere is an arena where there is one correct answer to each question and, thus, one that lends itself to regimes of examination.

9:30–9:50: eye exercises and calisthenics, done in unison as described in chapter 1.

As Gladys Chicharro-Saito notes (2008), the collective, performed-in-unison aspects of these movements are thought to improve the children's moral character.

9:55–10:35: period 3, English. The children all sit down before the warning bell. The head student collects homework done in exercise books and puts them on the teacher's desk. English Teacher Hu comes in and starts the class before the second bell. First a tape of native speakers reading a textbook English dialogue is played. Then the teacher gives her own rendition. Then the children read the dialogue again and again—first aloud, in unison as a class, then in pairs, in front of the class with each student taking on one of the dialogue roles. The teacher corrects, praises, and criticizes the students' performances, as need be.

Foreign language instruction is generally amenable to exemplary teaching methods. The educated native speaker is the ultimate model.

10:45–11:25: period 4, art. The lesson covers bird and flower paintings, a classic subject matter for Chinese traditional painting. The children get out their ink sets, water, and brushes and Art Teacher Li passes out paper. Teacher Li demonstrates how to paint a bird, one stroke at a time. First the eye, then beak, head, back, wing, tail, and legs. She emphasizes how to hold the brush, how to make the tip of the brush pointy by twisting it, and how to control the amount of ink on the tip of the brush and the flow of ink. There is a single correct way for each stroke and a single stroke for each part of the bird. The children then paint their own birds for the rest of the period, while Teacher Li walks around and gives advice. The children are a bit noisy, but all manage to complete a bird painting. Four or five of the paintings are quite good, but most of the children have not quite learned how to control the flow of ink.

Traditional Chinese painting, like calligraphy, requires mastery of the ink brush before all else. This requirement also encourages exemplary pedagogy, though it is done in a more relaxed style because art is not a key examination subject.

> **11:25–1:45**: return home for lunch.
>
> **1:50**: I arrive in the classroom, and again some girls are cleaning, sweeping the floor, and dusting. By 1:58, all the students and Teacher Zhang are in the classroom and the warning bell sounds.
>
> **2:00–2:20**: writing practice. The students sit at their desks and write characters. All must write at least two hundred characters (twenty characters ten times each) during this period. Teacher Zhang walks around checking the students' posture as they write.

Calligraphy and posture were emphasized together at every primary school I visited.

> **2:20–2:55**: period 5, science. Teacher Feng is one of the few male teachers at the school. The lesson for today is about rotational leverage as demonstrated with screwdrivers. The larger the diameter of the handle, the less strength is needed to turn the screwdriver. The teacher has brought in a board, many wood screws, and screwdrivers of various sizes and has student volunteers take turns trying the various screwdrivers and competing with one another in screwing in the screws for about twenty minutes before returning to the textbook and lecturing on the physics principles involved.

This lesson is the most hands-on and participatory of the day. It is similar to the types of lessons suggested in the education-for-quality literature discussed in the previous chapter. The lesson goes against the grain of the exemplary pedagogy enacted for most of the day.

> **3:05–3:40**: period 6, computer science. The computer lab is under repair so the students stay in the classroom while a teacher gives a lecture on computer safety, everything from avoiding electric shocks to computer viruses and hackers.

Here, circumstances force or allow the replacement of a hands-on activity with a lecture.

> **3:50–4:30**: activity period. This period is supposed to be reserved for physical activity, singing songs, or free reading in the library but is often taken over for some other pedagogic purpose. Today Teacher Zhang returns to class and has

the students practice the multiple choice questions for the impending public health exam. The school day ends at 4:30.

Again, exemplary activities are substituted for what is supposed to be the least exemplary part of the day. This happened in approximately one-third of the "activity periods" that I attended.

Literary Masculinity and the Cultivation of Self

Beyond schools, the imperial governing complex influences all aspects of social life through its structuring of the gendered desires associated with "literary masculinity." I take this term from Kam Louie's (2002) analysis of "talented scholar/beautiful woman" (*caizi jiaren*) stories and his theorization of the hybrid Chinese/English term "*wen* masculinity." This genre of writings "revolve[s] around the theme of winning the woman and passing the examinations, though not necessarily in that order" (Louie 2002:61). It reached its peak during the Ming and Qing dynasties (roughly 1400–1900) but had roots stretching back over two thousand years and has been reinterpreted in various ways throughout the twentieth and into the twenty-first centuries. A more recent twist on this genre can be found in the works of the contemporary Taiwanese intellectual/critic/playboy Li Ao. In his erotic novel *Mountaintop Love* (*Shangshan, Shangshan, Ai*), the protagonist, who shares many biographic details with Li Ao himself, seduces a beautiful young woman and then thirty years later her beautiful daughter. While the intellectual persona of the protagonist forms the starting point of the young women's attraction to him, the irresistible climax of his seductive technique is the tour he gives them of his extensive personal library (Li Ao 2001).

As important as contemporary novels of literary masculinity may be, just as pertinent for my purposes is an earlier genre of theatrical productions that brought the talented scholar/beautiful woman genre to the illiterate masses (Louie 2002:65–68). The popularity of the plays suggests that not only scholars were moved by stories of literate men passing the examinations and getting the girl. This popularity resonates with the educational desires of a relatively undereducated population depicted in this book.

As a social scientist rather than a literary scholar, I use the term "literary masculinity" with a necessary and purposeful multiplicity of meaning.

It simultaneously refers to the embodiment of literary virtues as a means for enhancing one's status in the world, the sexual desires enabled by this enhanced status, the literary representation of these desires, and the ways in which those literary representations inform (and indeed are cited within) the expressions of this desire in actual social worlds. The historical background for this desire is, of course, the imperial examination system, in which men, but not women, were allowed to achieve social and political power through success in literary endeavors. Though the imperial examination system is no more and men and women are equally able to attend college, the fantasies and ideals of literary masculinity continue to haunt the present. In contemporary Zouping schools, I was struck by the lack of a school counterculture, and especially the lack of any signs of a type of masculinity that anchored itself in rejecting academic ideals (Kipnis 2001a, 2001b). Though boys may have had, on average, worse handwriting than girls, they did not take pride in academic failure or consider academic success a feminine characteristic. In so far as I was able to discuss the matter, all the secondary school students I spoke to said that intellectual prowess and academic success were attractive characteristics for both male and female students, but especially for boys. When I asked high school students about bullying, responses varied over the extent to which bullying was a problem in Zouping schools, but all agreed that academically successful students were the least likely to be bullied. Moreover, I was unable to convince Zouping students of the social significance of categories like "nerds" and "geeks" in American high schools.

As applied to gender relations, literary masculinity should be seen in relative terms. Even in the talented scholar/beautiful woman genre, the "beautiful woman" often displayed considerable literary talents of her own and was certainly culturally refined. In contemporary Chinese marriage patterns, academic prowess is clearly valued in both sexes, but there is a strong tendency for men to have at least as much education as their spouses. In urban settings, women with Ph.D. degrees are sometimes jokingly referred to as "the third gender" because of the difficulty they have in finding spouses (Southwell-Lee 2010). But having too little education can also be a problem for women on the marriage market. In Zouping, more than one tertiary-educated but still unemployed and unmarried young women told me that they feared that if they took a (relatively high-paying) job in a local factory, their Quality, along with their desirability on the marriage market, would decline. At least until they were married, they said, they would prefer lower-paying but more cultivated jobs, such as

FIGURE 15. Banner with newlyweds' faces in front of a wedding banquet hotel. Clothes originally were bright red, the traditional wedding color. Photograph by the author.

working in a bookstore. A female college student from Zouping told me
that many women work hard in order to enter Peking University (along
with Qinghua University, the most prestigious in China) in order to find a
husband: "Once you are attending Peking U., you know that all the men
are desirable partners; the men know that the women can raise intelligent
children as well."

The citation of literary representations of literary masculinity is itself
common. The memorization of literary classics facilitates this citation. Consider two examples. Wedding ceremonies in twenty-first-century Zouping,
especially those in the county seat, are often run by commercial wedding
firms. These firms usually set up large (five meter by four meter) banners
with photos of the couple outside the hotel where the wedding banquet is
to be held. Often the couple is dressed in (what are imagined to be) traditional Chinese outfits for these photos or have their faces inserted into
backgrounds that include bodies dressed in such clothes. One of the more
common motifs for these photos is that of the "talented scholar" and the
"beautiful woman" (*caizi jiaren*). The couplet in the photo above reads "A
heavenly match of a talented scholar and a beautiful woman; Why envy
the immortals? Only this loving couple deserve your jealousy."

The second example is a ditty I heard recited on several occasions.

人生四喜	**The Four Joys of Life**[15]
久旱逢甘霖	A good rain after a long dry
他乡遇故知	Meeting old friends away from home
洞房花烛夜	Honeymoon night in the bridal chamber
金榜题名时	Seeing one's name on the Golden Honor Role
	[i.e., the list of people who passed the examination]

Three aspects of this ditty deserve comment. First, the fours events are significant to life in both the imperial era and the early twenty-first century. In Zouping I have witnessed the joy farmers express during a timely rain, the pleasure travelers take in meeting old friends, the happiness on the faces of newlywed couples, and the celebrations that occur after securing admittance to a top university. The ditty as whole thus convincingly frames contemporary life as part of an ongoing tradition. Second, the ditty places the joys of sexual awakening and educational achievement next to one another, connecting the pieces of a literary masculinity. Finally the ditty orders the pleasures from the most common to the most exceptional, placing examination success in the highest position, even more pleasurable than one's honeymoon night.

Certainly literary masculinity is not the only form of masculinity in China. Louie (2002) pairs it with martial (*wu*) masculinity, but more important here is to note that the playboy scholar is not the only prototype of literary masculinity. Also important are more prudent idealizations of literati who learned to keep their sexual desires confined to socially proper marital relations. Quite a few talented scholar/beautiful woman romances end with the talented scholar marrying the socially proper woman rather than the one he initially desires (Louie 2002:61–63). In this ideal, control of sexuality, a disciplined approach to the acquisition of literary knowledge, and moral character development come together. The contemporary strength of this masculine ideal can be seen in the plenitude of relatively uneducated but economically successful Chinese businessmen who attempt to compensate for the lack of educational opportunity in their youth by spending their later years pursuing cultural capital (and at least sometimes abstaining from the sex industry socializing that many associate with business in China).[16] Many Chinese universities have set up special courses for businessmen, known as "National Studies Classes" (*guoxueban*), which focus on traditional Chinese texts, leading the businessmen to study the same Confucian classics that the primary students in Zouping memorize. At Peking University, the most prestigious in China, businessmen from all over the country pay 26,000 yuan per year to attend National Studies Classes that meet for 3–4 days a month for one to two years (Billioud and Thoraval 2007:9–10). Several Shandong universities also offer such courses, and I met quite a few Zouping businessmen who had attended them. Nanlai Cao (2008, 2009) describes a slightly different route to literary masculinity taken by many successful businessmen in the city of Wenzhou. They pursue a Christian version of the literary male ideal. They declare the Bible the definitive intellectual/moral text, devote themselves to Bible study, give sermons on the Bible, and lead discussions on the wisdom contained in the Bible. Not surprisingly, while Wenzhou churches are sometimes socially diverse, including both successful businessmen and migrant workers, in mixed-class churches only successful businessmen can deliver sermons or lead Bible discussion groups. Women also rarely give sermons. Even though many Wenzhou "boss Christians" (*laoban jidutu*) have limited formal education, they maintain Bible interpretation and preaching as exclusively male and upper-class domains in order to bolster their literary masculinity (Cao 2008, 2009).

Exams, Meritocracy, and Legitimacy

The place of exams in contemporary PRC society is firmly entrenched. Not only are there exams for university entrance, senior middle school entrance, graduate school entrance, and almost every variety of diploma available, but outside of the education system exams are also widespread in the recruitment of employees in both the public and the private sector, and they are used by the government itself in the process of issuing various licenses and awards, as in the case of Zouping's "public health city" award described above. As in almost any other modern country, a main purpose of exams is to select the competent or, at least, to weed out the incompetent. However, to a far greater extent than elsewhere, exams are also seen as a way of fighting corruption and nepotism. Regardless of the accuracy of an exam as a measure of the qualities that a given employer or university desires, exams are seen as providing a check on the otherwise corrupt tendencies of those granted the power to make selection decisions.

Such attitudes go to the heart of personnel matters within the Party itself. The CCP is a huge organization with over seventy million members. The party-state's system of personnel hierarchy (*nomenklatura*) has fifteen grades, and these do not even include the majority of cadres working at the township and village level. Party leaders at any level of this hierarchy understand well the relative lack of checks on the power of cadres within their local contexts and, consequently, do not trust those below them to make selection decisions in an unbiased manner. In 1983 the Party center declared that by the year 2000 all cadres should be university graduates, all county-level leaders should hold an MA degree, and all cadres at the provincial level or above should hold a Ph.D. (Bakken 2000:64). As entrance to degree programs is by examination, degrees are evidence of meritocratic, impersonal examination success, which is held to prove overall Quality. Because some have gotten around these rules by obtaining illicit degrees,[17] the standard university entrance exam (the one for graduating senior middle school students and not the one for adults seeking to reenter educational institutions) has become the ultimate standard in trustworthiness. Many government jobs, in Shandong anyway, require applicants not only to have a university degree but also to have gotten that degree straight out of senior middle school, which demonstrates that their admittance to that degree program was the result of success on the university entrance exam. Though not all provincial-level leaders hold a Ph.D., in Shandong the CCP has come close to reaching the other two goals (though this was achieved in part before the requirement of attaining the degree straight out of senior middle school, when some cadres had access to degree programs outside of those governed by the university entrance exam system). Moreover, echoes of desires to enact the third can be seen in the four Ph.D. degree holders in the present Politburo (the group of twenty-five leaders at the head of the CCP) and in the scandals that have erupted because many complain that the degrees of three of them are false.[18] Regardless of the legitimacy of the Ph.D.'s, political desire to obtain or dispute the degrees itself demonstrates the imagined links between political legitimacy and meritocracy.

To battle corruption, the Shandong party-state has also regulated pay scales in state-owned enterprises in such a way that managers cannot raise the salaries of non-university-educated employees above a certain level. As a result, skilled workers (such as welders, electricians, and chemical technicians) have left state-owned enterprises to take up jobs in privately owned enterprises that pay much more. In December 2008, the party-state further tightened controls linking education levels to promotion possibilities for public servants (*Beijing Youth Daily* Staff 2008).

In the summer of 2008, when the results of the 2008 university entrance exams were reported and university admittance committees were processing applicants, a nationwide debate emerged over the relationship between exam scores and university admittance. In a story taken up by newspapers all over the country, it was reported that a Hubei Province senior middle school graduate, Zhang Mengsu, had received admittance and a full scholarship to a famous Singaporean university even though her score on the Chinese (Hubei Province version) university entrance exam was so low (445 points) that she would have been restricted to the lowest tier of China's universities. It was reported that though Ms. Zhang was not a good test taker, she had a bright, outgoing personality, as well as excellent oral English and oral Mandarin skills, and that these had enabled her to make a good impression in her interview with the Singaporean university recruiters. More important, she had won a provincial essay-writing contest, come in third place in district-wide oral English and computer English competitions, was head student in her class and editor of various student publications, had taken up paid employment during summer vacations since the end of ninth grade, and had regularly taken leadership positions in school activities. All of these activities took time away from her exam preparation. Though her teachers acknowledged that she had never been the school's best student in exam scores, they added that she was probably the best student in almost every other way. While later newspaper reports cast doubts as to whether she had in fact received the scholarship, it is the debate that this story led to rather than its veracity that interests me.[19]

On the one hand, almost all the opinion pieces related to this story (such newspaper reports are generally accompanied by several short opinion columns) praised the Singaporean university for being able to see beyond exam scores. These editorials argued that exam scores cannot capture a person's true "Quality" and that Ms. Zhang was clearly a rare talent. On the other hand, the editorial authors also stressed that while Singaporean society was advanced enough to have university admittance panels that could make impartial decisions, such was not the case in China. One writer said that if such powers were granted to admittance committees in China, then an "unchecked avenue for corruption" would be created. As a consequence, the Chinese public would never acknowledge the accomplishments of those admitted to college. Even reducing the required entrance exam scores by a few points for students who had clearly documented "special accomplishments" was supposedly looked upon with suspicion (*Qilu Wanbao* Editorial Staff 2008a).

In post-Mao China, exam-based selection procedures have become central to the battle against corruption. Exams are often seen as the only method that can produce social hierarchies that the public will accept as legitimate. While the editorial writers discussing the Zhang Mengsu case (and the Party leadership) hope that further economic development will lead to a Singapore-like situation, in which selection committees can supposedly be trusted, they feel that that stage of modernity has not yet been reached in China.

The Imperial Governing Complex Unraveled

While I have stressed how exemplarity, exams, authoritarian hierarchy, literary masculinity, and nation building overlap, they do not constitute a functioning cultural whole. The overlaps are imagined by those concerned with the conduct of conduct in the CCP leadership, education bureaus, and schools, and sometimes even by parents and students, and are also duly noted by critics of the regime. They are, however, just as frequently undone.

Calligraphy, for example, is more often seen as a practice of freedom, individual expression, and anti-authority than as one of imitating exemplary models. Because the medium of ink on paper (unlike oil painting) allows no correction, complete mastery of ink flow off of the brush is required, and beginners must devote considerable time to mastering the basic brush strokes. But this rote practice might be likened to a musician practicing scales. Once the basics are mastered, the stress is on the artistic flow of notes or brushwork, and even calligraphers whose cursive characters are barely recognizable are admired for the expressive energy that their work embodies (Yen 2005). Attachments to traditional Chinese culture and hatred for authoritarian educational structures are views that go together often enough. The writer/artist Feng Zikai (1898–1975), for example, published many cartoons and essays criticizing the way in which Chinese exam preparation regimes oppressively discipline students and turn education into a factory for mass-producing identical person/objects.[20] Yet at the same time, he felt that painting in the Western medium of oils was constrictive. A spontaneous banner written by his friend Ma Yifu elicited the following response from Feng:

> I particularly treasure Mr. Ma's calligraphy, above all his impromptu writing. That is not to say that the work he does when at leisure is not as good; but here

[my preference] is based on my personal theory of art. I feel that detailed brush-work can't express individuality, energy, or inspiration as readily as something done on the spur of the moment. In calligraphy, things created with careful brushwork conceal everything within and are not readily perceived, while in the case of off-the-cuff writing, the artist's ability is on immediate display; its individuality overwhelms you at first glance. That's why I don't like Western painting done in workmanlike oils, while I am thrilled by Chinese pictures that are executed with brush and ink. I have no interest in major creations that might take five or ten years to complete; rather I am delighted by paintings that are done spontaneously after a meal. (Cited in Barmé 2002:179)

It is further true that any of the individual governing or pedagogic prac-tices described in this chapter could be added or deleted at a given school without changing other practices. At one primary school I visited, a physi-cal education (PE) teacher told me how he had just moved away from a PE curriculum that emphasized uniform and rigorous physical training for everyone in the class to one in which the students were encouraged to do any form of physical activity that they wished. PE, he explained, is not an exam subject, so it is an area where the school could implement "happiness education" (*kuaile jiaoyu*). He added: "The idea is to make the students like physical activity so that they will do it for life. They can do whatever they like: jump rope, climb on the monkey bars, play basketball or ping-pong. As long as it is safe and we have the equipment they can do it." Yet at the same school, the number of Tang dynasty poems to be memorized by first-grade students had just been increased. Extending exemplarity in one area can thus be accompanied by reducing it in another. In short, the imperial governing complex is not an all-or-nothing phenomenon.

Examining the variety of ways that elements of the imperial govern-ing complex are implemented in other East Asian countries further demonstrates the historical accidents involved in some of these overlaps in contemporary Zouping. Singapore is a fascinating case because an author-itarian political structure and competitive, exam-based education system have been matched with the elimination of both Chinese language and traditional Chinese writings from the national curriculum. The demise of Chinese-language education in Singapore can be seen in the history of Nanyang University. In 1953, while the region was still a British colony, a group of Chinese businessmen established Nanyang as the first Chinese-language university outside of China, in order to serve the region's Chinese-language-educated high school graduates. However, during the 1960s and

1970s, Lee Kuan Yew, the Western-educated and autocratic first prime minister of Singapore and leader of the People's Action Party (PAP), worked to first anglicize and then dissolve the university. After a long struggle, in 1981 the university was taken over by the Nanyang Technological Institute, and the degrees, cultural capital, and careers of the previous graduates of the university were marginalized. The closure was justified by the political sensitivity of having a "Chinese university" in a country surrounded by Malay nations and by the fact that the entire Singaporean education system had switched to the English medium during the 1970s. This system-wide switch to English was itself justified by the importance of English as the language of commerce. Many former Nanyang graduates, however, believed that Lee's desire to marginalize left-leaning, Chinese-language-educated political competitors, as well as enemies made during the long struggle over Nanyang's status, greatly influenced the struggle over Nanyang University (Jianli Huang 2007; Lim 2009; van der Kroef 1964).

If Lee fought against Nanyang University and Chinese-language education during the 1960s and 1970s, it was not because of any doubts over the supposed racial supremacy of Chinese people. After resolving the Nanyang problem, in the 1980s he began to voice these views more and more baldly, declaring that 80 percent of individual success is genetically determined and that the academic successes of East Asians and Jews reflect the genetic superiority of their "races" (Barr 2000:185–206). Flatly contradicting typical "Confucian" views of the perfectibility of humans through practices of self-cultivation, Lee's views on race and eugenics led to a seemingly unique vantage on the social functions of exam-based meritocracy and holistic hierarchy. In response to those who argue that the examcentric education system is too stressful and competitive, resulting in extremely high rates of myopia, suicide, and a host of other problems (Lim 2009:232; Wee 1995), Lee counters that the extreme competition allows the state to select the genetically most endowed people as leaders. Without a mention of the forms of self-cultivation the system's discipline encourages (virtues that a more "Confucian" perspective might emphasize), Lee argues that those who succeed in Singapore's school exams have genetically superior abilities:

> [A good man] may not have disclosed what he is because he has not yet been put under severe stress. It depends on the qualities of the population, the genetic pool we have inherited. We get the leaders we are capable of throwing up. . . .

The subsequent results in University show one good brain in a thousand. These have more than average intelligence, more than average energy, more than average capacity. (Lee Kwan Yew, cited in Lim 2009:230)

Lee considers it crucial for Singapore's survival that the best leaders be selected from those with top university results and that the gene pool of the country as a whole be enhanced by encouraging those with good examination results to reproduce more frequently than others. As a consequence, he instituted Singapore's infamous family planning regime in which university-educated women are given financial incentives to have more children, while women who do not make it to college are given financial incentives to have fewer children (Lim 2009; Wee 1995).

While the CCP has paid little attention to Lee's biological determinism, the PAP's (and Lee's) authoritarian political system is often seen as a model to imitate. The PAP's history of fostering economic growth and limiting corruption without introducing either Western-style press freedoms or a system of democratic checks and balances that could threaten one-party rule is very attractive. The importance of a meritocratic, highly paid civil service to this system has especially received CCP attention (Duchatel 2008). And China's combination of authoritarian rule and economic success makes education in Chinese and about China potentially more attractive to the PAP now than it was during the 1960s, 1970s, and 1980s. Perhaps in the not-so-distant future, more Chinese-language options will be reintroduced into the Singaporean education system.

Taiwan in contrast has taken its imperial governing complex in a completely different direction. During the forty-year period between 1949 and 1989, the Nationalist Party combined authoritarian rule and an extremely competitive exam-based education system with efforts to become the world center of traditional Chinese-language education. The simplification of Chinese characters that took place in the PRC was rejected in part because reform of the writing system would make it more difficult for educated people to read the classics. Literary Chinese and classic writings were mandatory aspects of the curriculum, and many felt that by the 1970s, the top Chinese literary stylists in the world all came from Taiwan. Since 1989, martial law has been lifted, the island's political system has democratized, and trends in popular culture have emphasized how Taiwan is culturally distinct from China rather than a center of Chinese exemplarity. These political trends have affected the education system. An emphasis on multiculturalism has reduced the centrality of classical Chinese literature, and the Taiwanese education bureaucracy has attempted to make the system less centered on entrance exams and less competitive by creating alternative paths to university entrance. The latter of these reforms, however, has failed miserably. The competition to enter the best universities remains extreme. No reform to the university admittance system can get completely away from tests or grades of some sort, and middle-class parents especially are quick to direct their children to private schools or after-school programs whenever public school reformers try to make public school curriculums less devoted to the exams, tests, grades, or other measures that matter for university admittance. The introduction of a multicultural curriculum has simply increased the number of topics subject to study and testing. By all reports, the education system has become more competitive since the end of martial law.[21]

A detailed account of the education systems in Japan and Korea would be beyond the scope of this book, but a brief introduction helps round out the discussion. South Korea and Japan are now both democratic nations with vibrant public spheres in all media. In Japan, the writing of Chinese characters is central to everyday literacy and thus education. For girls, especially, handwriting is taken as evidence of a person's background and character (Miller 2005), and calligraphy is a highly admired art (Nakamura 2006). In South Korea, the formal written language contains no Chinese characters, though they are still used in some contexts, and high school students are still required to recognize a fair number. The education system in both countries, however, is extremely meritocratic, exam-oriented, and competitive. Anecdotal evidence and newspaper articles suggest that the South Korean system is among the most intense in the world. Michael Seth (2002) describes how the relatively egalitarian construction of the education system there (completing universal access to primary education before devoting too many resources to secondary education, and so on) resulted in an increase in the population able to compete for entrance to higher levels of education at each stage in the development of the system. When primary school was universalized, the competition for junior middle school was intense; when junior middle school was universalized, the competition for senior middle school became intense, and so on. In 2008, newspaper reports described senior middle schools in Korea where the students live at the school in order to prepare for university entrance exams sixteen hours a day, seven days a week, much as in secondary schools in Shandong (Choe 2008; Dillon 2008). One Korean parent said that success in the university entrance exams "determines seventy to eighty percent of a person's future," with admittance to one of the top three universities virtually guaranteeing a good career (Choe 2008). Newspaper reports also suggest that Korean men desire white-collar jobs more than blue-collar jobs not so much for their higher salaries as for their imagined links to educational credentials (Fackler 2008). To avoid the intensity of the educational competition in Korea, tens of thousand of Korean secondary students leave the country to attend middle school in the United States, Australia, England, and New Zealand (Onishi 2008). A Korean educational psychologist developed her own brand of "education-success correspondence theory" to explain the zeal for education there (Oh 2003). In Japan, the national examination system drives hordes of secondary students into daily after-school programs (*juko*) that specialize in preparing students for exam (Dierkes 2008). While a decline in the university-aged population in Japan may have led to a reduction in competition for university places, competition for the top universities is still quite intense. The classic research of Thomas Rholen (1983) on Japan's high schools during the early 1980s showed how hard Japanese students studied then. Only those at the very top or the very bottom of the secondary system— i.e., those who either had no hope of reaching college or those for whom school and exams were relatively easy—seemed to enjoy their secondary years. How much the Japanese system has mellowed is an open question, though surveys of math and science scores suggest that during the twenty-first century Japan has fallen behind students from Taiwan, Hong Kong, and South Korea; consequently, some Japanese parents complain that Japanese education has lost its emphasis on learning at an early age, memorization, and cramming (Fackler 2008).

Conclusion

The various aspects of the imperial governing complex discussed in this chapter—exemplarity, exam-based meritocracy, holistic hierarchy, literary masculinity, and nation building—manifest themselves in various ways in contemporary Zouping education and governing, conceptually overlap and reinforce one another, and can be said to have at least buttressed educational desire there. But they neither form a functional whole nor even seem essential to the production and maintenance of high levels of education desire. Looking more broadly across East Asia, we can see similar forms of educational desire in the absence of both the exemplarity associated with the learning of Chinese characters and traditional Chinese writings and the holistic hierarchy related to rigidly authoritarian political systems. And if we look even more widely at the patterns of educational attainment and striving of populations of East Asian descent in the United States, Australia, New Zealand, Malaysia, Indonesia, and elsewhere, we can see that high levels of educational desire can persist even without a rigid examination system and even in nations where projects of monocultural nation building through the education system have seemingly passed their peak. In contemporary East Asia, we can say that the social respect shown to exam success (not just by universities but also by employers, by publics selecting politicians, and by unmarried individuals seeking partners) is as much a cause of systems of exam-based meritocracy as an effect of them.

In short, while the imperial governing complex may be seen as closely related to the intensity of educational desire in contemporary Zouping, it cannot be considered its sole and direct cause. In the next chapter, then, we will move on to yet other forms of explanation for this intensity. Rather than examine local sociocultural patterns, the types of policies implemented in the PRC, or the historical legacies of the examination system extant in imperial China, we will turn our attention to the universalizable human attributes that educational intensity in Zouping draws upon.

The Universal in the Local: Globalized and Globalizing Aspects of Educational Desire

Three factors determine whether a given social phenomenon will take hold, spread, and become universal.[1] The first is how well it fits with what it biologically means to be human. To say that humans everywhere have customs relating to the sharing of food, for example, is to acknowledge that humans are social beings who need to eat to survive. The second is how well it fits with particular ecological, political, and/or economic conditions. If I argue that most children in industrialized societies attend school, I suggest that something about industrialized societies causes children to attend school. This cause may or may not be "functional." Attending school may be "useful" (economically? socially? psychologically?) in an industrialized society, or it may just appear that way to parents in industrialized society, or perhaps industrialized societies simply give rise to powers that compel parents to send their children to school. The third factor is how easily the technology, practice, or dynamic spreads from one group of humans to another, at least within particular ecological, political, or economic contexts. Here, as Bruno Latour argues (1994, 2005:63–86), it is worth noting the properties or agency that the phenomenon itself embodies that makes it attractive, useful, or troublesome for human users. In his terms, such properties or agencies are "mediators."

Especially important are those technological mediators that establish equivalencies between people. Such mediators subjectify people by enabling social exchange with anyone who shares a relationship to the same mediator (Latour 2005:191–218). Such mediators are attractive to those who adopt them precisely because they enable interactions beyond the boundaries of a culturally defined group. Currencies, languages, religions, legal frameworks, technological standards, systems of measurement, techniques of observation, and so on spread in part because they enable the empowering expansion of social worlds. In some cases, then, the universal makes its way into the local precisely because of circumstances that cause it to be locally desired.

The Nature of Social Desire and Hierarchy

Educational desire in Zouping, China, or East Asia is first of all a social dynamic. Reproduced in many individuals, it seems to spread like a contagion until it envelopes entire communities, as evidenced by the 100 percent affirmative responses I received when surveying parents about whether they wished their children to attend college. Educational desire has become what is commonly known in China as a social "fever" (re),[2] defined by David Palmer (2007), in relation to "qigong fever," as a social movement

> situated somewhere between the political campaigns or 'movements' (yundong) of the Mao era, and the fully commoditised consumer fads of capitalist societies; a 'fever' is a form of collective effervescence in China's post-totalitarian phase which occurs when official policies and informal signals sent from above correspond with, open spaces for, and amplify popular desire, which appropriates these spaces in unexpected ways, simultaneously complying with, appropriating, disrupting and mirroring the projects of state hegemony. (21–22)

Insights from two theorizations of the social logics of human desire in general, Deleuze and Guattari's *Capitalism and Schizophrenia* and Georges Bataille's *Accursed Share,* illuminate such fevers. Deleuze and Guattari's first useful point is that the interrelationships among social institutions, technologies of governing and acting, and desires are complex. The fact that educational desire is tied to phenomena like systems of writing, examinations, school buildings, and educational bureaucracies, to name just four of its mediators, makes it typical of the sorts of passions Deleuze and Guattari analyze. They label such complexes "assemblages" and note:

> Assemblages are passional, they are compositions of desire. Desire has nothing to do with a natural or spontaneous determination; there is no desire but

assembling, assembled, desire. The rationality, the efficiency, of an assemblage does not exist without the passions the assemblage brings into play, without the desires that constitute it as much as it constitutes them. (Deleuze and Guattari 1987:399)

That educational desire in Zouping might be seen as an assembled, assembling passion demonstrates the difficulty of separating it easily from the institutions, technologies, and traditions discussed in the previous three chapters. Like the chicken and the egg, educational desire is at once a consequence of the assemblage and a driving force in its reproduction.

Deleuze and Guattari's (1983) second useful point is that social organization depends on lack. Social production and reproduction by necessity rely upon human desire, and human desire ("an abject fear of lacking something" [27]) is structured through the social organization of lack. Such a conception of desire recalls the relation between educational desire and what in chapter 3 I called *suzhi* discourse. Governing with the goal of raising the nation's Quality depends on a conception of the nation as a whole, as well as individuals and communities within it, as lacking in Quality. Lack is especially marked in rural, uneducated, and impoverished persons, households, and communities, and thus intense passions may be born in such sites (Yan 2003b). That the standards determining what constitutes a "Quality" individual undergo constant inflation (from upper secondary school to university education, from undergraduate university education to graduate school levels, from any university education to degrees from the top universities only), and can be redefined by powerful institutions and individuals, only increases the insecurity that surrounds the lack and the intensity of the passion. But also, as argued in chapter 3, the discourses that define this lack are not simply the products of unidirectional, top-down, authoritarian governing. Rather these discourses emerge from fantasies deeply embedded in the wider society, circulate among various social classes and groupings, can be resisted by the formal institutions of government as much as the subjects of governing, and are sometimes turned against the powerful as well as the powerless.

The third insight to be gained from Deleuze and Guattari (1983) is that desire is mass-produced: "fantasy is never individual: it is *group fantasy*" (30; italics in original). They call potentially variable individual desires "molecular" and mass fantasy a "molar aggregate":

once desiring-production has spread out in the space of representation that allows it to go on living only as an absence and a lack unto itself . . . a *structural unity* is imposed on the desiring-machines that joins them together in a molar aggregate. (306; italics in original)

Let us recall the major traits of a molar formation or of a form of gregarious-ness (*herd instinct*). They effect a unification, a totalization of the molecular forces through a statistical accumulation obeying the laws of large numbers. . . . the statistical transformation of molecular multiplicity into a molar constella-tion is what organizes lack on a large scale. (342; italics in original)

Two aspects of this conception of a molar aggregate seem especially rele-vant to educational desire in Zouping. First, the "herd instinct" in humans makes the sharing of fantasies, desires, and passions desirable in itself. To share a passion with a group of others is to participate in the same social universe. Second, the manipulation of this passion is common in mass set-tings such as schools and crucial to the processes of nation building so evident in contemporary Chinese education. Educational administrators, curriculum designers, and teachers play on the desires of students to join a herd, to subjectify themselves in both the immediate group of their school-mates and the seemingly infinitely larger universe of the nation as whole. Especially for rural children, the attraction of becoming part of the great and glorious nation, as an equal member if one can just learn enough, seems easy to understand.

From Georges Bataille another set of insights emerge. Bataille ana-lyzes human hierarchies, of the sort that exist everywhere, according to the triple dynamics of economy, eroticism, and sovereignty. Eroticism relates to the possibilities of breaking the rules that humans devise to regulate sexuality. These rules form part of the code that on the one hand separates humans from animals, and on the other distinguishes the high from the low and justifies human hierarchies. As Bataille (1991) puts it:

certain basic behaviors, our way of eating for example, or of evacuating, or sexual activity subject to rules, distinguishes man from animals. From this point of view, each man is certainly superior to animals, but more or less so: the way in which he satisfies his animal needs is more or less human. (333)

Humans everywhere are consequently unequal, but in "civilized" societies, the code that justifies this inequality, that separates nature from culture, involves extensive efforts of cultivation and self-cultivation, in internal-izing the learnings that define civility. The hierarchies justified by degrees of civility define both what values are sovereign and who is held to best embody those values. In economic terms, the sovereign is that nonproductive excess upon which the surplus produced by human economies is expended. This nonproductive expenditure is always intimately, if contradictorily, related to the values that justify the sovereignty.

Bataille's philosophy draws attention to two dilemmas central to the dynamics of educational desire in Zouping. The first concerns the relationship between values and human hierarchy. Valuing anything—academic achievement, human Quality, self-cultivation, knowledge of Tang dynasty poetry—establishes a social hierarchy around that value. Calling knowledge of Tang dynasty poetry valuable, for example, automatically implies that those who master this knowledge are better than those who do not. But nation-based systems of education also need to treat the students that fill their classrooms as "equals" who will all become citizens of the same nation, regardless of their mastery of the content in question. The debates about the education-for-quality reforms in China in this sense resemble debates about education reform anywhere in the world—how to balance the production of learned persons with the egalitarianism necessary to allow "the masses" universally to embrace learning and become national citizens.[3] The second dilemma concerns whether the cultivation of Quality deserves to be seen as a sovereign value in its own right or as merely a tool in the pursuit of economic development. This dilemma informs the contradictory efforts of the CCP party-state to promote vocational education. On the one hand, it directs the investment of educational funds into vocational schools despite the unpopularity of these schools among parents. On the other hand, many of its schools place an unrelenting emphasis on academic success, and the Party's own recruitment and promotion procedures undermine the value of vocational degrees. The endless pursuit of Quality can be both a nonproductive pleasure that defines sovereignty within China and a tool of the ultimate economic sovereignty of development.

In short, aspects of educational desire in Zouping reflect universal dilemmas of human desire and social hierarchy, as well as dilemmas of the relationships between systems of education and social hierarchy in all modern societies. As Deleuze and Guattari suggest, human beings are passionate, social, tool using, and historically complex creatures, and their desires necessarily arise in social assemblages. Herd instincts are common and often manipulated through the production of lack. As Bataille suggests, establishing rules in human societies and the values related to those rules leads everywhere to the creation of social hierarchy and sovereignty.

Educational desire relates to the pursuit of sovereignty both as the pursuit of rank and as a form of expenditure whose value exceeds its usefulness to mere economic development.

Agrarian Discipline

Robert LeVine and Merry White (1986:75–77) have described a series of characteristics common to schooling in almost all agricultural societies that exist and existed across Eurasia, North America, and North Africa. These characteristics include several aspects of what was depicted as the imperial governing complex in the previous chapter, including the emphasis on memorization and modeling in the pedagogic process; the strict authority of the teacher, whose role is to embody model characteristics; the tendency to treat texts as sacred; and the assumption that the memorization of sacred texts leads to simultaneous moral and intellectual development.

Qu'ranic schools provide an excellent non–East Asian example of such pedagogic practices. The chanting of texts is common to Islamic schools from Indonesia to Morocco, as "young boys are taught to listen and repeat, to accumulate verses by memory, to write the words of the sacred text" (LeVine and White 1986:78). The average student can take close to eight years to memorize the whole Qu'ran (LeVine and White 1986:81). Understanding comes much later and is not considered to be the immediate cognitive reward that motivates students to work at studying. In part, students at Qu'ranic schools are motivated by strict discipline, and teachers often beat misbehaving boys. Memorization of the Qu'ran as a sacred moral text is naturally both a moral and an intellectual achievement, and elders with high levels of Qu'ranic knowledge have been respected throughout the Islamic world. Finally the teachers themselves are closely scrutinized to see whether they are the intellectual and moral exemplars that Qu'ranic teachers are supposed to be (LeVine and White 1986). In Morocco, at least, the moral emphasis on the virtues of memorization has spilled over into the state public school system (Boum 2008).

The spread of such systems of education across agricultural societies relates to both experiential and social structures of agricultural life. Obtaining food from farming requires laboring well in advance of harvesting. One must plow, sow, irrigate, and fertilize in the proper manner long before one can reap the benefits of one's labor. While there can be room for experimentation, farmers, especially poor ones, cannot risk depart-ing from time-tested methods. To do so might lead to crop failure and starvation. Copying exactly the farming techniques of another successful farmer, without at all understanding the reasons for those techniques, is perfectly acceptable. That disciplined, rote memorization and the imita-tion of ideal models are considered the most virtuous of pedagogic tech-niques in such societies hardly seems surprising (Bakken 2000; LeVine and White 1986).

Moreover, in agricultural empires, where the vast majority of people are farmers, social differentiation often centers on age/sex hierarchies rather than on occupational differentiation. These hierarchies contribute to making rote memorization a virtue. Young people are completely de-pendent on their elders for both the resources with which to farm and the knowledge of how to farm. Elders expect respect simply for being old, and morality rests on age-, gender-, and kin-based social roles rather than on abstract laws. Conforming with one's social role is as great a virtue as conforming with the proper techniques of agriculture. In such societies, intelligence is demonstrated by knowing how to artfully conform rather than how to innovate, a perspective that allows the easy blending of intel-lectual and moral virtues (LeVine and White 1986:38–44).

In most agricultural empires, pedagogy was associated with the reli-gious study of sacred texts, reinforcing the link between intellectual and moral development. In China, Confucian values of filiality and the exem-plary respect (filial piety) owed to superiors circulated across all levels of state and society. The relationship of an emperor to his subjects was thought of as parallel to that between fathers and sons, and the concept of filiality was held to encompass both (Rawski 1988; Zito 1997). LeVine and White (1986:77) argue that China's implementation of the imperial examination system made it different from other agricultural societies, in which schooling was primarily a religious activity. In China exams both sharply differentiated between winners and losers and linked study directly to social advancement. The relation of Confucian texts to the imperial bureaucracy made study as much secular as religious. While there is some truth in these arguments, the place of exemplarity in traditional Chinese education cannot be denied. In imperial China the emperor was positioned between heaven and earth and, thus, simultaneously sacred and secular. Confucian texts were held to be morally uplifting, and their memorization was thought to improve the morality of students. Their con-tent emphasized a filial piety appropriate to both familial and imperial contexts. Even if pedagogy was religious in most other agricultural societies, links between religious and state structures were also common, so the Chinese case is not really an exception. Even in modern school systems, as Véronique Benei (2008:46–48) argues, pedagogic rituals often draw from the predominate religious traditions of the surrounding society. In part, it is the blending of secular and religious ritual form that makes patriotic rituals compelling. As Amy Stambach (2010) argues, combining religious and pedagogic agendas remains a workable project in most parts of the world. Perhaps the most important distinguishing feature of the Chinese case was the tight links between educational success and worldly power, a feature that made cultural capital in imperial China more directly lucrative than it was elsewhere. It is this legacy that gives rise to a worldly literary masculinity and ties the virtues and dynamics of an agricultural era to the education system of rapidly industrializing modern society.

That the pedagogic traditions of agricultural societies around the world involved dynamics of moral exemplarity does not necessarily imply a uniform movement away from exemplarity during processes of industrialization. The interrelationships among industrialization, the development of state bureaucracies, the establishment of modern education systems, projects of nation building, and more localized cultural traditions are everywhere quite complex. In Europe and the United States these were gradual processes that took centuries and followed different paths in different places. The relative timing of different changes varied among countries, with the gaps between, for example, universalizing literacy through a few mandatory years of primary school and universalizing a full 12–15 years of preschool, primary, and secondary education ranging from a few decades to a couple of centuries. In China, the cultural legacies of the imperial examination system and the importance of exams in contemporary processes of governing may work to reproduce exemplarity. Any presumption of a move away from exemplarity as a uniform feature of modernization seems premature.

The Masculine and the Literary

In addition to providing space for exemplarity, pedagogy in agricultural societies was often patriarchal—reserved for or at least dominated by men. While such arrangements may have been common, literary masculinity itself has not dominated the globe, even if pockets of it have arisen in more than one cultural setting. One reason for this lack of predominance, especially in the Christian West, was the manner in which scholarly attributes linked to family structures. In Christian Europe, men of a studious, pious nature could become monks, but as a consequence of this choice they were supposed to remain celibate and were forbidden from marrying. Partially because of this manner of institutionalizing religious piety, dominant ideals of manhood and sexual desirability for men revolved around ideals of knighthood and chivalry, ideals that valued physical prowess and worldly domination above a studious, inward-turning piety.

In contrast, masculinity among East European Jews centered on the study of the Torah, and men who devoted their life to such study were not only able to marry but also idealized by women as husbands and sexual partners (Boyarin 1997). Such a situation more closely resembles that of imperial China. While imperial China did have celibate Buddhist monks, the much larger literati class was both expected to marry and considered desirable partners. Comparing the literary masculinities of the Jewish and Chinese imperial traditions brings out not only unique elements of each tradition but also the universalizable social conditions that enable literary masculinities to spread.

Perhaps the first universal that needs to be emphasized in relation to literary masculinity is the relative plasticity of gender ideals and sexual desire. While sexual dimorphism (the fact that human males are on average larger than human females) may be a biological universal, it does not necessarily follow that women are naturally attracted to large men with muscular physiques or that sexual fantasies of both men and women revolve around muscular men ravaging helpless women. Within both Jewish and Chinese traditions there are numerous narratives depicting female desire for sensitive, slender, pale, and studious boys. Consider the Yiddish folksong in which the lovelorn girl wishes her mother would bring

> a little bride-groom for me,
> With black hair and blue eyes,
> Let him be fit for Torah.
> And Torah as the Torah prescribes,
> He must learn day and night;
> Let him write me a letter,
> Let him remain a good little Jew.
> *Cited in Boyarin 1997:95*

Such desires compare well to those depicted in the most famous classical Chinese novel, *A Dream of Red Mansions,* in which Jia Baoyu, the main male character and focal point of much female attention, is introduced with the following description:

> His face looked as fair as if powdered, his lips red as rouge. His glance was full of affection, his speech interspersed with smiles. But his natural charm appeared most in his brows, for his eyes sparkled with a world of feeling. (Tsao 1978:47)[4]

The Jewish and Chinese institutions of literary masculinity differed in important ways, especially as one moved from boyhood to adulthood. For East European Jewish men, Talmudic study was a lifelong endeavor, and ideals of manhood placed men in the private interior spaces of the house so they could better study religious texts. Running businesses, playing hosts to guest, and circulating in public outside spaces were considered wifely responsibilities. For Chinese men, study was a means of becoming an official as well as an end in itself. Women rather than men were considered best consigned to the private, interior spaces of the home, while men ran businesses, traveled, and played the host. Consequently, even if study required retreating to inward spaces, such study was preparation for public, outward-facing roles.[5]

But the rise of modern, industrial societies in which schooling is universal and success in school leads to desirable masculine roles in the economy has allowed the similarities between the two traditions to seem more important than the differences. Success at school and in literary endeavors requires particular forms of bodily comportment, a distinct habitus. Sitting still, listening to the teacher, focusing on the text or intellectual problem rather than on one's immediate social environment are skills and habits that must be learned. An exclusive focus on such habits can lead to bodily attributes—small muscles, pale skin, shyness—that are undesirable for men in a cultural context where macho values prevail. In traditional Christian, European contexts, this sort of bodily comportment was related to monkhood and ineligibility for marriage. Later, with the rise of normative heterosexuality and homophobia in the Victorian era, the association of this sort of bodily disposition with ineligibility for marriage mapped onto denigrations of homosexuality (Boyarin 1997; Foucault 1988). But in both the Chinese and the Jewish traditions, the fear that such a disposition might somehow diminish the future masculinity and marriageability of boys is absent.[6] Industrial societies in which such fears are institutionalized give rise to ambivalent attitudes toward studious boys, an ambivalence that is well captured in the derogatory yet subtly complimentary slur "nerd" and in well-received literary works like Arthur Miller's *Death of a Salesman,* where Biff Loman, the high school football star, fails miserably in later life. Industrial societies in which such fears are not institutionalized, or subgroups within those societies without such fears, are much more likely to develop educational fevers.

Building Linguistic Nations

Though I argued in the previous chapter that nation building was historically linked to an "imperial governing complex" in China, nation building is, of course, more than just a specifically East Asian concern. Projects of nation building throughout the modern world involve pedagogic processes of moral regulation (Corrigan and Sayer 1985; Durkheim 1992), normalization (Foucault 1979), and the creation of nationwide mores of speaking, reasoning, writing, and social identification. They also universally lead to the institutionalization of compulsory education systems that resemble one another in many ways (Meyer and Ramirez 2003). The specificities of these processes, however, must always be analyzed in the context of the particular histories of individual nations (Corrigan and Sayer 1985) and of the political actions and alliances that cause a given country to adopt the linguistic mores that it does (P. Kerim Friedman 2005; Gramsci 1971).

In the case of contemporary Chinese nation building, three historical circumstances stand out. First is the sheer scale of the enterprise. A nation, or at least a normalized, national linguistic sphere, has never been constructed on such a scale. India, while approaching China in absolute population, has structured its education system around the predominate languages of individual states, with the result that eighteen separate languages are taught as first languages in Indian schools. The sheer number of Chinese language speakers and readers ensures that the Chinese nation-building enterprise will have global effects. Second is the long history of the Chinese state and its spoken and written languages of governing. The English term "Mandarin" for contemporary standard spoken Chinese both points to the historical continuity of this language with that of earlier eras and masks the linguistic transformations of the modern era. Mandarin is a translation of the old Chinese term *guanhua,* meaning literally the spoken language of imperial officials (i.e., mandarins). In the People's

Republic of China, Mandarin is now called *putonghua* (the spoken language of "ordinary" people). The political success of this renaming has meant that "the spoken language of imperial officials" has become the "spoken language of ordinary people."[7]

Third is the sociological relationship of Mandarin to local dialects in post-Mao China. In contrast to many parts of the world, where standard, national dialects are assumed to carry more prestige than more localized dialects, in China localized dialects often carry more prestige than the national language. When migrant workers leave poorer areas of the country to seek employment in wealthier places, they end up speaking standard Mandarin to their bosses and each other and are excluded from various spheres of local life by long-term local residents speaking their local dialect. Shanghai dialect in Shanghai, Wenzhou dialect in Wenzhou, Cantonese in Guangdong, and even Zouping dialect in Zouping have gained in prestige and local popularity as nonlocal-dialect-speaking migrants pour into these relatively wealthy places. Locals romanticize their dialects by claiming that intimate feelings can be expressed only in their local tongues and insist that their local dialects be given a place of prominence in various quasi-public institutions like churches, temples, and other sites of public (but not official) speech. This makes China an intermediate case in the debates over the roles of linguistic markets and nation building in the contemporary world.[8] On the one hand, the promotion of Mandarin as the national language in schools can be seen as having something to offer the rural masses as well as national elites. Claiming the "spoken language of ordinary people" as the national standard fights prejudice against the rural masses as uncivilized. It offers rural people a chance to trade up their status from that of "peasants" to proper national citizens. As such, the promotion of Mandarin should not be seen as a top-down imposition that merely solidifies elite interests. On the other hand, the historical links of standard Mandarin to the language of elite rule mean that the choice of Mandarin as the standard language cannot be seen as a simple derivative of popular sentiments.

Demographic Transition

At least since the pioneering work of Warren Thompson (1929), demographers and sociologists have noted and argued over the causes of demographic transition—the shift from patterns of high mortality and high

fertility observable in most agricultural societies to the patterns of low
mortality and low fertility observable in wealthy industrial societies. While
the medical advances that lead to declining mortality are relatively easy to
understand, there is no clear agreement over what leads to declining fertility. Economic pressures on households, the direction of intergenerational
wealth flows, the average age of marriage, educational levels of women,
the availability of contraception, political pressures to have fewer children,
and family structures (whether extended or nuclear) have all played a role
in one location or another, but with the exception of the educational levels
of women, none of these factors seems to be easily correlated with historical declines in fertility rates. Neither have any universal processes been
identified that specify the interplay of a subset of these factors as causing
fertility decline, though it is clear that children do not have the same role
in industrial societies as they did in agricultural societies (Caldwell et al.
2006; Hirschman 1994).

In places like rural Zouping, where the birth control policy kick-started
the process of fertility decline in advance of both high education levels for
women and sustained economic development, it is not so much the decline
in fertility itself that needs explaining as the gradually shifting norms of
child raising. How do parents come to desire fewer children, and, more important for this project, how do they become so invested in the academic
achievements of their children? These questions are related to, but not
quite the same as, ones that demographic transition theory attempts to answer. Nonetheless, demographic transition theorists' discussions of three
common patterns of the interrelation between the spread of mass education and changing attitudes toward children are illuminating. First, as the
years of compulsory education increase and child labor becomes illegal,
the ability of children to contribute to the household economy decreases
and, depending on how education is funded, the cost of raising children
increases, making it economically less viable to raise large numbers of
children. Second, as children spend more years in school, neither they nor
their parents imagine farming as an ideal future. If the parents are themselves farmers, their inability to provide a career path for their children
increases anxiety about each child's future. Third, if the school system
fosters a competitive environment, and if monetary investment in some
aspect of the child's schooling seems to yield a comparative advantage,
then the desire of parents to invest in their children's education grows.
If the government, school system or wider society value academic success in general, and devalue farming as an occupation, then the pressure

for such investment increases further (Ariès 1962, 1980; Caldwell et al. 2006:89–104; LeVine and White 1986).

All of these aspects of compulsory education facilitate a parental shift from "quantity" to "quality" in child-raising strategies. But just as important as the shift from quantity to quality is a shift from a model of delayed reciprocity in parent-child relationships to a model in which parents identify with the successes of their children. The prospect of a bit of old age care or respect in day-to-day relations is no longer the sole motivation for child raising. Rather "parents come to identify with the children in whom they had invested so much of themselves as well as their resources, and they were able to derive subjective satisfaction from the economic and reproductive careers of their children even in the absence of material support" (LeVine and White 1986:67).[9] In China, as in most developing nations with large surpluses of agricultural labor, the devaluation of farmers and farming aggravates this process. Farming parents come to imagine themselves as worthless. Their children become their "only hope," not just because they are singleton children (as depicted so wonderfully in Vanessa Fong's [2004b] book about urban Chinese families), but also because the parents themselves no longer have hope for their own lives.[10] In the words of Deleuze and Guattari, this is yet another path through which the construction of lack produces desire.

The hopelessness of farming parents is perhaps most easily read in the attitudes of their child-students, who often go to great lengths to deny their rural backgrounds. High school students in Zouping, for example, often change their names from three characters to two to hide their rural origins.[11] Many novels and television dramas portray university students of rural origins who attempt to hide their uncultured parents from their classmates. In the novel *Utopia,* for example, a university student's father comes to the city of Chongqing to work as "shoulder-pole man" (*bangbang*), carrying loads for city residents up and down the steep, staired walkways of the city on a shoulder-pole, in order to help pay for his son's tuition. When he sees his father on the street in front of a crowd, the student calls his father "shoulder-pole man" rather than dad, and a father-son conflict results (Xiao 2008:249–54).

As unfilial as such behavior might seem, it in fact masks another form of filial piety that itself masks the transformation in child-raising norms. In Chinese school settings, children are constantly urged by their teachers to study hard for the sake of their parents. When I asked Chinese students why they study so hard if they don't enjoy it, many replied that they saw their studying as a form of filial piety (*xiao*). Even the curriculum had a role in promoting this moral vision, with explicit lessons devoted to filial piety in both "thought and morality" (*sixiangpinde*) and literature classes. One of the Tang dynasty poems all Shandong sixth-grade students memorized in 2006, for example, was titled "Youzi Yin."[12] It describes an old mother sewing clothes for her son by candlelight so that he can spend all of his time studying and become an official in a faraway place. Students are asked to memorize the poem so that they can recite it with feeling, to imagine the sacrifices that their own parents make on behalf of their education, and to write essays about how they might repay their own debt to their parents by studying hard.

Charles Stafford (1995) describes how textbook examples of filial piety in Taiwan during the late 1990s likewise emphasized parents sacrificing so that their children may study. As in "Youzi Yin," the predominate gendered pattern of these examples involved "textbook mothers" sacrificing for their sons' academic success (Stafford 1995:70). But Stafford suggests that in Taiwan, such examples implied sacrifice by the family for the nation. In contemporary Zouping, parents, teachers, and students alike understand this sacrifice as a matter of familial self-interest rather than as a sacrifice by the family for the nation. In Zouping, educational success is above all a familial success, and the production of disciplined students is understood by parents, teachers, and students as the crafting of filial subjects. But the apparent continuity of filial piety here in fact masks a transformation in the meaning of filiality. Instead of paying their parents back for the effort and expense of raising them with respectful care in their old age, children participate in the projects of educational desire that their parents imagine for them.

Late Development and Diploma Disease

Ronald Dore first proposed the idea of a "diploma disease" in 1976. He suggested that late-developing nations were likely to experience a large gap between the incomes of those involved in the "traditional" and "modern" sectors of the economy, that this gap would cause young people to flock to schools in the attempt to pursue the credentials that would enable them to secure modern sector jobs, and that the desires of these young people would pressure the governments of these countries to expand the education system more rapidly than the modern sector of the economy itself. The final result would be more and more high-level graduates pursuing a limited number of modern sector jobs and a continual inflation in the level of diploma needed to pursue a particular type of job (Dore 1997). Jonathan Unger (1982) gives a more detailed elaboration of this thesis, including its impact on the education system:

> In such circumstances, many a young person's solution has been to strive for a yet higher education, to get above the crowds of competing job applicants. As this occurs, the reputation of a school and often the careers of its teachers become more dependent upon obtaining a respectable pass rate of students on the next higher level of schooling. With the school increasingly geared toward "prepping" its students in the subjects that are most important for such examinations, other school subjects receive short shrift. . . .
>
> A mad situation appears where the curriculum of even a rural primary school is influenced more by the manner of questions posed ultimately on university (and hence secondary school) entrance examinations than by the more practical need to prepare the village's sons and daughters for more modern roles within the village economy. . . .
>
> [E]ven those pupils from the cities who successfully climb up through the secondary schools . . . frustratedly end up swelling the ranks of the educated unemployed, having been provided with "credentials" that did not in the end "qualify" them for anything and having been instilled with attitudes and yearnings that incline then neither toward independent entrepreneurial pursuits nor gainful manual employment. (1–2)

The fit of Dore's theory with the situation of Zouping is limited, though it does seem to illuminate some of the dilemmas of Zouping's educators and students. Perhaps most difficult to assess is the relationship between securing credentials and future salary.[13] On the one hand, it is fair to say that the extremes of wealth and poverty in China as a whole are as large as those anywhere in the developing world. On the other hand, within Zouping itself, those extremes are relatively muted. In 2006, factory laborers in Zouping made as much as all but the upper echelon of government workers; the truly impoverished in Zouping suffer diminishing income most commonly because of health care issues, not their lack of a diploma, and the most wealthy have left the county to live in other, more upscale locales. Yet when I asked Zouping residents why they thought that parents so universally wished for their children to attend college, "Because we are poor" was a common answer. Certainly the people who answered this way were poor compared with me, but even though I was their interlocutor, the examples they gave made it clear that the poverty they were referring to was not simply one in comparison with myself. Rather they were thinking of both the experiences within their own families of a few decades ago, when many experienced starvation, and the extremes of wealth and status that they had seen on television or through travel, both within their own country and abroad. Images of great wealth and dreams for their children's future came from Beijing, Shanghai, or even New York and Paris rather than Zouping. Moreover, wealth and poverty were not simply about monetary income but tied to a desire for modernity itself, conceived as a type of prestige. To have a nonmanual, comfortable job was to have a modern job, even if it paid no more than farming. Factory labor was a poor second to office work. Though considered more modern than farming, and though most young people took factory jobs over farming, such jobs offered little prestige. In short, in Zouping it is not the "income gap" alone that separates the "modern" and the "traditional" sectors of the economy. Outside of China, ethnographers have noted the imagined links between education and modernity in many other places, including Africa (Fuller 1991) and India (Benei 2008).

Two more modifications need to be made to Dore's narrative to apply it to contemporary Zouping. First, we should note that the "modern sector" in Zouping and China more broadly is developing rapidly and that young people in Zouping will not suffer for lack of preparation for the "village economy." Whatever their future holds, the majority of them will not live and work in villages after they graduate. Second, we should acknowledge that in addition to being desired for the sake of wealth and modernity, educational success in China is valued as an end in itself, as a nonreducible form of value.

Despite these caveats, aspects of Dore's thesis do illuminate education fever in Zouping. Pressures for exam success clearly do penetrate all the way down the system, though efforts on the part of the education bureau in implementing the education-for-quality reforms may have reduced them at the primary school level. Perhaps most important, even if the gaps between high- and low-status employment are not primarily monetary in places like Zouping, and even if educational success offers prestige independent of monetary awards, the hope for prestigious, "modern sector" white collar jobs does increase pressure on the education system in Zouping, Shandong, and China more broadly. This hope leads parents to press for more university places but not more vocational training, and local cadres to do everything they can to provide opportunities for academic success.

The percentage of people obtaining university degrees is skyrocketing throughout China, and inflation in the credentials necessary to obtain any job is apparent. Positions in the local party-state that in the 1980s went to people with senior middle or even junior middle school diplomas now require a university degree. To move easily from a county like Zouping into a white-collar job in large cities like Shanghai and Beijing now requires a master's degree. Even Zouping factories require junior middle school graduation certificates, and many prefer senior middle school certificates as well. One of Zouping's possible futures—as a place filled with well-educated young people who end up working in factories—is fully anticipated by Dore's thesis. Whether such people will feel unfulfilled because they (or their parents) once dreamed that college would lead to white-collar jobs may become a pressing practical question.

Modernization theories of one form or another (and here I include most theories of demographic transition as well as Dore's diploma disease thesis) are rightfully criticized for narrating unitary paths from a single past (usually agrarian) to a singular present/future—modernity. Agrarian societies were never exactly alike. Pathways toward industrialization have not been unitary, and, perhaps more important, modernity itself is always a doubly moving target: what is considered modern from a native, "emic" perspective varies over time and space and even according to point of view within a particular spatiotemporal context; second, what is labeled as modern from a "scientific," "etic" perspective also evolves along with technological, social, political, and economic change. Consider what LeVine and White (1986) say about demographic transition in "the West":

> Each secular trend [of demographic transition] showed at least two surges, often 80 or 100 years apart. Fertility began its major decline in the nineteenth century, but fell sharply after World War I. Infant mortality dropped after 1900 but continued to decline thereafter until it reached present levels. The spread of primary schooling was primarily a nineteenth century phenomenon, but secondary schooling as a mass process did not occur until the twentieth century. New concepts of the child and education arose between the mid-seventeenth and early nineteenth centuries but did not have their major institutional impact until a great deal later. In each case the socio-economic and ideological conditions affecting the consciousness of parents were different by the time the later surge occurred, and different social forces were mobilized to advance the trend . . .

secular trends cannot be treated as single historical events and ... the tele-scoping of historical process that seems to occur in 'late-developing countries' cannot be treated as replicating a trend that took centuries in Europe. (72)

Despite the fact that narrating a single theory of modernization is im-possible, the very fact that industrialization, urbanization, the institution of compulsory education, and demographic transition have occurred in all of the world's wealthy countries suggests that it would be equally wrong to treat every country or society as a unique phenomenon. At the very least, two widespread processes must be given a role to play in the expansion of educational desire in Zouping. First, the gap in prestige, value, and income between what is perceived as modern and what is denigrated as tradition structures the social organization of lack and stimulates desire for educational advancement. Second, the reduction in the number of chil-dren in conjunction with the expansion of the education system encour-ages parents to treat children as "projects" whose achievements are their own rather than solely as sinks of reciprocal gift giving who repay parents with respect and old-age care.

Governing and Audit

Modernization theories are universal because they trace that which can be universalized in the experience of "modernized" countries and imagine how it might happen (or did happen later) in the "late-developing" coun-ties. A less teleological discussion of universals must be prepared to go in the other direction as well. Is there anything in the experience of Zouping or China that might have spread to the lives of or be indicative of pos-sible futures for those who are already living in "modernized" countries? The place of examinations in wider cultures of governing and audit is one arena in which China seems to hold a leading position.

This topic has recently received considerable discussion and debate in the discipline of anthropology (Collier 2005; Gledhill 2004; Kipnis 2008a; Power 1997; Strathern 2000). As Michael Power (1997:4–6) notes in his book *The Audit Society: Rituals of Verification,* in Great Britain, Europe, and the United States, the lines between formal financial audits and other forms of assessment blurred during the "audit explosion" of the 1980s and 1990s. Bureaucratic measures to assess employee performance, organiza-tion conformity with official regulations, or the extent to which certain policy objectives have been achieved were and are increasingly described as "audits." The politics of auditing can be intense, as the terms and formal procedures of such audits have considerable consequences for those who are audited. Moreover, the terms of an audit often become "a tail that wags the dog" of organizational goals and dynamics (Power 1997: 91–122). Originally coined in the title of a volume edited by Marilyn Strathern (2000), the term "audit cultures" has been used to describe both the "rituals of verification" that are applied in assessing the performance of employees or subordinated people and collectivities in hierarchical organizations, and the organizational cultures of which these rituals are a constitutive part.

As the term suggests, Western anthropologists imagine that the procedures of such rituals of verification arose in the Western fields of accounting and audit. Their spread is further seen to be part of the wider diffusion of "neoliberal" procedures of governing "from the West to the rest," a viewpoint that I have criticized at length elsewhere (Kipnis 2008a). Here I would like to suggest a modified genealogy of modern audit cultures—one that starts with multiple roots in the imperial cultures of Chinese examination systems, religions, and business accounting.

The very word used in Chinese to refer to "audits"—*kaohe* 考核 (perhaps more accurately translated into English as "assess" or "assessment")—speaks to the genealogical links of performance auditing to examinations in China. The base meaning of the first character, *kao,* is "to give or take an examination or quiz." As with the English word "examine," secondary meanings of the word refer to inspections or investigations that have something to do with verifying facts. Compounds like *kaocha* 考察 (inspect, investigate) *kaogu* 考古 (archaeology, or making a factual investigation of historical circumstances), or *kaoju* 考据 (a form of textual research into the accuracy of previous interpretations) all speak to the ideational links between examinations and wider processes of examining. Despite these references to factual investigation in the nonhuman realm, compounds with the character *kao* are especially used when the target for the examination is a human being and the examinee has something to gain or lose as a result of the examination. Medical examinations, university entrance exams, criminal investigations, and employee assessments are all forms of *kao.* Like contemporary procedures of audit, *kao* implies a power relation in which a superior "examines" an inferior.

Chinese ideas of assessment have historical links to ancient religious and business practices as well. Buddhist and Daoist moral account ledgers date back to the fourth century. By the late twelfth century, such ledgers had developed elaborate point systems. These ledgers are still published today and work by listing standard good and evil deeds (*gong* 功 and *guo* 过) and the positive or negative numeric value of each deed.

> For example, one seventeenth-century ledger allots one hundred merit points to a man who saves the life of another, but deducts one hundred from the account of a man who "hoards rice rather than distributing it to the needy in times of famine." Ledgers usually include a simple one-month calendar, on which the user is to record his daily tally. (Brokaw 1991:4)

In some Chinese temples, oversized abacuses—the traditional tool of accounting in Chinese business—are displayed as reminders of the heavenly accounting of good and evil deeds that all must face.

While not relying on such an elaborate numeric point system, the grading of examinations in the imperial system was by necessity a highly regulated form of comparison. One historian describes the standardization of exam essays as follows:

> Baguwen 八股文 (eight-legged essays) and Shitieshi 试帖诗 (standard exam poems) were two standardized testing formats for essay and poetry. Both of them had to be written to conform to particular rules, including rules on the number of sentences; format length and style of each component; rules for rhyming, symmetry and tonal balance and "couplet" styles. There were also strict limits on the total number of words for the overall essay. (Yu and Suen 2005:21)

Strict rules about procedures for registering for exams, taking exams, and scoring exams were also set. Outstanding phrases or passages were marked with circles or dots, and the density of circles or dots served as a proxy for a numeric score. Each essay was scored by two examiners; if their opinions differed, a third scorer was called in as arbitrator (Suen and Wu forthcoming).[14] In sum, imperial China had a rich legacy of historical techniques for assessing people that has informed procedures of assessment in Republican China, during the Maoist decades and today. These procedures had multiple origins—in imperial examinations, in business accounting, and in religions—and from quite an early date relied upon standardized, numeric procedures for evaluation.

Borge Bakken (2000:245) has suggested that the contemporary "Chinese must be the most thoroughly evaluated people of us all." The lives of

Zouping's students and teachers provide ample support for this assertion. Students in all grade levels in Zouping's schools are given standardized exams in every subject twice a year except for physical education. The textbooks, exams, and teaching curriculum are designed together. For the students, test results really matter only when they are entering senior middle school and college. But the tests at the end of each semester are designed to be similar to these critical examinations and are generally good predictors of a student's eventual results. For teachers, every examination is tightly linked to performance evaluation and salary bonuses. Teachers' evaluations are based not only on the class averages of their students but also on the rate at which they enable "late-developing students" to catch up with the class average and the rate at which they enable "advanced" students to continue to excel.

The numeric point systems for major exams make fine distinctions. Top scores on the university entrance exams and senior middle school entrance exams vary from year to year and according to the exam taken (the senior middle versus university and, within the university exams, sciences versus humanities), but usually range from 550 to 750 points. Cutoff scores for entrance to various universities and senior middle schools are drawn by the point, so the difference of a single point out of a total of more than 500 is often significant.

In Zouping, as throughout Shandong, it is possible to attend an elite senior middle school if one's score is slightly too low by paying a onetime fee (12,000 yuan in Zouping in 2007). Many of the thousands of students who pay this fee each year missed the cutoff score by just one point; for such students, one point out of more than 500 cost their families 20 percent more than the average annual income for a Zouping adult. In the Shandong city of Qingdao in 2007, these fees were regulated as follows: students who were between 1 and 10 points below the cutoff score paid 10,000 yuan to enter the senior middle school of their choice; those between 11 and 20 points below the cutoff score paid 15,000 yuan; those between 21 and 30 points below the cutoff score paid 18,000 yuan; no one more than 30 points below the cutoff score was legally admitted.

Elaborate point systems are also established for less significant competitions, such as the yearly contests between classes at a given middle school. One large high school with roughly fifty classes at each grade level established a thousand-point system and issued a twenty-page rulebook about the awarding of points. Five hundred of the thousand points were awarded on the basis of exam results—specifically the proportion of students on each exam who scored above various cutoff scores. Another three hundred points were allotted to discipline in the classroom. Points were deducted for a wide range of infringements such as lateness or fighting, while bonus points were awarded for each member of the class who was evaluated as a "civilized student" or who did good deeds such as turning in valuables found around the school to the proper authorities. The final two hundred points were allotted to discipline out of the classroom (in settings like the cafeteria or on field trips) and to interclass athletic competitions.

Evaluation systems for teachers are even more complicated. At one junior middle school teachers were evaluated on a one-hundred-point system. Sixty points were based on the exam results of students, but allocating these points required the exams to be analyzed in more than ten different ways, including class average, number of students scoring high enough to make the honor role for the entire county, percentage of students in class exceeding the county average for the exam, number of students who went from more than 15 percent below average to above average, and so on. Bonus points were awarded for students tutored outside of class who did well on exams, and teachers who were homeroom leaders would receive extra points if the class as a whole did well in all of its exams. In addition to exam results, ten points of the teacher's score were based on student evaluations, ten points on contribution to education reform (which was evaluated on seven different points, such as articles published in teaching journals or on websites, lectures given on teaching methods, active participation in school-wide teacher forums, and keeping a theoretical diary about teaching methods), ten points on professional performance (grading homework thoroughly and on time, not being late, evaluations of one's class by senior teachers, turning in thorough lesson plans and other reports on time, and so on), and ten points on political discipline and morality (not hitting or abusing students or accepting bribes, not expressing improper or "negative" political opinions in class, handling relationships with students, colleagues, and school leaders in an appropriate manner). Detailed rules on how to award points for these latter categories were also specified. For example, four of the ten points for political discipline and morality were to be assessed by the principal, three through a secret ballot of colleagues with whom one shared an office, and three by a committee of five different types of school administrators who sat between the principal and the teachers in the school hierarchy. After every teacher was awarded a score on the basis of this system, a quota system for awards was set as follows. The top 20 percent of teachers were categorized as excellent and given bonuses or raises; the next 30 percent were declared good and were eligible for smaller bonuses if enough money was available; the next 45 percent were declared passing but were not eligible for bonuses; the bottom 5 percent were declared failing and faced mandatory demotion or dismissal.

At many senior middle schools, at least before the 2008 round of reforms, large monetary bonuses (sometimes exceeding a teacher's annual salary) were given to teachers whose students did well on the university entrance exams. The manner of apportioning such bonuses was again very detailed and usually required the analysis of exam scores in over a dozen different ways. To be eligible for these bonuses, teachers had to teach third-year classes (i.e., classes with students who would take the university entrance exam). Only those teachers who scored in the top 30 percent in the regular evaluation system (similar to the one for the junior middle school described above) are permitted to teach third-year classes.

Complex numeric evaluation schemes are not limited to the education system but exist in many other fields as well, including the assessment system for communist cadres. One of China's preeminent rural sociologists, Zhao Shukai, recently completed a detailed research project on governance in China's townships, in which his research team systematically interviewed cadres in twenty townships across ten provinces about many aspects of governing including the "accountability system" (*wenze tixi*) through which their performance is audited.[15] According to Zhao's study, at the county level cadres are given specific numeric targets for economic and social development, such as the percentage of children of a certain age who attend school. Regardless of whether a given county meets its targets in a given arena, it will have its numeric score compared with those of other counties. The promotion of leading cadres is largely determined by these scores. At the township level, every aspect of work is given a numeric evaluation, and the promotion prospects of leading cadres as well as salary bonuses for all workers are directly tied to the numeric evaluations. As Zhao (2007) describes it:

> The enormous and complicated system of audits that confronts county leaders includes three types of targets. The first are economic development targets, including tax collection, increases in agricultural output, peasant income, the individual and private sector, and success in attracting outside investment. The second consists of targets for the construction of "spiritual civilization," such as building up the legal system, social stability ([lack of] petitions and

Falun Gong activity), united front work, ideological construction, promoting civilized behavior, environmental protection and subscriptions for newspapers and publications. The third consists of targets for party construction, such as organizational construction, building up party work style and clean government, democratic elections, propaganda work, ideology and political awareness. At the end of each year, county authorities send down personnel to conduct inspections. This large contingent of inspectors . . . inspects and assesses townships one by one. The township workers must fill in forms, which the inspectors then verify. (64–65)

The manner in which many of the items described above are quantified can seem quite far-fetched. For example, "ideological construction" might be measured by the number of official slogans written on the display walls of villages, or the number of subscriptions to official party newspapers (so township governments waste considerable amounts of money on subscription fees for papers that pile up, unread, on the floor of offices), or by the number of pages of "theoretical essays on Marxism" written by township cadres (so townships hire specialized essay writers to churn out writings the contents of which no one, not even the cadre whose name is put on the title page, reads) (Zhao 2007:66). For more serious items, such as quotas for the legal birth of a second child under the birth control policy, "yellow card warnings" or even "one-vote vetoes" (*yi piao foujue*) apply. Failure to meet the quota of a one-vote veto audit item results in the blockage of all promotion, no matter how well a given cadre does on other items. Some township cadres face up to ten one-vote veto items. Despite the inspections, many numerical targets are faked. For example, a prefecture desiring to spur dairy production set quotas for the number of milk cows farmers in a given township should own. When the inspectors came, the township officials simply took them to one village where there were many dairy cows and made up numbers for the rest (Zhao 2007:66). Collusion with village cadres enabled the township officials to pull this deception off. Other numeric targets lead to "formalism" (*xingshizhuyi*), in which the outward form of the target is met without really undertaking the task that the target is supposed to measure, as in the case of the newspaper subscriptions or essay writing described above. In still other cases, quotas result in serious efforts to comply with policy directives from above, as is often but not always the case with the birth control policy (Zhao 2007:64–73).[16]

The use of numeric measurements to evaluate township cadres relates to a desire to fight corruption and push cadres to properly serve the masses by enacting "scientific administration" (Zhao 2007:66). But the result is that leading cadres direct most of their attention upward, to the superiors who carry out the audits and their procedures for doing so, rather than downward toward the needs of the masses that they are supposedly serving (Zhao 2007:73).

Power argued that audit procedures have threatened to become the "tail that wags the dog" of organizational goals in many Western settings. In the Chinese instances it seems rather that the tail has become the dog. That is to say, auditing or, to translate more precisely, assessing and examining (*kao*) procedures explicitly become the organizing framework for the entire field that they claim to assess. Athletic competitions perhaps provide the best analogy for this dynamic. Sports like basketball, soccer, gymnastics, swimming, or track and field might be taken as indicators of the imagined quality designated by the abstract concept "athletic ability." Perhaps the lovers of a particular sport would claim that their sport is a better measure of this idealized abstraction than other ones. Few serious participants in a given sport, however, would claim that improving their "athletic ability" is their ultimate goal. Rather their goal is to become a better soccer or basketball player, a better swimmer, runner, or gymnast. The field in which they attempt to excel is defined by the way of keeping score in a particular sport (which of course is influenced by changes in rules, equipment, and so on). In the same manner, education and cadre performance in China are fields largely defined by the university entrance exams and the cadre accountability system. While some may lament this fact, and others may argue about whether the university entrance exams really measure "human Quality," or whether the cadre assessments really measure the extent to which a cadre has served the masses without corruption, no one involved in these fields can afford to behave in a manner that reflects such questioning.

George W. Bush's No Child Left Behind (NCLB) initiative has led to an increase in both the frequency of and the stakes involved in standardized testing in the United States. As a result of this policy, all states must administer standardized tests in reading and math annually to children in grades three through eight and once to children in grades ten through twelve. Schools that fail to demonstrate continually improving class averages are subject to funding cuts and other punishments. The policy has been roundly criticized by anthropologists interested in education in the United States (see, for example, the entire March 2007 issue of *Anthropology and Education Quarterly*), especially for the way in which the emphasis on standardized testing influences teacher behavior and school curriculums (e.g., McDermott and Hall 2007). Supporters of the law often put forth arguments for the need for "accountability" in education and see the standardized tests as a way of subjecting both teachers and schools as a whole to greater public scrutiny. I do not wish to enter the debates around NCLB here, but rather wish to make two points. First education policy in NCLB and indeed everywhere links exams to accountability, demonstrating the general applicability of the linguistic logic embedded in the Chinese character *kao*. The logic that links examinations in schools to performance evaluation in large organizations to accounting principles in business is likely to be noted in any society that has schools, exams, bureaucracies, and money—which is to say any "modern" society. Second, post-NCLB levels of standardized testing in the United States still pale in comparison to those in Zouping and China more broadly. If one wishes to imagine what the future might look like in the United States if pro-NCLB education reformers are allowed to continue their reforms, then China may not be a bad place to look.

By placing China on the cutting edge of developments in world patterns of governing, I wish to call into question vantages on modern education that place too much emphasis on its Western origins. Meyer and Ramirez (2003), for example, argue that the world institutionalization of education has led to an increasing isomorphism of national education systems over time, an argument I will address in greater detail in the next chapter. Here I wish to point out that they see Western nations as the sole originators for the models that are spreading around the world (Ramirez 2003). Thus they miss the position of nations like China at the vanguard of some of the changes that are occurring around the world. Countries like the United States may (perhaps justifiably) refuse to acknowledge that they are copying Chinese models when they strengthen regimes of testing and teacher audit, but the very fact that there may be more to this isomorphism than copying models suggests that the diffusion of cultural models from the West has been overemphasized in the discussion of global similarities in educational governing.

Competitive Dynamics

A related universalizable aspect of education in Zouping is the competitive dynamic that emerges when entrance exams are taken as the raison d'être for education. In so far as this is the case, the analogy with sports or other competitive games is relatively precise. In any high-stakes or professional-level sport, the competition rapidly evolves to the limits of human endurance—that is to say, if more training helps, then the competitive environment, as mediated through whatever coaches, managers, and trainers exist for a given sport, pushes all serious athletes to train as much as their bodies can stand. Fortunately for athletes, in physical training appropriate rest is essential and overtraining is counterproductive, so athletes are spared from training sixteen hours a day, seven days a week. Unfortunately for Chinese secondary students, the only physiological limits on studying appear to be a need for a modicum of sleep (but perhaps not even eight hours a day) and an occasional five- or ten-minute break to stretch and rest one's eyes. Consequently, the boot-camp-like regimes of Shandong's secondary schools become an almost unavoidable strategy. The 2008 attempts of the Shandong Education Bureau to limit this competition by restricting the ways in which principals and teachers can force students to study resembles the American NCAA (National Collegiate Athletic Association) attempts to limit practice times for collegiate athletes so that they will have enough time to devote to their studies. The counterstrategies that American collegiate athletes (and their coaches) and Shandong secondary students (and their parents and teachers) might use to get around these regulations are also roughly comparable.

The intensity of the competition deepens the bodily imprint of schooling endeavors. The ingrained psychological and physiological effects of a youth spent studying become more and more apparent. Chinese educational psychologists, for example, worry about increasing introversion among Chinese youth, while high levels of myopia are apparent to all. Literary masculinity strengthens as a cultural force simply because it becomes the easiest physical option for young men whose youth is spent competing for university places and whose bodies and minds are shaped in that environment.

Are all education systems destined someday to reach the level of competitive intensity evident in contemporary China? I suspect not, in part because strong traditions of literary masculinity are not universal. Nevertheless, given the proper social environment, the pressures that drive competitive systems to extremes are universalizable, and similar dynamics of competition do appear to be emerging in pockets of the educational systems of non–East Asian first world nations. SAT scores at elite American universities have increased over the past five decades even as they have declined among the test-taking population as a whole (in part because a greater proportion of the population takes the test).[17] It is not that students are getting smarter but just that larger numbers of them are getting better at doing whatever it takes to present themselves as excellent candidates according to the rules of the admissions game in the United States. Similar dynamics, no doubt, emerge in corners of most of the world's education systems. As with examinations and audit, China would need to be considered as a vanguard in the emergence of these cultural patterns.

Conclusion

In presenting aspects of universalizability in the pressures that have led to a feverish level of educational desire in Zouping, I am in no sense presenting an argument that other places in the world necessarily exhibit, have exhibited, or will exhibit similar assemblages of desire. Even as elements of educational desire in Zouping—exemplarity, literary masculinity, demographic transition and the psychology of investing in children, diploma disease, audits and competitive dynamics—have existed outside of Zouping, China, and East Asia, and may yet spread further given the right circumstances, it is unlikely that all the elements will come together in the same way as they have come together in contemporary China. It is probably also true that I could have lengthened this chapter by adding more universalizable elements or shortened it by discussing fewer, though I have tried to include the most salient ones. Rather, my point has been twofold. First, I wish to demonstrate that explanations of educational desire that rely solely on conscious local, provincial, or national-level policies of governing or imperial East Asian governing legacies can offer only a partial picture of what is happening in places like Zouping. More important, for people who are not from Zouping, Shandong, China, or East Asia, they conceal what about educational desire in Zouping can speak to their own experiences and circumstances. "Cultural" and "universalistic" explanations of a given social phenomenon should be seen not as incompatible alternatives but rather as different and complementary lenses that mutually enrich the understanding of the social dynamics to which they are applied.

CHAPTER SIX

Conclusion

I have taken the spatiotemporal frames of the preceding four chapters—the local, the national, the East Asian, and the universalizable—as four different perspectives for analyzing and understanding the governing of educational desire rather than as competing, mutually exclusive explanations. Educational desire in Zouping is simultaneously, in at least some of its aspects, local, national, East Asian, and universalizable. However, I do not mean to imply that all of the governing dynamics discussed in these four chapters are equally useful for explaining educational desire. The first task of this conclusion, then, is to put the pieces of the first four chapters together into a more coherent narrative.

From the broadest comparative perspective, five universalizable aspects of educational desire clearly come together in Zouping, China, and East Asia: rapid, late industrialization; demographic transition; literary masculinity; nation building; and exemplarity. Rapid industrialization in densely populated, formerly agrarian societies potentially devalues the labor of farmers. The mass numbers of people with farming skills but little nonfarming experience make the skills of those people relatively worthless in wider labor markets. This economic devaluation is often exacerbated by ideologies of modernization in which "peasants" are labeled as backward and nonfarming occupations are considered as "advanced" and "modern." Farming parents who lack both connections to urban areas and skills valuable to the secondary and tertiary economic sectors can come to see education as the only way out of this low-status trap for their children. In places that have experienced a demographic transition—where birthrates are low and parents have relatively few children—both the desire to treat children as projects and the relatively large economic, emotional, and temporal resources available to each child increase the probability of high levels of educational desire.

These processes may be inhibited among social groups in which the pursuit of the literary excellence necessary for educational success is seen as somehow diminishing the masculinity needed for young men to attract partners. The potential devaluation of education among such groups affects not only the educational efforts of boys but also the overall social valuation of educational success, as societies generally do not highly value activities that are seen as primarily female domains.

In nation-states where leaders or the populace at large believes the nation itself to be under threat, citizens may value education beyond its economic utility for its potential to build monocultural and seemingly patriotic populations. Traditional forms of exemplarity can be useful to such nation-building efforts. Turning the educationally successful into exemplars has the potential to widen educational desire among the population.

The legacies of the imperial governing complex, along with the competitive dynamics of modern East Asian history, have caused these five universalizable factors to come together in productive ways in all East Asian states. Throughout East Asia, Confucian traditions, especially when linked to examination systems, have given rise to cultural idealizations of strong forms of literary masculinity. In addition, examination systems provide a method of legitimating social and political hierarchies that can seem desirable (at least compared with the alternatives of nepotism or completely open democracies) to both authoritarian leaders and the wider populace. Literary masculinities and exam-based methods of legitimizing hierarchies mutually reinforce one another and enhance educational desire. High levels of educational desire intertwine with both rapid industrialization and rapid socioeconomic differentiation in mutually reinforcing ways. Industrialization feeds desire for degrees, while the existence of a highly educated populace increases the potential for further industrialization. Success in education (as measured by exams) is pursued as a way out of the feelings of lack generated by low socioeconomic status. Educational success, in turn, serves to legitimate the hierarchies that reproduce status differentiation. Processes of demographic transition can also interact with educational desire in mutually reinforcing cycles. The more parents treat their children as projects of educational development, the greater the collective social pressures to treat children as such projects, and the higher the level of competition in the education system. The higher the level of competition, the more resources must be devoted to each child to ensure success. The higher the level of resources needed for each child, the less parents desire to have large families.

In modern East Asia, the legacies of colonialism, both Western and Japanese, have made building strong nation-states a priority of political leaders and nationalist intellectuals. The development of competitive education systems can be seen as a tool of nation building in three ways. First, those concerned with human resources might argue that enhancing the educational level of the national labor pool promotes economic development. Second, those concerned with national coherence in the face of ethnic differentiation within the nation's borders and threats from outside those borders might see education systems as providing a tool to build unified, monocultural, patriotic populations. Finally, those concerned with maintaining the power of a particular regime might see expanding educational opportunities (in the name of strengthening the nation) as a method to increase political legitimacy. Many different sectors of the state thus find something to be gained from encouraging educational development and manipulating the education system, though conflicts among different bureaucracies over priorities can emerge. Competitive examination systems also enhance the value of exemplary teaching methods, and encouraging the use of such teaching methods can be attractive to bureaucrats concerned with nation building and patriotism. While teaching Chinese characters and classical Chinese culture may likewise elicit a reliance on exemplary teaching methods, it does not seem to be an essential element for reproducing educational desire, though it may reinforce tendencies toward a reliance on exemplary teaching methods and, hence, the value of exemplarity in wider modes of governing. Similarly, though authoritarian governments may believe exemplarity to be useful to their projects of reproducing absolute hierarchies and stymieing political change, it is clear that exemplary teaching methods in schools do not necessarily produce compliant adolescent and adult subjects and, moreover, that high levels of educational desire can be reproduced in the absence of authoritarian states.

In contemporary China, these factors have come together in a distinct and forceful way. The birth control policy not only gave a boost to the social forces unleashed by the processes of demographic transition but also provided the state with the language of raising the Quality (*suzhi*) of the population. This language both reflected nationalist desires to build a strong nation that could compete with other nation-states in the region and around the globe and provided educational bureaucrats and parents throughout China a means of connecting educational desire with nationalism. By pursuing educational advancement, students and their parents have been strengthening the nation as well as their individual families.

The language of improving the Quality of the population has been seized upon by a wide range of state cadres, education bureaucrats, and even teachers and principals to further a contradictory mix of educational priorities and agendas. These agendas have been as diverse as promoting unquestioning acceptance of the leadership of the Chinese Communist Party, encouraging independent, entrepreneurial thinking, championing traditional culture, and promoting vocational education. While each of these agendas has led to concrete governing actions in classroom settings, none has been powerful enough to counter the force of a mass drive for examination success by students, parents, teachers, principals, and local cadres. Only when they find a way of swimming with the currents unleashed by the drive for exam success have these other agendas surged ahead.

Policies that directly influence the social and political value of exam success also affect educational desire in China. Here the language of improving human Quality has again been important. As the CCP has attempted to enhance the power and control of its central leaders, it has argued that it can prevent corruption and ensure good governing without the checks and balances of democracy by selecting leaders of "high Quality." This is more than just rhetoric: the Party has made serious attempts to force those in charge of personnel decisions all the way down its ranks to pay close attention to educational credentials. By defining human Quality in this way, however, and by linking educational credentials so tightly to exam success, the CCP has reinforced the importance of examination results. In addition, by expanding university enrollments during the late 1990s and early 2000s, the party-state has made at least the dream of attending college a real possibility for perhaps a majority of the families of Chinese children. Though few will gain admittance to the most elite tier of Chinese universities, the overall expansion of enrollments encourages greater numbers of students to seriously play the university entrance exam game.

Finally, though not directly related to educational issues, the national policies that have governed the expanding devaluation of "peasant" status in contemporary China deserve some attention. While a devaluation of agricultural labor in densely populated, industrializing nations is commonplace, the processes of devaluation have been exacerbated in contemporary China in two concrete ways. First, the household registration policy has devalued the citizenship of those without residential rights in urban areas. As almost all forms of state welfare attach closely to the jurisdiction of an individual's household registration, "peasants" (the official designation for people with registrations located in rural villages) have been denied access to a great variety of health, education, employment, and welfare privileges. The fact that shifting one's household registration from a rural to an urban area becomes easier if one secures a university or master's degree has linked the privileges of urban citizenship directly to educational success. Second, from the end of the Maoist era to the mid-2000s, infrastructural investment has greatly favored urban areas. While the current generation of Party leaders, Hu Jintao and Wen Jiabao, has promised to reverse that trend and has made some initial steps in that direction, the infrastructural gap between rural and urban China remains large.[1]

In Shandong and Zouping, local governing dynamics also exist that have strengthened educational desire. Shandong in general and Zouping in particular are relatively developed places in eastern China that have exhibited a relatively high degree of compliance with the birth control policy. Consequently, there has been enough money for most local governments to build decent schools and for most households to dream of sending their (usually one or two) children to college. The relatively low birthrate has further sped the effects of demographic transition on parental ambitions for their children. In addition, economic development in Shandong has followed the "state corporatist" model, placing a greater portion of revenues and prestigious jobs under the control of government or quasi-government institutions. As these institutions emphasize credentials when hiring, economic incentives to compete in the university entrance exam game are larger than elsewhere.

As much of the above discussion has implied, the "causes" and the "effects" of educational desire are deeply intertwined. Various demographic trends, patterns of economic development, and societal tensions can be seen as both a cause and an effect of educational desire, and some may in fact interact with educational desire in mutually reinforcing cycles. Most of this book has focused on the possible causes of high levels of educational desire; here, switching to a discussion of the possible effects of this desire enables a wider consideration of the importance of the topic of this book.

Demographically, while low birthrates and small family sizes may elicit high levels of educational desire, it is also true that high levels of educational desire can lower birthrates. The developed nations and districts of East Asia have the lowest fertility rates in the world. In a ranking of the total fertility rates for the 225 countries of the world for which data were available, Japan, South Korea, Taiwan, Singapore, Hong Kong, and

TABLE 2. **Bottom Seven Countries in the World by Total Fertility Rate in 2009**

Rank	Country	Total Fertility Rate
219	Japan	1.21
220	South Korea	1.21
221	Northern Mariana Islands	1.15
222	Taiwan	1.14
223	Singapore	1.09
224	Hong Kong	1.02
225	Macau	0.91

Macau accounted for six of the bottom seven nations (with only the tiny Northern Mariana Islands—total population of roughly eighty thousand people—joining the East Asian nations in the bottom grouping).[2] All of these countries have fertility rates significantly under the replacement level of 2.1.

While the causes of low fertility rates are heatedly debated by demographers and are doubtlessly multiple and complex, it would be foolish not to consider the pressures brought to bear by high levels of educational desire. On the one hand, high educational levels for women are everywhere correlated with low fertility rates, as women with higher degrees desire careers as well as families and struggle to find the time and energy to pursue both. On the other hand, the amount of effort it takes to raise a child who can compete in East Asian schools can be daunting. To get a head start, children must be tutored as much as possible when young. After reaching school age, money must be spent on educational activities and children must be shuttled back and forth to these activities. Parents must regularly discipline children to do extreme amounts of homework every night and must spare their children from significant housework so that they can focus on their studying. In those East Asian contexts where women receive little aid from their governments and husbands to complete these tasks, it is not surprising that fertility rates are low. Such mothers are caught between educational experiences that prepare them for careers other than motherhood and forms of motherhood that demand exceptional effort and hinder careers.

In contemporary Zouping, the institutionalization of boarding schools has reduced some of the time pressures on Zouping families. The pressures of high levels of educational competition, however, still reach Zouping households. These households both shoulder high levels of educational expenses and spare their children from housework. Moreover, if the state

FIGURE 16. Mother supervising son's homework in urban Shandong. Adapted from cover of Linping Liu et al. (1997).

continues to retreat from high levels of institutionalized supervision of student homework (as begun in the 2008 education-for-quality reforms), then more of this burden will likely fall on parents. In sum, one probable effect of high levels of educational desire is a continued decline in fertility rates. The birth control policy itself will likely become easier to enforce and will perhaps soon be seen, at least in provinces like Shandong, as no longer necessary by the PRC government.

Educational desire also reinforces China's unrelenting urbanization. Children who spend twelve, fifteen, or nineteen years in schools do not generally desire farming careers, though there will always be both exceptions to this rule and people who have no other options. Young people who desire urban lives are both a necessary condition for the expansion of urban areas (though not a sufficient one) and a driving factor behind the shape of China's urban labor markets. All urban labor markets in China are influenced by the drive of young rural people to join them, though in many sectors urban governments establish rules to exclude rural migrants.

Educational desire may additionally be seen as a factor in the quest for economic development, though it is not always a simple positive. While China will clearly have an ample supply of tertiary-educated workers in the future, the desire for academic success may also lead to a shortage of skilled technicians.

Educational desire also influences the development of Chinese nationalism and national identity. During the post-Mao era, the relationship between traditional Chinese culture and the ruling regimes in Taiwan and the People's Republic of China has been reversed. While Taiwan has abandoned an exclusive emphasis on traditional Chinese literary culture, and explicitly embraced the pursuit of a curricular multiculturalism, the PRC has increasingly emphasized the teaching of Chinese classics in order to claim for itself the nationalist mantle of the true home and defender of Chinese culture. At the same time, the PRC has positioned itself as the primary teacher of Chinese as a second language to foreign students. The relative difficulty of learning written Chinese and the feverish pursuit of this difficult task by contemporary Chinese students increasingly link PRC nationalism with identities based in Chinese literary competence. As Chinese economic success leads more non-Chinese citizens to study Mandarin, the level of effort required to become literate in Chinese characters at the level of an average PRC citizen becomes higher, impossibly so for all but a handful of non-Chinese nationals. While the predominance of English as a global language has guaranteed a degree of multiculturalism and tolerance of foreign languages and cultures among Chinese students (often more than among citizens of Anglophone nations), I would not be surprised at the eventual emergence of a form of nationalist pride based in a superior mastery of the Chinese literary tradition. Such pride would be reinforced by the types of linguistic ideologies discussed in chapter 4, where literacy in Chinese characters is taken as evidence of an overall mental, moral, and physical superiority. This pride would be further buttressed by the position of Mandarin as a global but not multinational language. There is perhaps no other language in the world that attaches so closely to a single nation-state yet still attracts so many foreign students.

This sort of pride is already evident within China in some of the less tolerant attitudes expressed toward ethnic minority cultures and languages. Where Han Chinese students study together with students from other ethnic groups who do not value Chinese language education to the same extent, stereotypes about their stupidity and laziness emerge. The existence of affirmative action policies reinforces such stereotypes. Among secondary students striving for university admittance, affirmative action for ethnic minorities elicits disgruntlement among the majority Han Chinese, as such policies do everywhere in the world. But it is not only students and parents who express such sentiments. In my visits to schools in the peripheral regions of China, including Xinjiang and Inner Mongolia, I have been surprised at how easily Han teachers make unsolicited statements about the laziness and stupidity of "Mongols" or "Uygurs" and their unwillingness to work or study hard. These teachers resent the relative ease with which targeted groups get into college as well as what they see as the undeserved high rank of their teacher colleagues of targeted backgrounds. Such attitudes have a long history in China, as the work of William Jankowiak (1993:33–40) on ethnic stereotypes in Huhhot demonstrates.

The Han Chinese project of civilizing and normalizing minority populations by teaching them the "national" (i.e., Han majority) language and culture further (and somewhat ironically) enhances ethnic consciousness, though in different ways for different groups of people. As Mette Hansen (1999) demonstrates, for minority ethnic groups who long ago accepted Mandarin as the language of education and literacy in Chinese characters as the measure of an educated person, mainstream education can strengthen ethnic consciousness by providing the means for expressing ethnicity within the Chinese political system; for ethnic groups whose own literary traditions and writing systems make standard Chinese education seem like the imposition of an ethnically other state, the very medium of the education system serves to reinforce minority ethnic identity.

Outside of China, where Chinese diasporic students often exhibit greater dedication to academic success than those of other ethnic backgrounds, the links of Chinese ethnic identity to educational desire are also foregrounded. Such is the case in the United States, where East Asian students are often stereotyped as model minorities for their educational successes,[3] and in Australia, where elite private schools formerly dominated by European students have become increasingly East Asian. Many of these schools have simultaneously experienced an increase in their levels of academic competitiveness and a decrease in their footballing prowess, as the Asian students and parents are more likely to emphasize the former at the expense of the latter. This pattern has led to some tension between the predominately European alumni of these schools and the East Asian communities that now seek to educate their children there over the relevance of athletic excellence to admission policies. In Malaysia, affirmative action policies that favor Malays over Chinese in university admission are a source of considerable ethnic tension (Crouch 2001). Similar tensions may be found in other Southeast Asian nations as well.

High levels of educational desire also shape the forms of social and political hierarchy and, hence, governing in China. Not only does the Party attempt to legitimate itself by claiming high levels of educational success for its members, but also, perhaps more significantly, many forms of (relatively)[4] public evaluation and performance audit take the form of scoring on a point system that is very similar to the university entrance exam. It is not simply, as argued in the previous chapter, that exams form part of the historical repertoire from which the designers of modern audit techniques draw, but also, in a more sociological vein, that the experience of being "examined" in schools as a child, especially in the manner generated by Chinese educational culture, makes examination-based forms of performance audit, or forms of audit that are scored like exams, seem reasonable, to adult examiners and examinees alike.

In sum, the demographic, economic, social, and political effects of high levels of educational desire are every bit as diverse as the sources of this desire. Are there any ethical or policy lessons that may be derived from analyzing these effects?

At the most general level, educational desire should be neither worshiped nor condemned. As the work of Bataille suggests, it is not possible to value anything—from academic achievement to democracy, truth and justice to even equality itself—without setting up some form of hierarchy that distinguishes people on the basis of the extent to which they embody or embrace the valued ideals. It is difficult to imagine a world that celebrates the expressive beauty of Chinese poetry, art, and calligraphy but does not denigrate boys with sloppy handwriting, that admires excellence in science and humanities but produces no school dropouts, or that promotes the pursuit of excellence in any form of human endeavor without also promoting forms of discipline that can be taken to destructive and self-destructive extremes.

Skepticism is also justified toward many of the ethical claims made by educational researchers writing in either defense or criticism of traditional Chinese pedagogic methods or contemporary Chinese modes of education. While I am sometimes sympathetic with the liberal critics of authoritarian and exemplary classroom teaching techniques, I doubt very much that these techniques do as much harm as their critics claim. I do not believe that exercises in memorization stifle creativity, that preventing the questioning of pro-Party writings in classroom settings produces politically passive adults, or that "teaching to the test" alienates students from impoverished backgrounds. While I would not endorse the unnecessary enforcement of particular political views in the classroom, I accept that memorization, exemplarity, and discipline have an important place in educational settings. Strict school systems are often the most egalitarian, as lax discipline in school settings simply means that the discipline required for school success is unevenly applied—more in families with the patience and resources to do so themselves and less elsewhere.

School discipline at an early age is also necessary to the production of scholarly adults. Such a position has been supported by some of the most politically radical of social theorists. As Antonio Gramsci (1971) suggests:

> In education one is dealing with children in whom one has to inculcate certain habits of diligence, precision, poise (even physical poise), ability to concentrate on specific subjects, which cannot be acquired without the mechanical repetition of disciplined and methodological acts. (37)

Or as Jules Henry (1963) argues:

> In some areas of modern education theory (especially inside the heads of my education majors) democracy, permissiveness, originality, spontaneity, impulse release, learning, thinking and adjustment to life are all mixed up together, so that, without any historic perspective at all, students come to me with the conviction that criticism of permissiveness is an attack on democracy itself. They have not been taught that the schoolrooms in which the originators of our American democracy received instruction were places of great discipline. . . . China is unparalleled in the tyranny with which schoolmasters ruled, yet China has given the world great poetry, drama, painting and sculpture. . . . What, then is the central issue? The central issue is love of knowledge for its own sake. . . . Creative cultures have loved the 'beautiful person'—meditative, intellectual and exalted. (260–61)

But if I do not find the liberal critics of school discipline convincing, neither do I believe the champions of memorizing classics. I do not agree with the scholars discussed in chapter 4, who argue that the rote memorization of Chinese classics improves the moral character of young schoolchildren, or that it raises their overall level of Quality. Indeed, I do not accept that there is such a thing as Quality. Any educative system must strike a series of creative compromises between instilling the discipline necessary for some to excel and many to feel competent and admitting, in the end, that there is something arbitrary about what is learned. Excelling at school must be valued, but forms of excelling or just getting by that do not involve school success should also have a place.

Such a (non)conclusion requires a position of neutrality in the large debates over styles of education, but it does not imply that I have no opinions regarding particular pedagogic practices or policies. I find the recent policies to enhance vocational education in Shandong well thought out. Paying for good vocational schools, even if they are currently unpopular among parents and students, both makes good economic sense given China's emerging position as a world manufacturing center and provides a valuable fallback for those students who find the level of competition in the academic track too high. Zouping's implementation of the education-for-quality policy during the late 1990s and early 2000s, when junior middle schools were given quotas of places at the senior middle schools in order to reduce the level of competition among schools and enable principals to reduce study times, likewise was an apt compromise between the demands of equity and excellence. The more recent, Shandong-wide efforts to limit competition at senior middle schools, however, seem destined simply to shift the competition to the private sector and give an undue advantage to relatively wealthy and urban students. In short, creative policy solutions will involve making timely compromises between competing ideals rather than following a particular ideological agenda.

In addition, as Jules Henry suggests, we should differentiate between the sort of political authoritarianism that demands either silence or the forced, ritualistic enunciation of particular political views and the discipline required to embody certain skills or memorize particular bodies of facts—whether linguistic, mathematical, scientific, or historical. The former is always distasteful, though when enacted in school settings it does not seem to produce unreflective adults. The latter may certainly be overdone but very often is pedagogically productive.

What the future holds for education in China is difficult to predict, but a few trends deserve comment. First of all it is difficult to imagine that anything completely novel will occur. Even before the 1980s, China had already been exposed to wave after wave of "revolutionary" and "imported" education philosophy—Maoist, Russian, European, Japanese, American, and European (Hayhoe 1984). Much of what has been espoused in the name of "education for quality" is essentially a rehashing of the ideas of John Dewey that were first introduced to China in the 1920s. Moreover, as Gita Steiner-Khamsi (2004a, 2004b) argues, the politics of global educational borrowing, more often than not, amount to little more than the use of international rhetoric in local policy debates. That changes would not be new, however, does not imply that no changes can occur. Educational funding could become more or less egalitarian. Various topics and readings could receive more or less emphasis in the curriculum. Teachers could be given lighter or heavier workloads. But the structural constraints generated by high levels of educational desire will limit the extent of many types of changes. Here, the cases of Taiwan and South Korea are illustrative. Both of these countries underwent revolutionary changes in the political sphere without being able to move away from extremely competitive exam-driven educational systems. If a democratic revolution were to sweep the CCP from power in China, the school curriculum would undoubtedly change, but not the examcentric nature of the system.

Finally is the issue of what lessons a study of educational desire can provide for the subdiscipline of the anthropology of governing. In an argument that strikes me as revealing the typical strengths and weaknesses of much of the "globalization" literature, Meyer and Ramirez (2003) suggest that a series of interrelated global models of educational practice, all of Western origin, are coming to dominate the world. All countries implement surprisingly similar systems of education. Everywhere, governments think it imperative to educate all citizen-children, in schools with age-graded classrooms, in language arts, mathematics, and sciences. There is certainly much truth in these arguments, but also several lacunae. As Kathryn Anderson-Levitt (2003) points out, arguments about global educational isomorphism fail to capture the contentious debates about education that emerge within nation-states all over the globe. Others have argued that distinctive national traditions of such debates have arisen in many countries (Schriewer and Martinez 2004). Rather than simply frame the problem as one of global isomorphism versus national distinctiveness, I have tried to look at educational desire from the intersection of the concepts of culture, governing, and emplacement. The intersection of these concepts privileges neither isomorphism nor national difference. More important, it sees the processes that lead to both similarity and variation as multiple and overlapping. Cultural traditions of governing of *distinctive* national origins can converge in similar patterns of debate and behavior in different countries, while institutions of a singular origin can be reinterpreted locally in strikingly distinctive ways. Above all, I have insisted that practices of governing, of conducting conduct, have emerged all over the world, and it is to the multiplicity of such traditions that we must turn to understand both similarities and differences in political and educational practice.

This multiplicity of traditions requires grappling with the term "culture." I began this book with Michael Fischer's definition and reassertion of the importance of this concept. Let us return to this definition and twist it in new ways. Fischer (2007) states:

> Culture is (1) that relational . . . , (2) complex whole . . . , (3) whose parts cannot be changed without affecting other parts . . . , (4) mediated through powerful and power-laden symbolic forms . . . , (5) whose multiplicities and performatively negotiated character . . . (6) is transformed by alternative positions, organizational forms, and leveraging of symbolic systems . . . , (7) as well as by emergent new technosciences, media, and biotechnical relations. (1)

Missing from Fischer's definition are processes of valuation and governing. Educational desire is first of all an embodied reaction to social processes of valuation. It is relational because in specifying what is to be valued (educational success), processes of valuation also designate who is to be valued. Because these processes designate who is to be valued, the governing of educational desire becomes political in a double sense. First, this governing plays a central role in the legitimation of social and political hierarchies. Second, it determines priorities for processes of social regulation, for how children should be disciplined—that is, the conduct of conduct.

Processes of valuation are always relative matters. Perhaps there are very few people in the contemporary world who would not desire educational success. But the question is to what degree is this value taken. How willing are the governed to sacrifice other valued qualities for it? In this sense, processes of valuation are also, as seen from the outside, arbitrary. There is no easy explanatory logic for why one thing is valued over another. If there were, then everyone would value that thing equally and its valuation could not be considered a cultural attribute. The only explanations for why one thing is valued over another are social and historical.

Governing, the conduct of conduct, is central to cultural processes of valuation because it is an attempt to inculcate processes of valuation in a bodily manner. The habits of being a good student, of internalizing certain linguistic and physical skills and of desiring to excel at those skills, lead to the reproduction of educational desire both because the internalization can lead to the unreflective acceptance of a particular way of doing things and because the inculcation of these habits during childhood acts as a subconscious template that is drawn upon when students grow up to raise their own children. In the end, it is the imbrication of culture with processes of governing and valuation that makes the content of the culture significant, both in a temporal sense (being able to persist over significant periods of time) and in a political sense (being involved in contentious, power-laden processes that define human hierarchies).

For much of the world, whether we like it or not, the realities and stereotypes attached to educational desire will define what it means to be Chinese or East Asian. Political, demographic, and economic dynamics both within and outside of China will be affected by it. Ignoring the processes of cultural valuation associated with this desire can only impoverish what social science might offer the world.

Notes

Chapter One

1. But see Li Quansheng (2003) for a description of a village where these calculations have been voiced more explicitly.

2. Perhaps one of the best recent summaries of these issues is Brightman (1995). See also Clifford (1988).

3. One of the most explicit examples of such a presumption lies in the glossary of Mitchell Dean's (1999) textbook on governmentality, which defines governmentality as "the different ways governing is thought about in the contemporary world which can in the large part be traced to Western Europe from the sixteenth century. Such forms of thought have been exported to large parts of the globe owing to colonial expansion and the post-colonial set of international arrangements of a system of sovereign states" (209–10). More subtle expressions of this assumption persist as well. Aihwa Ong and Li Zhang (2008:7) present an insightful discussion of the compatibility of forms of self-cultivation and authoritarian governing in contemporary China, but they tend to reduce the impetus behind the self-cultivation to neoliberalism, in part by writing that "Foucault defines governmentality—or the 'conduct of conduct'—as a modern technique," thereby neglecting some of the more traditional sources of this governing combination. I stress that here I am interested in the practical application of Foucault's ideas rather than in interpreting his *oeuvre*. Whether the limitation of governmentality style analyses to practices of modern, Western origins is a fault derived from Foucault's writing or from the way he has been read by more recent theorists is an issue that holds little interest for me.

4. Judith Farquhar and Qicheng Zhang (2005) provide a marvelous portrayal of how traditional Chinese theories of governing manifest themselves in the practices of self-cultivation among contemporary Beijing residents. Kipnis (2008a) describes how traditional Chinese treatises on governing echo in contemporary practices of governmental audit. François Jullien (1995) and Chee-han Lim (2009) provide

suggestive ways of thinking about the differences between Chinese and Western traditions of theorizing about governing.

5. Past and present leaders use the language of "teaching" or "educating" (*jiao*) the people when they mean forcing them to accept particular practices and institutions.

6. Greenhalgh (2008), for example, describes how rocket scientists disastrously gained the upper hand in the design of the birth control policy.

7. See Kipnis (1997:12–20, 2002a, 2002b) for discussions of the political constraints experienced during this earlier research.

8. In Zouping, compensation for villagers who lose their land to urban expansion has been quite high. Overall, the vast majority of people living in such villages find their economic situation improved after losing their land. There is compensation for thirty years of lost agricultural production and compensation for lost houses and house sites. In addition, some village committees retain the rights to bits of collective land that enable the village as a whole to derive income from building shopping malls or rental housing. For a description of a place where former villagers have made out extremely well, see Anita Chan et al. (2009:330–75). For more troubling cases see Sargeson and Song (2010).

9. The provision of education for the children of migrant workers is a vexed issue in China, as the public schools in the largest cities are rarely willing to accept students who are not local residents. In smaller cities, however, the situation can be more favorable, and in Zouping schools were built specifically to accommodate the children of migrant workers, or at least those who had full-time jobs at the largest of the local factories. At the time of my last visit in October 2009, at one excellent, large public primary school, 70 percent of the children were from households whose parents had migrated to Zouping for work at the local factories. For a depiction of the types of difficulties migrant worker children can face in larger cities, see Woronov (2003).

10. In China and Korea, dynasties selected elites through examinations on the classics of the neo-Confucian canon, while in Tokugawa Japan the study of Confucian classics and the establishment of schools for this study were a common elite practice. The Confucianism thus learned was itself a philosophy of governing, and training elites in Confucian texts was an aspect of the Confucian governing espoused in this literature.

11. See Perry (2007) for an excellent discussion of the continuing relevance of Leninism for a discussion of contemporary Chinese governance. Elsewhere, I have criticized at length the application of the category neoliberalism to the Chinese practices of governing associated with "suzhi discourse" (Kipnis 2007).

12. Abelmann (2009) provides a compelling description of the impacts of these stereotypes on Korean American students at the University of Illinois. Her portrayal, however, also demonstrates how social scientists concerned with such stereotypes reject the possibility of reasonable discussion about the social fact of the relationships of culture and ethnicity to educational desire.

Chapter Two

1. Trenchant anthropological critiques of modernity include those by Escobar (1995) and Fabian (1983). In the anthropology of China, those by Yang (2008) and Schein (2000) are compelling.

2. Figure from the 2008 Zouping Statistical Yearbook (Zouping Bureau of Statistics 2009:310). This calculation does not include 100,000–200,000 migrant workers from outside the county who live mainly in the county seat.

3. My household survey revealed that average incomes for working rural adults in Zouping in 2005 were about 10,000 yuan. In 2006 the exchange rate was roughly 8 yuan per $US. For more on Zouping's economic development, see Walder (1998) and Kipnis (2001b).

4. The economic relationship between employment opportunities and securing degrees is explored at greater length in chapter 5.

5. I suspect an ideological bias toward the young in this area. There is an implicit assumption that since China has been "modernizing" so rapidly, recent graduates have more "scientific" knowledge than earlier ones. While it is true that young recent graduates usually speak better standard Mandarin than their older counterparts, I am not so convinced that they are necessarily better teachers.

6. Of course, some parents might still have preferred a small, poorly equipped local school to a better equipped facility further away. But my surveys suggest that such parents were a minority. See Kipnis (2006a).

7. These figures are drawn from interviews and the county yearbooks (Zouping Gazetteer Office 1997:349–50, 2004:392). All nonfootnoted figures are derived from interviews with officials in Zouping's educational bureaucracy.

8. For English language analyses that echo these criticisms, see Murphy (2007) and Rong and Shi (2001).

9. As a kin term, *waisheng* literally means members of the younger generation who have been born "outside" of one's patriline, in this case referring to the man's sister's children.

10. For more on the lack of anti-intellectual culture in Zouping's school, in particular the absence of the school countercultures written about so often with regard to British and American schools, see Kipnis (2001a, 2001b).

11. Earlier retirement ages for women are common across the state sector in China. In practice, in some cases it is considered a benefit that women earn because of their heavier loads of housework, while in other cases it becomes a form of institutionalized sexism.

12. For example, see the front page of the May 9, 2006 *Binzhou Daily*.

13. I have not done formal research in Canberra, but I have made presentations about Zouping schools in Canberra middle schools and asked if anyone studied as hard as the Zouping students did. Never did anyone answer affirmatively. I have also spoken with many Canberra university students and observed how hard my

son and his friends study. None of these sources of information suggest that anyone in Canberra studies in the manner that the majority of Zouping students study.

14. For more on state corporatism versus entrepreneurialism, see Chih-jou Jay Chen (2004:1–29).

15. During the 1990s, many analysts assumed that the household registration system was a legacy of the Maoist era that was doomed for extinction. For recent discussions of the continued importance of the household registration system in the twenty-first century, see Fei-ling Wang (2005) and Kam Wing Chan and Buckingham (2008).

16. Data cited in Kipnis (2001b) shows that, at least during the 1990s, rural students from Shandong applied for college with more steadfastness than the national average. I have not been able to find updated versions of this data.

17. In my own tours of counties outside of Zouping, I found only one that had built a state-of-the-art secondary vocational school. Because of the shortage of vocational schools and Shandong's booming industrial economy, this school was able to arrange employment for 98 percent of its graduates. At the same time, because of the rapid increase in university graduates, many university graduates complain of underemployment (the *New York Times* reported a 30 percent unemployment rate among 2006 university graduates [French 2007]). The lack of enthusiasm for vocational education extends to the tertiary level as well. In 2005, Shandong's official education website declared that in order to respect the desires of parents, all of the money available for expanding university places in 2005 would be channeled into four-year universities (*benke*) and none to vocational short-course places (*zhuanke*) (www.shandong-edu.net, accessed October 10, 2005).

18. See Kipnis (2001b) for a slightly older discussion of the desire for education in rural China.

Chapter Three

1. For more on the role of local experimentation in Chinese policy making, see Heilmann (2008). On the importance of models, see Bakken (2000).

2. According to Susan Greenhalgh and Edwin Winkler (2005:226–29), Shandong is a province with a high level of compliance with the policy, Jiangsu and Hubei actually experience fewer births than policy allows (as many rural couples decline to have a second child when their first is a daughter), while the southern provinces of Anhui, Guangdong, Guizhou, Fujian, and Jiangxi are sites of higher son preference and noncompliance.

3. Zhang (2007) discusses recent changes in parental childbearing preferences in a village in rural Hubei Province.

4. *Zi* can mean son or child while *nü* means daughter. Thus, sometimes the first half of the saying stands alone, referring to children of both genders, while at other

times the entire saying is spoken, implicitly suggesting that appropriate forms of grandeur for boys and girls differ. In Chinese mythology dragons and phoenixes are both powerful creatures, but phoenixes are also considered beautiful, making their power more feminine.

5. See articles and letters to the editor in the July 12–15, 2008 editions of the *Qingdao Zaobao* (*Qingdao Morning News*), particularly those listed under the headline "Jiazhang PK Xuexiao: Xiaofang Shoushang Shei Fudan," *Qingdao Zaobao*, July 14, 2008, 13.

6. The ability of local government in rural areas to levy fees and taxes indiscriminately has been severely curtailed over the first few years of the twenty-first century. So such fees and taxes are largely a problem of the past. See Linda Chelan Li (2007) for one discussion of this reform.

7. For further discussion of education funding in China, see Kipnis and Li (2010).

8. I take this insight from the excellent dissertation of Qinghong Lin (2009). Unlike Lin, however, I argue that during the 1980s and 1990s, popular uses of this term shifted further. See Kipnis (2006b). The general topic of "*suzhi* discourse" has attracted considerable attention from anthropologists and other scholars, and debates have emerged over the extent to which this policy should be seen as a form of neoliberalism, a position I have argued against (Kipnis 2007). Other important writings on this topic include Anagnost (2004), Bakken (2000), Cao (2009), Greenhalgh and Winckler (2005), Jacka (2009), Judd (2002), Sigley (2009), Sun (2009), Tomba (2009), Woronov (2009), and Yan (2003a).

9. Most senior middle school students specialize in either humanities or sciences, reflecting the structure of the university entrance exam. There are, however, dedicated university places for students specializing in art, music, athletics, and even areas like fashion modeling (for the exceptionally tall, thin, and beautiful of both sexes) and becoming an astronaut. In Zouping and elsewhere in Shandong, the senior middle schools I have visited all had courses for students specializing in art, music, and athletics. Some also had an occasional course devoted to pursuing university places in one of the more specialized areas, like fashion modeling. In general, senior middle school principals are quite strategic about the way in which they offer such courses. If the principal feels that the school may secure more university places by offering a particular course, then he or she will do so. Entrance requirements for such courses vary but will generally include a minimal score on the senior middle school entrance exam and demonstration of potential in the specialized area.

10. Woronov (2008) depicts a similar example in a Beijing primary school.

11. By 2005, when I revisited the same schools, a compromise had been enacted throughout the county school district. All schools had spaces devoted to scientists and Marxist heroes as well as space devoted to model student artwork.

12. Note that the words I have translated as "moral" and "ideological" here have

a common element. A more literal translation of the two Chinese terms would be "moral thinking *suzhi*" and "political thinking *suzhi*."

13. A written text for this lesson can be found in the ideology and politics textbook for the first semester of the second year of senior middle school (Xiaoxue Sixiang Pinde He Zhongxue Sixiang Zhengzhi Jiaocai Bianxie Weiyuanhui 2003:118–26). The lesson is famous enough to have become a source of humor for irreverent satirists like Wang Shuo (2000:228).

14. In particular see Mao's essay "On Contradiction" (Mao 1975:vol. 1, 341).

15. Note that Mao Zedong thought is not what Mao thought or wrote but rather the official interpretation of Mao's writings by the contemporary Party propaganda apparatus. There is, of course, much room for reading Mao's writings on education in an anti-authoritarian, even anarchist manner.

16. This policy was reaffirmed in September 2009. See Xu Jie (2009) for newspaper coverage.

17. This information was compiled from telephone interviews with lower-level officials in Shandong and a series of speeches and articles available on the official website of the Shandong Education Bureau (www.sdedu.gov.cn, accessed March 3, 2008). These articles include "Several items that need to be made clear in the implementation of education for quality" ("Tuijin suzhijiaoyu luoshi guifan xuyao mingque ruogan juti wenti"); "Fully realize the regulations on senior middle school curriculum, Actually implement senior middle school education for quality" ("Quanmian luoshi gaozhong kecheng fangan, Zhashi tuijin gaozhong suzhi jiaoyu"); "Comrade Zhang Zhiyong's speech at the special training meeting on education for quality for senior middle school principals throughout the province" ("Zhang Zhiyong tongzhi zai quansheng gaozhong xiaozhang suzhi jiaoyu zhuanti peixun huiyishang de jianghua").

18. See the article "Weifan Suzhi Jiaoyu, 25 Xiaozhang Shou Qu," *Qingdao Zaobao*, July 10, 2008, 21.

19. This example also should caution against overemphasizing the degree of change involved in the opening of new spaces for self-governing, called "neoliberalism" by some scholars (e.g., Ong and Zhang 2008).

20. Lily Chumley (2009) has done fascinating research on the private schools that opened up for preparing for the specialized university entrance exam in fine arts.

21. In Chinese these are known as *tiao-kuai* relationships. The *tiao* are the vertical lines of administration that go up and down through various levels of government (townships, counties, prefectures, provinces) within bureaus like the education bureau or the public security bureau. The *kuai* are the local governments themselves, which include, most centrally, the Party secretary of a given locality and all the people and departments that report directly to him (or, rarely, her). The *tiao* and *kuai* have separate sources of funding, budgets, and lines of authority. For a recent discussion of *tiao* and *kuai* in relation to policing, see Tanner and Green (2007).

22. This twisting could be seen as what James Scott (1985) has famously described as an everyday form of resistance. A more exact theorization of this form of resistance can be found in Børge Bakken's (2000) discussion of "ways of lying" under authoritarian regimes.

23. State Council Decision on Expanding Vocational Education (Guowuyuan Guanyu Dali Fazhan Zhiye Jiaoyu de Jueding) (2005 #35). Accessed on March 10, 2008, at http://www.gxgzgz.com/ReadNews.asp?NewsID=177.

24. Ministry of Education (Jiaoyu Bu), "Introducing the Current Situation of Our Country's Vocational Education Reform and Expansion" ("Dangqian Woguo Zhiye Jiaoyu Gaige Fazhan Qingkuang Jieshao"). Accessed March 10, 2008, at http://www.moe.edu.cn/edoas/website18/info21282.htm.

25. Xing and Li (2009:207) also argue that vocational school graduates have lower unemployment rates than university graduates.

26. After taking the university entrance exam and receiving their scores, students then fill out the universal application form. Cutoff scores are announced for the three tiers of universities. Students will also know the admission scores from previous years for specific programs at specific universities. Despite this knowledge, selecting which department and university to apply to still involves an element of risk. The score needed for a specific program could change from one year to the next, and if a student lists a program for which his or her score is not good enough as the top choice, then the student may not be admitted anywhere as some programs accept only students who put them as top choice.

Chapter Four

1. I originally called these legacies "the Confucian complex," but this term caused considerable offense to scholars interested in treating Confucianism as a philosophy instead of practices of governing that are often implemented in an authoritarian fashion. They rightfully suggest that Confucianism should not be reduced to the way in which some power holders abuse Confucian precepts or practices.

2. The historical literature on Confucian education during the Qing dynasty and earlier, and the imperial examination system and its demise during the early twentieth century, is too large to review here. For a brief introduction to some explicit attempts to recreate classic Confucian institutions during the twentieth and early twenty-first centuries, see Billioud and Thoraval (2007).

3. For more on the efforts to turn "peasants" into Chinese, see Murphy (2004).

4. I lump the ideographic and pictographic together here because they are often merged in popular imagination (Yen 2005:137). Strictly speaking, pictographs are stylized pictures. For example, the Chinese character for woman/female (女) derives from a stylized picture of a kneeling women and is thus a pictograph; the

character meaning good (好) is a woman next to a child: thus the idea for good has something to do with the connection between women and children and this character is an ideograph. The character for mother-in-law (婆) has the pictograph for a woman on the bottom and a character that rhymes with mother-in-law on the top, so it combines phonetic with pictographic/ideographic elements as the majority of characters do.

5. See Yen (2005:135–40) for a summary of some of these debates.

6. Poem by Li Bai; the translation is by François Cheng, D. A. Riggs, and J. P. Seaton (Cheng 1982:112).

7. These students tended to invert or misplace elements of characters in a pattern that might (controversially) be compared to dyslexia in English-language writing. Psychologists debate the extent to which such problems should be labeled with the term dyslexia across different writing systems. Some psychologists even suggest that different parts of the brain are used when writing Chinese characters and Western words, so that the problems that people have with the different writing systems reflect different types of ailments. See Schmid (2008).

8. Following linguistic anthropologists like William Hanks (1996:192–197), and Susan Gal (1989), I use the term language ideology to refer to assumptions about language use that relate to social hierarchies, i.e., that make speaking or writing in particular languages, dialects, styles, or manners a form of cultural capital.

9. Literary representations of the importance of handwriting are also numerous. One of my favorites takes place in the Wang Anyi novel *Age of Enlightenment* (*Qimeng Shidai*). A father, not satisfied with his son's handwriting, requires him to use the father's writing as a model. The son discovers both that his father's excellent handwriting seems feminine and that his own handwriting in some way resembles that of his father. The son begins to realize other ways in which his personality resembles his father's (Wang Anyi 2007:287).

10. Such articles run regularly in the health and education sections of the *Qilu Evening News*. See, for example, page B4 of the November 11, 2005 edition for a full-page ad, or page A7 of the September 3, 2005 edition for some shorter sponsored stories and ads.

11. Billioud and Thoraval (2007:15–17) discuss the popular movement to introduce Confucian classics to primary school students in China more broadly.

12. The Hong Kong–based educational psychologists Watkins and Biggs (Biggs and Watkins 2001; Watkins and Biggs 2001) argue that the "Chinese learner" is a paradox. From the point of view of Western educational psychologists, the rote-learning pedagogic strategies Chinese students are exposed to are terrible. Yet they still manage to excel. Watkins and Biggs argue that cultural conceptions of student participation account for this paradox.

13. The novelist Wang Shuo, for example, has satirized a famous lesson regarding Mao Zedong thought, internal and external contradictions, and the chicken and the egg. See chapter 3.

14. The textbook chapter for this lesson is in *Guofang Jiaoyu* (Guofang Jiaoyu Weiyuanhui 2005:46–52).

15. Thanks to Chen Liang for writing out the characters for me.

16. For more detail on such socializing, see Xin Liu (2002) and Zheng (2004).

17. A discussion of the methods by which officials obtain illicit degrees and a series of recommendations of the steps that should be taken to combat this form of corruption were published in the Chinese news weekly *Liaowang* (Outlook Weekly) by Li Song (2007).

18. Li Keqiang's degree is accepted, but those of Li Yuanchao, Liu Yandong, and especially Xi Jinping have been questioned. The questions revolve around the facts that some of the dissertations that led to the degrees cannot be found in the relevant departmental libraries and that some of the degrees were obtained during periods when the degree holders already had full-time political posts, and thus during periods when they should not have had the time to write a dissertation. See, for example, discussions on the website China Economic Forum (Jingji Zhongguo Luntan), http://bbs.econchina.org.cn/bbs/dispbbs.asp?boardID=38&ID=9397& page=5, accessed August 20, 2008.

19. I was traveling around China when this story was reported and saw references to it in newspapers in three cities in Shandong, as well as Urumqi, Shanghai, and Beijing. The story is listed as being initially published in the Wuhan newspaper *Chutian Dushi Bao*. I collected versions of the story in the *Shandong Evening News* (*Qilu Wanbao*) and *Qingdao Morning News* (*Qingdao Zaobao*) (*Qilu Wanbao* Editorial Staff 2008a, 2008b; *Qingdao Zaobao* Editorial Staff 2008). These articles contain editorial comments as well as the initial article.

20. See, for example, the cartoons in Geremie Barmé's (2002:130, 198) wonderful biography.

21. This discussion of Taiwan relies on interviews I conducted in 2001 with Taiwanese normal university teachers, P. Kerim Friedman's dissertation (2005: 27–59, 128–33), an open letter from one hundred scholars regarding Taiwan's education reform in 2003 (Open Letter 2003), a response from Taiwan's National Policy Foundation (Xue 2003), and Kunjin Huang (2009).

Chapter Five

1. As described in the introduction, to say that certain practices, technologies, and social dynamics are universal is to say not that they exist everywhere but that they demonstrate a certain potential for universalization (Chakrabarty 2000; Collier and Ong 2005; Dean and Hindess 1998). Even this potential can be limited in my conception of the term. I mean to include not only phenomena that could spread anywhere but also those that seem to emerge in or spread to a range of societies that share a few basic features—such as agricultural empires or rapidly

industrializing nations. The main criterion is that their spread does not depend upon particular, culturally defined traditions of governing, interpreting, reading, teaching, or writing.

2. Ellen Hertz (1998:71-93) and Jing Wang (1996) provide interesting analyses of stock market and high culture fevers. See Zhou (1993) for a discussion of feverlike social action in general.

3. This contradiction has been noted by many other educational theorists in slightly different terms. Bradley Levinson and Dorothy Holland (1996) have written eloquently about comparative processes of the cultural production of the learned person. Jules Henry (1963:260-61) writes of the links between the production of creative people and the thoroughness of institutionalized discipline in various school systems and the resultant contradictions this relationship causes for liberal American educators who wish to promote democracy, creativity, and permissiveness all at once. Stig Thøgersen (1990) describes the conflicts between the mass production of citizens and the selection of elites as common to all modern systems of education.

4. Notoriously, Jia Baoyu was not a disciplined student (always neglecting the books of the official canon); but he was literary, sensitive, and absolutely uninterested in anything that might be considered macho.

5. The female inside, male outside dichotomy is common in agricultural societies. The reversal of this pattern in East European Jewish communities perhaps relates to the fact that such communities were not necessarily agricultural and that Jewish communities in Eastern Europe were minorities excluded from the affairs of state. For more on this dichotomy in China, see Judd (1994), Kipnis (2002b), Rofel (1994), and Wolf (1985).

6. As described in the previous chapter, there is an association between boys and hyperactivity and bad handwriting in Zouping, and this association no doubt resonates with the fact that there are both martial and literary masculinities in China. The key point, however, is that in China the relative strength of literary masculinity ensures that studious boys are not stigmatized.

7. Some of the complex history of this transformation is captured by Elisabeth Kaske (2008).

8. In such debates, Pierre Bourdieu is often criticized for a position that emphasizes only the role of national dialects as prestige languages in which some people accumulate symbolic capital more easily than others while ignoring the politics of the interrelations among several dialects that may exist in a given national space. Gramsci is credited for emphasizing the historical political processes by which some dialects are promoted over others in a given national space. See P. Kerim Friedman's dissertation (2005:239-61) for an excellent summary of these debates.

9. In Zouping, the trend away from expectations that children would provide care in old age was evident in the house-building practices described in chapter 2.

In the past few years, wealthier villages at least have begun building old age homes in anticipation of a generation of retired farmers whose children have moved to the city. The building of these homes has received financial and policy support through the recent national push to build a "new socialist countryside."

10. Such a situation contrasts sharply with that depicted by theorists of continuing fertility decline in fully industrialized nations. There, the possibilities of higher educational and career pursuits cause young people to postpone their own childbearing desires (Caldwell et al. 2006:312).

11. In three-character names, the middle character is often a "generation name" that designates a person's generational place in a long-continuing patriline (all members of a given generation of a patriline share a single middle name). As lineages were and in some places are important institutions in rural communities, three-character names can indicate rural origins. See Kipnis (1997) for more on generation names.

12. The poem and accompanying didactic material may be found in the sixth-grade first-semester literature textbook (Renmin Jiaoyu Chubanshe Xiaoxue Yuwen Shi 2005:77–81).

13. The general literature on the economic returns of education is vast (e.g., Psacharopoulos 1973). Fleisher and Wang (2005) apply some of the econometric techniques of this literature to China. I do not find the conclusions of this type of research convincing, at least when it is applied to China, because the value of various degrees changes so quickly in reform-era China and because the data do not distinguish carefully enough among various types and tiers of university.

14. The imperial examination system has elicited vast amounts of scholarship. For a review essay discussing recent books on this topic, see Lee (2006).

15. For details on this research project, see Kipnis and Smith (2007). Zhao himself took posts in rural governments at the county level to better understand the complexities of local governance in China. The understanding derived from this experience informed both the types of questions he asked and the methods he used to approach cadres.

16. For a description of a Chinese locality where birth control quotas are routinely faked, see Xiyi Huang (2007:177–78).

17. Demerath (2009) provides a fascinating ethnography of the intensity of academic competition among elite American high school students. For one account of the increased difficulty of getting into Harvard, see Winerip (2007).

Chapter Six

1. See Chengfang Liu et al. (2009) for a discussion of the recent wave of catch-up infrastructure investment in rural China over the past few years.

2. These data come from the CIA world factbook online, https://www.cia

.gov/library/publications/the-world-factbook/rankorder/2127rank.html, accessed March 13, 2009.

3. Francis Hsu (1971) long ago wrote about the cultural sources of Chinese students' academic achievements in the United States.

4. That is to say, "public" at least to the members of the organization within which the procedures are applied.

References

Abelmann, Nancy. 2009. *The Intimate University: Korean American Students and the Problem of Segregation*. Durham: Duke University Press.

Anagnost, Ann. 2004."The Corporeal Politics of Quality (Suzhi)." *Public Culture* 16 (2): 189–208.

Anderson, Benedict. 1991. *Imagined Communities: Reflections on the Origin and Spread of Nationalism*. London: Verso.

Anderson-Levitt, Kathryn M. 2003. "A World Culture of Schooling?" In *Local Meanings, Global Schooling: Anthropology and World Culture Theory*, ed. K. M. Anderson-Levitt, 1–26. New York: Palgrave Macmillan.

Ariès, Philippe. 1962. *Centuries of Childhood*. London: John Cape.

———. 1980. "Two Successive Motivations for the Declining Birth Rate in the West." *Population and Development Review* 6 (4): 645–50.

Bai, Limin. 2006. "Graduate Unemployment: Dilemmas and Challenges in China's Move to Mass Higher Education." *China Quarterly* (185): 128–44.

Bakken, Børge. 2000. *The Exemplary Society: Human Improvement, Social Control, and the Dangers of Modernity in China*. New York: Oxford University Press.

Barmé, Geremie R. 2002. *An Artistic Exile: A Life of Feng Zikai (1898–1975)*. Berkeley: University of California Press.

Barr, Michael D. 2000. *Lee Kuan Yew: The Beliefs behind the Man*. Surrey: Curzon.

Barry, Andrew, Thomas Osbourne, and Nikolas Rose, eds. 1996. *Foucault and Political Reason: Liberalism, Neo-liberalism, and Rationalities of Government*. Chicago: University of Chicago Press.

Bataille, Georges. 1991. *The Accursed Share: An Essay on General Economy*. Trans. R. Hurley. 3 vols. Vols. 2 and 3. New York: Zone Books.

Beijing Youth Daily Staff. 2008. Guojia Guifan Gongwuyuan Zhiwu Dingji Renmian Tiao ren. *Nanjing Ribao*, 1.

Benei, Véronique. 2008. *Schooling Passions: Nation, History and Language in Contemporary Western India*. Stanford: Stanford University Press.

Biggs, John B., and David A. Watkins. 2001. "Insights into Teaching the Chinese Learner." In *Teaching the Chinese Learner: Psychological and Pedagogical*

Perspectives, ed. D. A. Watkins and J. B. Biggs, 277–300. Melbourne: Australian Council for Educational Research.

Billioud, Sebastien, and Joel Thoraval. 2007. "Jiaohua: The Confucian Revival in China as an Educative Project." *China Perspectives* 2007 (4): 4–20.

Boum, Aomar. 2008. "The Political Coherence of Educational Incoherence: The Consequences of Educational Specialization in a Southern Moroccan Community." *Anthropology and Education Quarterly* 39 (2): 205–23.

Boyarin, Daniel. 1997. *Unheroic Conduct: The Rise of Heterosexuality and the Invention of the Jewish Man.* Berkeley: University of California Press.

Brightman, Robert. 1995. "Forget Culture: Replacement, Transcendence, Relexification." *Cultural Anthropology* 10 (4): 509–46.

Brokaw, Cynthia J. 1991. *The Ledgers of Merit and Demerit: Social Change and Moral Order in Late Imperial China.* Princeton: Princeton University Press.

Caldwell, John C., et al. 2006. *Demographic Transition Theory.* Dordrecht: Springer.

Cao, Nanlai. 2008. "Constructing China's Jerusalem: Christians, Power and Place in Contemporary Wenzhou." Ph.D. diss., Australian National University.

———. 2009. "Raising the Quality of Belief: Suzhi and the Production of an Elite Protestantism." *China Perspectives* 2009 (4): 54–65.

Chakrabarty, Dipesh. 2000. *Provincializing Europe: Postcolonial Thought and His torical Difference.* Princeton: Princeton University Press.

Chan, Anita, Richard Madsen, and Jonathan Unger. 2009. *Chen Village: Revolution to Globalization.* 3rd ed. Berkeley: University of California Press.

Chan, Kam Wing, and Will Buckingham. 2008. "Is China Abolishing the Hukou System?" *China Quarterly* (195): 582–606.

Chau, Adam Yuet. 2008. "An Awful Mark: Symbolic Violence and Urban Renewal in Reform Era China." *Visual Studies* 23 (3): 195–210.

Chen, Chih-jou Jay. 2004. *Transforming Rural China: How Local Institutions Shape Property Rights in China.* London: RoutledgeCurzon.

Cheng, François. 1982. *Chinese Poetic Writing: With an Anthology of Tang Poetry.* Trans. D. A. Riggs and J. P. Seaton. Bloomington: Indiana University Press.

Chicharro-Saito, Gladys. 2008. "Physical Education and 'Embodiment' of Morality in Primary Schools of the People's Republic of China." *China Perspectives* 2008 (1): 29–39.

Choe, Sang-hun. 2008. "A Taste of Failure Fuels an Appetite for Success at South Korea's Cram Schools." *New York Times,* August 13.

Chumley, Lily Hope. 2009. "Compulsion, Intimacy and Art-Test Prep-Schools." Paper presented at 2009 IUAES meetings. Kunming, China.

Clifford, James. 1988. *The Predicament of Culture: Twentieth-Century Ethnography, Literature, and Art.* Cambridge: Harvard University Press.

Collier, Stephen J. 2005. "Budgets and Biopolitics." In *Global Assemblages: Technology, Politics and Ethics as Anthropological Problems*, ed. A. Ong and S. J. Collier, 373–90. Malden, MA: Blackwell.

Collier, Stephen J., and Aihwa Ong. 2005. "Global Assemblages, Anthropological Problems." In *Global Assemblages: Technology, Politics and Ethics As Anthropological Problems*, ed. A. Ong and S. J. Collier, 3–21. Malden, MA: Blackwell.

Corrigan, Phillip, and Derek Sayer. 1985. *The Great Arch: English State Formation as Cultural Revolution*. New York: Blackwell.

Crouch, Harold. 2001. "Managing Ethnic Tensions through Affirmative Action: The Malaysian Experience." In *Social Cohesion and Conflict Prevention in Asia*, ed. N. J. Colletta, T. G. Lim, and A. Kelles-Viitanen, 225–62. Washington, DC: World Bank.

Cui, Xianglu, ed. 1999. *Suzhi Jiaoyu: Zhong Xiao Xue Jiaoyu Gaige de Xuanlu*. Jinan: Shandong Jiaoyu Chubanshe.

Dean, Mitchell. 1999. *Governmentality: Power and Rule in Modern Society*. London: Sage Publications.

Dean, Mitchell, and Barry Hindess. 1998. "Introduction: Government, Liberalism, Society." In *Governing Australia: Studies in Contemporary Rationalities of Government*, ed. M. Dean and B. Hindess, 1–19. New York: Cambridge University Press.

Deleuze, Gilles, and Felix Guattari. 1983. *Anti-Oedipus*. Vol. 1 of *Capitalism and Schizophrenia*. Trans. R. Hurley, M. Seem, and H. R. Lane. Minneapolis: University of Minnesota Press.

———. 1987. *A Thousand Plateaus*. Vol. 2 of *Capitalism and Schizophrenia*. Trans. B. Massumi. Minneapolis: University of Minnesota Press.

Demerath, Peter. 2009. *Producing Success: The Culture of Personal Advancement in an American High School*. Chicago: University of Chicago Press.

Dierkes, Julian. 2008. "Japanese Shadow Education: The Consequences of School Choice." In *The Globalisation of School Choice?* ed. M. Forsey, S. Davies, and G. Walford, 231–48. Oxford: Symposium Books.

Dillon, Sam. 2008. "Elite Korean Schools, Forging Ivy League Skills." In *New York Times*, April 27.

Dore, Ronald. 1997. *The Diploma Disease: Education, Qualifications and Development*. 2nd ed. London: Institute of Education of London.

Duchatel, Mathieu. 2008. "Singapore: The Chinese Path to Political Reform?" *China Perspectives* 2008 (1): 96–97.

Durkheim, Emile. 1992. *Professional Ethics and Civic Morals*. Trans. C. Brookfield. New York: Routledge.

Englund, Harri. 2002. "Ethnography after Globalism: Migration and Emplacement in Malawi." *American Ethnologist* 29 (2): 261–86.

Escobar, Arturo. 1995. *Encountering Development: The Making and Unmaking of the Third World*. Princeton: Princeton University Press.

Fabian, Johannes. 1983. *Time and the Other: How Anthropology Makes Its Object*. New York: Columbia University Press.

Fackler, Martin. 2008. "Losing an Edge, Japanese Envy India's Schools." In *New York Times*, January 2.

Farquhar, Judith, and Qicheng Zhang. 2005. "Biopolitical Beijing: Pleasure, Sovereignty, and Self-Cultivation in China's Capital." *Cultural Anthropology* 20 (3): 303–27.

Fei, Xiaotong. 1992. *From the Soil: The Foundations of Chinese Society, A Translation of Fei Xiaotong's Xiangtu Zhongguo*. Trans. G. Hamilton and W. Zheng. Berkeley: University of California Press.

Ferguson, James, and Akhil Gupta. 2002. "Spatializing States: Toward an Ethnography of Neoliberal Governmentality." *American Ethnologist* 29 (4): 981–1002.

Fischer, Michael J. 2007. "Culture and Cultural Analysis as Experimental Systems." *Cultural Anthropology* 22 (1): 1–65.

Fleisher, Belton M., and Xiaojun Wang. 2005. "Returns to Schooling in China under Planning and Reform." *Journal of Comparative Economics* 33 (2): 265–77.

Fong, Vanessa L. 2004a. "Filial Nationalism among Chinese Teenagers with Global Identities." *American Ethnologist* 31 (4): 631–48.

———. 2004b. *Only Hope: Coming of Age under China's One-Child Policy*. Stanford: Stanford University Press.

Foucault, Michel. 1979. *Discipline and Punish: The Birth of the Prison*. New York: Vintage Books.

———. 1983. "The Subject and Power." In *Michel Foucault: Beyond Structuralism and Hermeneutics*, ed. H. L. Dreyfus and P. Rabinow, 208–226. 2nd ed. Chicago: University of Chicago Press.

———. 1988. *The History of Sexuality*. Trans. R. Hurley. New York: Vintage Books.

———. 1991. "Governmentality." In *The Foucault Effect: Studies in Governmentality*, ed. G. Burchell, C. Gordon, and P. Miller, 87–104. London: Harvester Wheatsheaf.

French, Howard W. 2007. "China Scrambles for Stability As Its Workers Age." In *New York Times*, March 22, A1, A8.

Friedman, Edward, Paul Pickowicz, and Mark Selden. 1991. *Chinese Village, Socialist State*. New Haven: Yale University Press.

Friedman, P. Kerim. 2005. "Learning 'Local' Languages: Passive Revolution, Language Markets, and Aborigine Education in Taiwan." Ph.D. diss., Temple University.

Fuller, Bruce. 1991. *Growing Up Modern: The Western State Builds Third World Schools*. New York: Routledge.

Gal, Susan. 1989. "Language and Political Economy." *Annual Review of Anthropology* 18: 347–67.

Gao, Yuan. 2005. "Xiaoxue Jiaoyu 'Yin Sheng Yang Shuai.'" In *Qilu Wanbao* (Jinan), October 19, A7.

Gates, Hill. 1996. *China's Motor: A Thousand Years of Petty Capitalism*. Ithaca: Cornell University Press.

Geertz, Clifford. 1980. *Negara: The Theatre State in Nineteenth-Century Bali*. Princeton: Princeton University Press.

Gledhill, John. 2004. "Neoliberalism." In *A Companion to the Anthropology of Politics*, ed. T. Nugent and J. Vincent, 332–48. Malden, MA: Blackwell.

Gold, Thomas. 1985. "After Comradeship: Personal Relations in China since the Cultural Revolution." *China Quarterly* (104): 657–75.

Gordon, Colin. 1987. "The Soul of the Citizen: Max Weber and Michel Foucault on Rationality and Government." In *Max Weber, Rationality and Modernity*, ed. S. Lash and S. Whimster, 293–316. London: Allen & Unwin.

———. 1991. "Governmental Rationality: An Introduction." In *The Foucault Effect: Studies in Governmentality*, ed. G. Burchell, C. Gordon, and P. Miller, 1–52. London: Harvester Wheatsheaf.

Gramsci, Antonio. 1971. *Selections from the Prison Notebooks*. Ed. and trans. Quintin Hoare and Geoffrey Nowell Smith. London: Lawrence and Wishart.

Greenhalgh, Susan. 1990. "The Evolution of the One-Child Policy in Shaanxi." *China Quarterly* 122: 191–229.

———. 1993. "The Peasantization of the One-Child Policy in Shaanxi." In *Chinese Families in the Post-Mao Era*, ed. D. Davis and S. Harrell, 219–50. Berkeley: University of California Press.

———. 2008. *Just One Child: Science and Policy in Deng's China*. Berkeley: University of California Press.

Greenhalgh, Susan, and Edwin A. Winckler. 2005. *Governing China's Population*. Stanford: Stanford University Press.

Guan, Zhaoxia. 2003. "Tan Xiandai Nongmin Suzhi Jiaoyu." *Xinyang Nongye Gaodeng Zhuanke Xuebao* 13 (1): 77–78.

Guofang Jiaoyu Weiyuanhui. 2005. *Guofang Jiaoyu, Liu Nianji*. Changsha: Quanguo Youxiu Chubanshe.

Guojia Jiaoyu Weiyuanhui, ed. 1992. *Shiyi Jie San Zhong Quanhui Yilai Zhongyao Jiaoyu Wenxian*. Beijing: Jiaoyu Kexue Chubanshe.

Hanks, William F. 1996. *Language and Communicative Practices*. Boulder: Westview Press.

Hansen, Mette Halskov. 1999. *Lessons in Being Chinese: Minority Education and Ethnic Identity in Southwest China*. Seattle: University of Washington Press.

Hayhoe, Ruth. 1984. "The Evolution of Modern Chinese Educational Institutions." In *Contemporary Chinese Education*, ed. R. Hayhoe, 26–46. London: Croom Helm.

Heilmann, Sebastian. 2008. "From Local Experiments to National Policy: The Origins of China's Distinctive Policy Process." *China Journal* (59): 1–32.

Henry, Jules. 1963. *Culture Against Man*. Harmondsworth: Penguin.

Hertz, Ellen. 1998. *The Trading Crowd: An Ethnography of the Shanghai Stock Market*. Cambridge: Cambridge University Press.

Herzfeld, Michael. 2005. *Cultural Intimacy: Social Poetics in the Nation-State*. 2nd ed. New York: Routledge.

Hindess, Barry. 1996a. *Discourses of Power: From Hobbes to Foucault*. Cambridge, MA: Blackwell.

————. 1996b. "Liberalism, Socialism and Democracy: Variations on a Governmental Theme." In *Foucault and Political Reason: Liberalism, Neo-liberalism, and Rationalities of Government*, ed. A. Barry, T. Osbourne, and N. Rose, 65–80. Chicago: University of Chicago Press.

Hirschman, Charles. 1994. "Why Fertility Changes." *Annual Review of Sociology* 20: 203–33.

Hsu, Francis. 1971. *The Challenge of the American Dream: The Chinese in the United States*. New York: Wadsworth.

Huang, Jianli. 2007. "Nanyang University and the Language Divide in Singapore: Controversy over the 1965 Wang Gungwu Report." In *Imagery of Nanyang University: Reflections on the River of History*, ed. G. K. Lee, 165–220. Singapore: Global Publishing.

Huang, Kunjin. 2009. "Education in Taiwan in 2007." In *The China Educational Development Yearbook*, Vol. 1, ed. D. Yang, 321–32. Boston: Brill.

Huang, Xiyi. 2007. *Power, Entitlement and Social Practice: Resource Distribution in North China Villages*. Hong Kong: Chinese University Press.

Ivy, Marilyn. 1995. *Discourses of the Vanishing: Modernity, Phantasm, Japan*. Chicago: University of Chicago Press.

Jacka, Tamara. 2009. "Cultivating Citizens: Suzhi (Quality) Discourse in the PRC." *Positions: East Asia Cultures Critique* 17 (3): 523–35.

Jankowiak, William R. 1993. *Sex, Death, and Hierarchy in a Chinese City: An Anthropological Account*. New York: Columbia University Press.

Jenner, William F. 1992. *The Tyranny of History: The Root of China's Crisis*. London: Allen Lane, Penguin Press.

Jie, Sizhong. 2004. *Zhongguo Guomin Suzhi Weiji*. Beijing: Zhongguo Changan Chubanshe.

Judd, Ellen R. 1994. *Gender and Power in Rural North China*. Stanford: Stanford University Press.

————. 2002. *The Chinese Women's Movement between State and Market*. Stanford: Stanford University Press.

Jullien, François. 1995. *The Propensity of Things: Toward a History of Efficacy in China*. Cambridge, MA: Zone Books.

Kahn, Joel S. 2001. "Anthropology and Modernity." *Current Anthropology* 42 (5): 651–79.

Kaplan, Sam. 2006. *The Pedagogical State: Education and the Politics of National Culture in Post-1980 Turkey*. Stanford: Stanford University Press.

Kaske, Elisabeth. 2008. *The Politics of Language in Chinese Education, 1895–1919*. Leiden: Brill.

Kipnis, Andrew B. 1995. "Within and Against Peasantness: Backwardness and Filiality in Rural China." *Comparative Studies in Society and History* 37 (1): 110–35.

————. 1997. *Producing Guanxi: Sentiment, Self, and Subculture in a North China Village*. Durham: Duke University Press.

———. 2001a. "Articulating School Countercultures." *Anthropology and Education Quarterly* 32 (4): 472–92.

———. 2001b. "The Disturbing Educational Discipline of 'Peasants.'" *China Journal* (46): 1–24.

———. 2002a. "Practices of Guanxi Production and Practices of Ganqing Avoidance." In *Social Connections in China: Institutions, Culture and the Changing Nature of Guanxi*, ed. T. Gold, D. Guthrie, and D. L. Wank, 21–36. New York: Cambridge University Press.

———. 2002b. "Zouping Christianity as Gendered Critique? The Place of the Political in Ethnography." *Anthropology and Humanism* 27 (1): 80–96.

———. 2003a. "Neo-Leftists versus Neo-Liberals: PRC Intellectual Debates in the 1990s." *Journal of Intercultural Studies* 24 (3): 239–52.

———. 2003b. "Post-Marxism in a Postsocialist Perspective." *Anthropological Theory* 3 (4): 457–80.

———. 2006a. "School Consolidation in Rural China." *Development Bulletin* (70): 123–25.

———. 2006b. "Suzhi: A Keyword Approach." *China Quarterly* (186): 295–313.

———. 2007. "Neoliberalism Reified: Suzhi Discourse and Tropes of Neoliberalism in the PRC." *Journal of the Royal Anthropological Institute* 13 (2): 383–99.

———. 2008a. "Audit Cultures: Neoliberal Governmentality, Socialist Legacy or Technologies of Governing?" *American Ethnologist* 35 (2): 275–89.

———. 2008b. *China and Postsocialist Anthropology: Theorizing Power and Society after Communism*. Norwalk, CT: Eastbridge.

———. n.d. "Subjectification and Education for Quality in China."

Kipnis, Andrew B., and Shanfeng Li. 2010. "Is Chinese Education Underfunded?" *China Quarterly* (202): 327–43.

Kipnis, Andrew B., and Graeme Smith. 2007. Guest editors' introduction. *Chinese Sociology and Anthropology* 39 (2): 3–7.

Kraus, Richard C. 1991. *Brushes with Power: Modern Politics and the Chinese Art of Calligraphy*. Berkeley: University of California Press.

Latour, Bruno. 1994. "On Technical Mediation—Philosophy, Sociology, Genealogy." *Common Knowledge* 3 (2): 29–64.

———. 2005. *Reassembling the Social: An Introduction to Actor-Network Theory*. New York: Oxford University Press.

Lee, Thomas H. C. 2006 "Imagining the Chinese Examination System: Historical Nature and Modern Usefulness." *China Review International* 13 (1): 1–12.

LeVine, Robert A., and Merry I. White. 1986. *Human Conditions: The Cultural Basis of Educational Development*. Cambridge: Cambridge University Press.

Levinson, Bradley, and Dorothy Holland. 1996. "The Cultural Production of the Educated Person: An Introduction." In *The Cultural Production of the Educated Person: Critical Ethnographies of Schooling and Local Practice*, ed. B. Levinson, D. Foley, and D. Holland, 1–56. Albany: SUNY Press.

Li, Ao. 2001. *Shang Shan, Shang Shan, Ai*. Taibei: Li Ao Chubanshe.

Li, Linda Chelan. 2007. "Working for the Peasants? Strategic Interactions and Unintended Consequences in Chinese Rural Tax Reform." *China Journal* (57): 61–88.

Li, Quansheng. 2003. "Nongcun 'Pazi Chenglong' Xianxiang Fenxi: Yi Dong Kuang Cun Weili." *Qingnian Yanjiu* 2003 (6).

Li, Song. 2007. "Zhenfang Guanyuan Xueli Zaojia Fantan." *Liaowang* (Outlook Weekly) 2007 (45): 10–12.

Lim, Chee-han. 2009. "Purging the Ghost of Descartes: Conducting Zhineng Qigong in Singapore." Ph.D. diss., Australian National University.

Lin, Qinghong. 2009. "Civilising Citizens in Post-Mao China: Understanding the Rhetoric of *Suzhi*." Ph.D. diss., Griffith University.

Liu, Chengfang, et al. 2009. "Infrastructure Investment in Rural China: Is Quality Being Compromised during Quantity Expansion?" *China Journal* (61): 105–30.

Liu, Linping, Rongguo Zhang, and Xiangdong Fang, eds. 1997. *Ai de Wuqu: Zhongxiao Xuesheng Chengzhang Wenti Bei Wanglu*. Beijing: Zhongguo Renshi Chubanshe.

Liu, Xin. 2002. *The Otherness of Self: A Genealogy of the Self in Contemporary China*. Ann Arbor: University of Michigan Press.

Louie, Kam. 2002. *Theorising Chinese Masculinity: Society and Gender in China*. Cambridge: Cambridge University Press.

Ma, Qinhe. 2001. "Nongcun Suzhi Jiaoyu Zhi Ben Shi Tigao Jiaoshi Suzhi." *Suzhou Jiaoyu Xueyuan Xuebao* 2001 (3): 60–61.

Mao, T'se-tung. 1975. *Selected Works of Mao T'se-Tung*. 5 vols. Beijing: Foreign Languages Press.

Mauss, Marcel. 1967 [1925]. "The Gift: Forms and Functions of Exchange in Archaic Societies." Trans. I. Cunnison. New York: W. W. Norton.

McDermott, Ray, and Kathleen D. Hall. 2007. "Scientifically Debased Research on Learning, 1854–2006." *Anthropology and Education Quarterly* 38 (1): 9–15.

Meyer, John W., and Francisco O. Ramirez. 2003. "The World Institutionalization of Education." In *Discourse Formation in Comparative Education*, ed. J. Schriewer, 111–32. New York: P. Lang.

Miller, Laura. 2005. "Japanese Girls' Orthographic Rebellion." *Anthropology News* 46 (9): 60.

Mo, Gong. 2005. " 'Suzhi Jiaoyu' Neng Peiyang Chu Xiandai Gongmin Ma?" *Nanfang Zhoumo* (Guangzhou), May 18, D27.

Murphy, Rachel. 2004. "Turning Peasants into Modern Chinese Citizens: 'Population Quality' Discourse, Demographic Transition and Primary Education." *China Quarterly* (177): 1–20.

———. 2007. "Paying for Education in Rural China." In *Paying for Progress in China: Public Finance, Human Welfare and Changing Patterns of Inequality*, ed. V. Shue and C. Wong. London: Routledge.

Nakamura, Fuyubi. 2006. "Creating New Forms of 'Visualised' Words: An Anthropological Study of Contemporary Japanese Calligraphy." Ph.D. diss., Oxford University.

Nie, Hongping Nannie. 2008. *The Dilemma of the Moral Curriculum in a Chinese Secondary School.* Lanham, MD: University Press of America.

Oh, Ookwhan. 2003. Review of *Education Fever* by Michel J. Seth. *Acta Koreana* 6 (2): 176–80.

Ong, Aihwa, and Li Zhang. 2008. "Introduction: Privatizing China: Powers of the Self, Socialism from Afar." In *Privatizing China: Socialism from Afar*, ed. L. Zhang and A. Ong, 1–19. Ithaca: Cornell University Press.

Onishi, Norimitsu. 2008. "For English Studies, Koreans Say Goodbye to Dad." *New York Times*, June 8.

Open Letter. 2003. Jiao Gai Wan Yan Shu, vol. 2008. Taibei. http://fcu.org.tw/~swin/series/20031122/200311122–2.html. Accessed March 30, 2010.

Palmer, David A. 2007. *Qigong Fever: Body, Science, and Utopia in China.* New York: Columbia University Press.

Perry, Elizabeth J. 2007. "Studying Chinese Politics: Farewell to Revolution?" *China Journal* (57): 1–22.

Pieke, Frank N. 2004. "Contours of an Anthropology of the Chinese State: Political Structure, Agency and Economic Development in Rural China." *Journal of the Royal Anthropological Institute* 10 (3): 517–38.

Power, Michael. 1997. *The Audit Society: Rituals of Verification.* New York: Oxford University Press.

Psacharopoulos, George. 1973. *Returns to Education: An International Comparison.* Amsterdam: Elsevier Scientific Publishing.

Qilu Wanbao (Shandong Evening News) Editorial Staff. 2008a. "Jiaru Luqu Difen Nüshengde Shi Guonei Gaoxiao." *Qilu Wanbao* (Jinan), July 14, A02.

———. 2008b. "Nüsheng Leyu Zhuren Bei Guowai Daxue Luqu." *Qilu Wanbao* (Jinan), July 14, B02.

———. 2009. "Qian Tong Song Lunyu." *Qilu Wanbao* (Jinan), September 29, A1, A5.

Qingdao Zaobao (Qingdao Morning News) Editorial Staff. 2008. "Guowai Daxue Luqu Zhang Mengyusu Yidian Duo." *Qingdao Zaobao,* July 16, 21.

Rabinow, Paul. 1984. Introduction. In *The Foucault Reader*, ed. P. Rabinow, 3–29. New York: Pantheon Books.

Ramirez, Francisco O. 2003. "The Global Model and National Legacies." In *Local Meanings, Global Schooling: Anthropology and World Culture Theory*, ed. K. M. Anderson-Levitt, 239–54. New York: Palgrave Macmillan.

Rawski, Evelyn S. 1988. "The Imperial Way of Death: Ming and Ch'ing Emperors and Death Ritual." In *Death Ritual in Late Imperial and Modern China*, ed. J. L. Watson and E. S. Rawski, 228–53. Berkeley: University of California Press.

Renmin Jiaoyu Chubanshe Xiaoxue Yuwen Shi, ed. 2005. *Yuwen, Di Shiyi Ce.* Jinan: Renmin Jiaoyu Chubanshe.

Rofel, Lisa. 1994. "Liberation Nostalgia and a Yearning for Modernity." In *Engendering China: Women, Culture, and the State*, ed. C. K. Gilmartin, G. Hershatter, L. Rofel, and T. White, 226–49. Cambridge: Harvard University Press.

Rohlen, Thomas P. 1983. *Japan High Schools*. Berkeley: University of California Press.

Rong, Xue Lan, and Tianjian Shi. 2001. "Inequality in Chinese Education." *Journal of Contemporary China* 10 (26): 107–24.

Rose, Nikolas. 1996. "Governing 'Advanced' Liberal Democracies." In *Foucault and Political Reason: Liberalism, Neo-liberalism, and Rationalities of Government*, ed. A. Barry, T. Osbourne, and N. Rose, 37–64. Chicago: University of Chicago Press.

Rosen, Stanley. 1989. "Value Change among Post-Mao Youth. The Evidence from Survey Data." In *Unofficial China: Popular Culture and Thought in the People's Republic of China*, ed. E. P. Link, R. Madsen, and P. Pickowicz, 193–216. Boulder, CO: Westview.

———. 1994. "Chinese Students in the Nineties Adjusting to the Market." *China News Analysis* 1994 (August 1–15): 1–12.

Said, Edward W. 1978. *Orientalism*. London: Routledge and Kegan Paul.

Sargent, Tanja Carmel. 2009. "Revolutionizing Ritual Interaction in the Classroom: Constructing the Chinese Renaissance of the Twenty-first Century." *Modern China* 35 (6): 632–61.

Sargeson, Sally, and Yu Song. 2010. "Land Expropriation and Women's Entitlements in Peri-Urban China." *China Journal* (64):19–45.

Schein, Louisa. 2000. *Minority Rules: The Miao and the Feminine in China's Cultural Politics*. Durham: Duke University Press.

Schmid, Randolph E. 2008. "Study: Dyslexia Differs by Language." *Washington Post*, April 7.

Schriewer, Jürgen, and Carlos Martinez. 2004. "Constructions of Internationality in Education." In *The Global Politics of Educational Borrowing and Lending*, ed. G. Steiner-Khamsi, 29–53. New York: Teacher College Press.

Scott, James C. 1985. *Weapons of the Weak: Everyday Forms of Peasant Resistance*. New Haven: Yale University Press.

Seth, Michael J. 2002. *Education Fever: Society, Politics, and the Pursuit of Schooling in South Korea*. Honolulu: University of Hawaii Press.

Shandong Sheng Tongji Ju, ed. 2006. *Shandong Statistical Yearbook 2006*. Beijing: Zhongguo Tongji Chubanshe.

Shandong Yanjiu Ketizu. 1998. "Guanyu Ren de Suzhi ji qi Jiegou de Fenxi yu Yanjiu." *Shandong Jiaoyu Keyan* 1998 (2): 4–8, 20.

Sigley, Gary. 2009. "Suzhi, the Body, and the Fortunes of Technoscientific Reasoning in Contemporary China." *Positions: East Asia Cultures Critique* 17 (3): 537–66.

Silbergeld, Jerome, and Dora C. Y. Ching, eds. 2006. *Persistence/Transformation:*

Text as Image in the Art of Xu Bing. Princeton: Department of Art and Archaeology, Princeton University with Princeton University Press.

Southwell-Lee, Meiling. 2010. "Women with Money, Women with Minds: Social Status, Gender and Marriage Choices among Elite Urban Women in China." Ph.D. diss., Australian National University.

Stafford, Charles. 1995. *The Roads of Chinese Childhood: Learning and Identification in Angang.* Cambridge: Cambridge University Press.

Stambach, Amy. 2010. *Faith in Schools: Religion, Education, and American Evangelicals in East Africa.* Stanford: Stanford University Press.

Steiner-Khamsi, Gita. 2004a. "Conclusion: Blazing a Trail for Policy Theory and Practice." In *The Global Politics of Educational Borrowing and Lending*, ed. G. Steiner-Khamsi, 201–20. New York: Teacher College Press.

———. 2004b. "Introduction: Globalization in Education: Real or Imagined?" In *The Global Politics of Educational Borrowing and Lending*, ed. G. Steiner-Khamsi, 1–11. New York: Teacher College Press.

Strathern, Marilyn, ed. 2000. *Audit Cultures: Anthropological Studies in Accountability, Ethics, and the Academy.* London: Routledge.

Suen, Hoi K., and Qiong Wu. Forthcoming. "The Keju Examination System of China from a Modern Psychometric Perspective." In *Essays on the Historical Civil Service Exam System of China*, ed. T. Curran. Lewiston, NY: Edwin Mellen Press.

Sun, Wanning. 2009. "Suzhi on the Move: Body, Place and Power." *Positions: East Asia Cultures Critique* 17 (3): 617–42.

Tanner, Murray Scot, and Eric Green. 2007. "Principals and Secret Agents: Central vs. Local Control over Policing and Obstacles to 'Rule of Law' in China." *China Quarterly* (107): 644–70.

Thøgersen, Stig. 1990. *Secondary Education in China after Mao: Reform and Social Conflict.* Aarhus: Aarhus University Press.

———. 2002. *A County of Culture: Twentieth-Century China Seen from the Village Schools of Zouping, Shandong.* Ann Arbor: University of Michigan Press.

Thompson, Warren S. 1929. "Population." *American Sociological Review* 34 (6): 959–75.

Tomba, Luigi. 2009. "Of Quality, Harmony, and Community: Civilization and the Middle Class in Urban China." *Positions: East Asia Cultures Critique* 17 (3): 591–616.

Tsao, Hsueh-chin. 1978. *A Dream of Red Mansions*, vol. 1. Trans. H.-y. Yang and G. Yang. Beijing: Foreign Language Press.

Unger, Jonathan. 1982. *Education under Mao: Class and Competition in Canton Schools, 1960–1980.* New York: Columbia University Press.

van der Kroef, Justus M. 1964. "Nanyang University and the Dilemmas of Overseas Chinese Education." *China Quarterly* (20): 96–127.

Vogel, Ezra F. 1965. "From Friendship to Comradeship: The Change in Personal Relations in Communist China." *China Quarterly* (21): 46–60.

Walder, Andrew G. 1998. "Zouping in Perspective." In *Zouping in Transition: The Process of Reform in Rural North China*, ed. A. G. Walder, 1–31. Harvard Contemporary China series, 11. Cambridge: Harvard University Press.

Wang, Anyi. 2007. *Qimeng Shidai*. Beijing: Renmin Wenxue Chubanshe.

Wang, Fei-ling. 2005. *Organizing through Division and Exclusion: China's Hukou System*. Palo Alto: Stanford University Press.

Wang, Jing. 1996. *High Culture Fever: Politics, Aesthetics, and Ideology in Deng's China*. Berkeley: University of California Press.

Wang, Shuo. 2000. *Please Don't Call Me Human*. Trans. Howard Goldblatt. New York: Hyperion East.

Watkins, David A., and John B. Biggs. 2001. "The Paradox of the Chinese Learner and Beyond." In *Teaching the Chinese Learner: Psychological and Pedagogical Perspectives*, ed. D. A. Watkins and J. B. Biggs, 3–23. Melbourne: Australian Council for Educational Research.

Wee, Vivienne. 1995. "Children, Population Policy and the State in Singapore." In *Children and the Politics of Culture*, ed. S. Stephens, 184–217. Princeton: Princeton University Press.

Winerip, Michael. 2007. "Young, Gifted, and Not Getting into Harvard." *New York Times*, April 29.

Wolf, Margery. 1985. *Revolution Postponed: Women in Contemporary China*. Stanford: Stanford University Press.

Woronov, Terry. 2003. "Transforming the Future: 'Quality' Children for the Chinese Nation." Ph.D. diss., University of Chicago.

———. 2008. "Raising Quality, Fostering 'Creativity': Ideologies and Practices of Education Reform in Beijing." *Anthropology and Education Quarterly* 39 (4): 401–22.

———. 2009. "Governing China's Children: Governmentality and 'Education for Quality.'" *Positions: East Asia Cultures Critique* 17 (3): 567–89.

Xiao, Xian. 2008. *Wu Tuo Zhi Bang*. Beijing: Zhongguo Haiguan Chubanshe.

Xiaoxue Sixiang Pinde He Zhongxue Sixiang Zhengzhi Jiaocai Bianxie Weiyuanhui, ed. 2003. *Sixiang Zhengzhi: Er Nianji Shang*. Beijing: Renmin Jiaoyu Chubanshe.

Xin San Pian Keti Zu. 2003. "Jiangsu Nongcun Jiaoyu Xiandaihua Diaoyan Baogao." *Jiaoyu Yanjiu* (283): 18–26.

Xing, Hui, and Shiwei Li. 2009. "Vocational Education Reform in China." In *The China Educational Development Yearbook*, vol. 1, ed. D. Yang, 203–14. Boston: Brill.

Xiong, Lumao, and Chuanjun He. 2002. "Muqian Nongcun Suzhi Jiaoyu Cunzai de Wenti Jiqi Duice." *Changsha Daxue Xuebao* 16 (1): 20–22.

Xu, Jie. 2009. "Chang Jiaqi Jian Zhong Xiao Xue Bu Zhun Bu Ke." *Qilu Wanbao* (Jinan), September 29, C04.

Xue, Chengtai. 2003. "Chong Jian Lian Quan, Jiaogai Wanyan Shu Shimo." Taiwan National Policy Foundation.

Yan, Hairong. 2003a. "Neoliberal Governmentality and Neohumanism: Organizing Suzhi/Value Flow through Labor Recruitment Networks." *Cultural Anthropology* 18 (4): 493–523.

———. 2003b. "Spectralization of the Rural: Reinterpreting the Labor Mobility of Rural Young Women in Post-Mao China." *American Ethnologist* 30 (4): 578–96.

Yang, Mayfair Mei-hui, ed. 2008. *Chinese Religiosities: Afflictions of Modernity and State Formation.* Berkeley: University of California Press.

Yen, Yuehping. 2005. *Calligraphy and Power in Contemporary Chinese Society.* New York: Routledge.

Yu, Lan, and Hoi K. Suen. 2005. "Historical and Contemporary Exam-Driven Education Fever in China." *KEDI Journal of Educational Policy* 2 (1): 17–33.

Zeng, Lin. 2005. "Zen Yang Rang Haizi Xie Yishou Hao Zi." *Qilu Wanbao* (Jinan), November 3, C1.

Zhang, Hong. 2007. "From Resisting to 'Embracing?' the One Child Rule: Understanding New Fertility Trends in a Central China Village." *China Quarterly* (192): 855–75.

Zhao, Shukai. 2007. "Rural Governance in the Midst of Underfunding, Deception and Mistrust." *Chinese Sociology and Anthropology* 39 (2): 8–93.

Zheng, Tiantian. 2004. "From Peasant Women to Bar Hostesses: Gender and Modernity in Post-Mao Dalian." In *On the Move: Women and Rural-to-Urban Migration in Contemporary China*, ed. A. M. Gaetano and T. Jacka, 80–108. New York: Columbia University Press.

Zhou, Xuegang. 1993. "Unorganized Interests and Collective Action in Communist China." *American Sociological Review* 58 (1): 54–73.

Zito, Angela. 1997. *Of Body and Brush: Grand Sacrifice as Text/Performance in Eighteenth-Century China.* Chicago: University of Chicago Press.

Zouping Bureau of Statistics. 2009. *Zouping Tongji Nianjian* (Zouping Statistical Yearbook) *2008.* Zouping: Zouping Bureau of Statistics.

Zouping Ertong Jingdian Daodu Xiehui. 2004. *Ertong Jingdian Daodu Duben: Gao Nianji Ban.* Binzhou: Zouping Jiaoyu Yinshua Chan.

Zouping Gazetteer Office. 1992. *Zouping County Gazetteer* (*Zouping Xianzhi*). Beijing: Zhonghua Shuju.

———. 1997. *Zouping Nianjian* (Zouping Yearbook) *1986–1995.* Jinan: Qilu Chubanshe.

———. 2004. *Zouping Nianjian* (Zouping Yearbook) *1999–2003.* Binzhou: Shandong New China Printers.

Index